FOR
THOSE
I LOVED

FOR THOSE I LOVED

MARTIN GRAY

WITH MAX GALLO

Translated from the French by Anthony White

Foreword by David Douglas Duncan

Illustrated

LITTLE, BROWN AND COMPANY/BOSTON/TORONTO

T11/72
FIRST ENGLISH LANGUAGE EDITION

Library of Congress Cataloging in Publication Data

Gray, Martin.
    For those I loved.

    Translation of Au nom de tous les miens.
    1. World War, 1939-1945--Personal narratives,
Jewish. I. Gallo, Max, 1932-   II. Title.
D810.J4G7213   940.53'15'0693   72-7301
ISBN 0-316-325767

Published simultaneously in Canada
by Little, Brown & Company (Canada) Limited

PRINTED IN THE UNITED STATES OF AMERICA

The monies Martin Gray receives from the sale of this book he will use to carry on the work of the Dina Gray Foundation, which is dedicated to the protection of human life.

TO ALL CHILDREN

Preface

> "And the Lord said to Satan: 'Behold he is in thy hand, but yet save his life.' So Satan went forth from the presence of the Lord, and struck Job . . ."
>
> **BOOK OF JOB**

MARTIN GRAY wanted to tell the story of his life. He needed to speak for his relatives long since gone, for himself, and for his foundation. He needed to tell others what his life had been like. The first time I saw him, he told me he wanted to write a book that would be a monument to his family, to his people, to all his people — those of the ghetto and those of Tanneron.

I had already written a few books, I knew something about words and was familiar with the history of the period; so I agreed to undertake this work with him.

Both of us were apprehensive about it at first. Life had taught Martin Gray to be cautious and modest, which made it difficult for him to talk to me. He doubted that words could give a true picture of what his struggles had been, the sorrow he had experienced, and the reasons he had to keep on living.

I was worried, too, because this kind of work was new to me and it dealt with the phenomenon of history's crossing paths with one man's incredible fate. That is why I wanted to write this book. Martin Gray had been through the convulsions of our heroic and barbaric age. He was bearing witness to his martyred and indestructible people, but he was also suffering the eternal and cruel tribulations of Job.

We saw each other every day for months. In Paris, at Les Barons, at night, often, because Martin devoted his daytime hours to the Dina Gray Foundation. I questioned him; I made tape recordings; I observed him; I verified things; I listened to his voice and to his silences. I discovered the modesty of this man and his indomitable determination. I measured in his flesh the savagery and barbarism of the century that had produced Treblinka. I felt a tumultuous destiny bearing down on me. I had to make cuts: every step of this life contained a story in itself. I kept only the essential parts. I rewrote, confronted the facts, sketched in the background, attempted to re-create the atmosphere. I used words. And I used every impression that life had ever left in me. Because little by little I thrust myself into Martin's life; little by little I clung to this other person's skin. This sounds extreme, but it is true: I was this other person, the waif from the ghetto and the escapee from Treblinka and Zambrow, the immigrant discovering the United States, the man in love.

This book was not written easily nor with the indifference of a professional. Martin Gray did not live that way and he never spoke that way. His life is a commitment and I tried to write this book as Martin Gray conducted his life.

I see no special merit in this. It is easy to move words around on a page, easy to feel sorrow and joy behind a typewriter, easy to relive what others have paid for with their blood.

But I had to do so to remain faithful to this voice and to those for whom this book was conceived and to try to convey to others the emotions I felt and the lesson I learned when I came face to face with a real man.

MAX GALLO

Paris
July 1971

Foreword

MARTIN GRAY never talked about himself — not before the fire. Never a word revealing where he came from or about his family, or how he lost one eye. For some reason — perhaps it was his accent — I always assumed he'd been born in Russia. But then there were references to Berlin and counterespionage and the American army, and that small-boy grin when he confessed to mass-producing *haute époque* chandeliers in the basement of his Third Avenue antique shop; chandeliers designed by his luminously beautiful Dutch wife, Dina, who rode herd on the taciturn little Puerto Rican in the basement where the master-pieces were assembled and gilded for New York's Gold Coast *décorateurs*.

My wife, Sheila, and I first met Martin and Dina one afternoon eight or nine years ago — anyway, Nicole was only an infant and the other children hadn't yet arrived, so it must have been nearly ten years ago — when we were exploring the mimosa-mantled ridgeline of Tanneron a few miles west of our home, here on the south coast of France. Ten years ago, Tanneron was just another of the obscure by-passed hill towns on the Riviera, a village of strawberry farmers, mimosa cultivators, stranger-wary wild boar hunters, one schoolteacher — and the Martin Grays, who lived in a three-hundred-year-old fortress of a farmhouse in the saddle of the ridge just south of town. When Sheila and I first met them they were camping out in two rooms; the rest of the place was a shambles of fallen tiles, cobwebs, timbers that might have been useful when building the Great Pyramid of Giza, and murky attics lighted only by cracks in the roof . . . a place where one might easily be crippled forever by falling through a floor or two. A marvelous place. It was easy to share Dina's love for it, and their excitement when she shoved aside ink drawings of elaborate delicacy (chandeliers) for others of stark simplicity and sweeping imagination, her dreams of what the house would eventually become. Martin's finger always poked at the drawings, and always stopped a millimeter short of smudging them. That great house, Les Barons, was finished just in time to shelter the ashes of Dina and her four children when Martin brought them home after the fire.

And it was only after they died that Martin began to talk about himself — a cataract of words. The dam holding back a thousand unbearable lifetimes finally broke.

This is his story.

DAVID DOUGLAS DUNCAN

Castellaras, France

Contents

V. FATE

Maps

FOR
THOSE
I LOVED

Before My Head Bursts . . .

I'M alive. Often it's not easy. Yesterday I had a visit from another journalist: I'm getting to know them. They wear the right expression, they look sad, but they keep asking questions, darting glances in every direction, opening doors, they want to know, grief's no hindrance, it's their job. I'm reminded of Pinkert — king of the dead — and his men, who loaded up their little carts each morning with the corpses left on the pavements of the ghetto: ragged children with red, swollen ankles; men who'd been stripped of their clothes and covered with sheets of paper; little girls clutching pathetic gray dolls which no one had dared take from them. Pinkert's men, caps pulled down over their eyes, white armbands with the Star of David low on their right sleeves, were doing their job. They took the bodies and piled them on top of each other, then they got between the shafts of the carts, and with a heave pulled them towards the cemetery and the mass grave. They chatted: sometimes, when they managed to get a slice of bread, that bread that tasted like plaster, they were happy. They whistled, passed remarks from cart to cart, but the Blues — the Polish policemen — who had no scruples about killing children, couldn't understand Pinkert's men. Shocked and contemptuous, they shook their heads. "Jewish swine," they repeated, and made only token searches of the carts on which the emaciated bodies lay piled, arms poking stiffly out.

The journalist yesterday morning wasn't a professional. He tried to pull it off, with his notebook and his tape recorder, but there he was in front of me, unable to move, paralyzed, hardly daring to glance at me, whispering and walking on tiptoe. I prefer the professionals, they know what suffering and life and death are all about.

But that guy, with his little black moustache, he was ignorant, and what's more, he hurt me. In spite of his nervous smile, he was really hurling silent questions in my face: "What on earth are you doing talking to me, sitting around in this room? Why are you alive? Aren't you ashamed?" He shook his head as he looked at the photos of my family: of Dina, my wife, which I showed him, I had to; and of my children, Nicole, Suzanne, Charles and Richard, smiling, which I pushed across to him. He kept the photo with all five of them in the field in front of the house, Suzanne standing with her arms raised, Dina hugging Richard, and he didn't say a word. He just shook his head. I wanted to grab him by the neck, sling him out, hurt him, and I wanted to beat my head against the wall. I'd have liked to take my head and throw it as hard as I could, like a grenade, at the house which Dina and I had rebuilt for our children. My head would burst, once and for all, and leave me in peace.

But no, there I was facing that journalist, who occasionally glanced up and then looked quickly down, as if to say, "I've seen you, you're alive, they're dead, and I haven't the guts to face their death and your life." I felt that, deep down inside him, he was afraid, afraid of letting me see what he was thinking: "Why aren't you dead too, like them? Aren't you ashamed of still being alive? Your life is a scandal."

I knew he was thinking that because, for months, ever since October 3, 1970, I'd been saying the same words over and over to myself. As soon as my head began to empty of sounds, thoughts of my wife and children would drown me. Then, like yesterday morning, with that journalist, I would feel like beating my head against a wall. My head would throb so hard it hurt. I'd bite my cheeks, my lips, to stop myself screaming. I felt like rending myself, tearing open my breast with my hands, I felt like yelling: "I'm alive!" I would yell, and I could hear my cry, it was like the cries from the cellars of the Gestapo headquarters on Szucha Alley in Warsaw, cries of horror that I uttered too.

It's mostly in the evenings that I feel this way, hating life, the life which remains to me. I turn on the radio, twiddle the knob until my ears can no longer stand the hubbub of words, which are so loud you can't hear them anyway, or of music which has ceased to be music. I calm down, immersed in the waves: the noise is excruciating and the physical pain a relief. I can think about them. See them again as they were. On October 2, the day before the fire, they ran towards me, waving their school satchels above their heads. It was a mild day, the sky was clear and bright: it hadn't rained for months and the mistral was starting to blow. I took a photo that day. There it is, in front of me. The next day, my life was in ruins; a wisp of black smoke hung above Tanneron. I hadn't seen such tall flames since the Warsaw ghetto was on fire.

So once again I was left on my own: once again there was nothing left of my life but myself. I'd got away from the fields of rubble, I'd got away from the sewers, I'd got away from Treblinka and all my people had vanished. But I was twenty then, I carried a gun, the forests of Poland were vast; and my hatred, like a spring, drove me day after day to kill in order to live. Then after the loneliness came peace: my wife, my children. And then that fire, Tanneron in flames, the crackling of the fire, the stench and the heat, like Warsaw. Everything was taken from me, everything that seemed to have been granted me: my wife, my children, my life. For the second time nothing was spared but myself.

I spent days and nights just trying to realize that it was true. I wanted to be through with the living self that clung to my flesh. I wanted this fresh beginning to end. Friends looked after me — men whose job it is to have to do with war and witness death and who spend their time pondering the mysteries of man's fate, like the soldier snatched from death's door who fell off the gangway of the ship that was to carry him happily back to the United States and who died on the quay. I kept going, from day to day, and I'm alive. It's those who haven't known suffering who are the most astonished. Like that journalist yesterday whom I showed to the door, still shaking his head, looking at the tree with my children's swings hanging from the branches. I haven't yet read what he's going to write. It will be nothing out of the ordinary, because he wouldn't dare admit what he thinks: that it's scandalous to have survived, that he doesn't understand. Too bad. He's the kind who can't understand why hundreds of thousands of us, from the ghettos of Warsaw, Zambrow and Bialystok, went to their deaths, and why we still kept fighting, and how, in spite of everything, some of us survived. He wouldn't understand how we could have buried or even how we could have touched the thousands of dead bodies in Treblinka, the children with staring eyes and lolling heads, on whom we threw spadefuls of yellow sand. He wouldn't understand how, in spite of that, I and others got away, and found the strength to start living again, and had children. He wouldn't understand why I'm still alive today, striving to prevent more fires and senseless deaths. If he seems to understand, it's just on the surface. I forgive him, I've no quarrel with him. He's never known suffering and I hope he never does.

But then I who have survived, with my head that feels like bursting in the evenings and yesterday with that journalist, I don't understand either how I can still be here, collecting documents, fighting for the Foundation, obtaining interviews from ministries to get aid for the struggle which I've undertaken. I no longer carry a gun as I did in the Polish maquis, but now and then I feel the same strength within me. At times I don't understand myself.

That's another reason why I want to describe what my life, our life, was like. So that on the day when my head finally bursts, others may know, and so that our life, my people's life, may endure.

I

Survival

1

I Was Born with the War

I was born with the war. The sirens wailed, the bombers
skimmed the rooftops, their shadows glided across the road, and
in the streets people were running, clutching their heads.

I was born with the war: we went downstairs to the cellar, the
walls were shaking and flakes of white plaster fell on our hair. My
mother was deathly pale, my eyes stung, women screamed. Then
there was a momentary lull, until the fire engines sounded their
horns and the women started screaming again.

September 1939: the month of my real birth. I know almost
nothing of the previous fourteen years. I can't search my memories, I don't want to. Why bother to recall that pleasant time?
We'd run through the streets behind the *droshkas* to the square
in the old town, in the heart of Warsaw. My father would take me
by the hand and we'd go to the factory. The machines were from
America: he'd show me, impressed in the steel, the name of the
firm and the town, Manchester, Michigan . . . I'd walk proudly
at my father's side between the machines. My father would pick
up a stocking or a glove. He'd make me decipher the trademark,
7777, our trademark, we were partners in a large factory, we sold
stockings and gloves all over Poland and abroad, and I had relations in the United States too, a grandmother living in New York.
Sometimes we'd go along Jerusalem Avenue to Poniatowski
Bridge over the Vistula. We'd cross Krasinski Gardens. Jews
would be bargaining with each other. They always seemed to be
wearing the same dark overcoats, they were poor. But I didn't

know what poverty was. I didn't even really know that we were Jews. We observed the major holidays but there were Catholics in our family. We were between the two religions. To me my father, tall, straight-backed and so firm of hand, seemed as if he were himself the origin of the world. We'd come home, I'd linger in Ogrod Saski, the last gardens before you reach Senatorska Street. Home. My father would open the door: I can still recall the sweet fragrance, my two younger brothers shouting. My mother would be there and the table set for supper. This was before my birth, long before, an era of fine weather which ended in the summer of 1939.

Suddenly, the war. My father is in officer's uniform, he clasps me by the shoulders, and I realize that I'm almost as tall as he is. We leave my mother and my brothers at home and set off together for the station. In the streets, everything has already changed: groups of soldiers, trucks, the first lines outside the shops. We walk side by side in the road, shoulder to shoulder, he's stopped holding my hand: I'm a man. He shouts something to me from the window of the train which I can't hear, then I am alone in the street. I think this was the day we had the first raid: I watched the bombers, silver with black crosses, flying low in groups of three.

"In here."

A Polish policeman yells in my direction from a porch where some terrified passersby are huddling. I begin to run down the empty street: I must get home, I don't have to obey anyone. I saw my father shouting something from the train. I've got to be as strong as he is. My mother pushes me down to the cellar: the plaster falls, we're suffocating, women are sobbing and wailing. After the alert, we see from the window the first fires, in the working-class areas, in the direction of the Praga marketplace. I begin to read the papers: France, England, America, everyone's sure to help us. We're going to fight to the end, the Germans will never enter Warsaw. I listen to the mayor's proclamations on the radio: Warsaw will never surrender. My mother's crying, my two brothers playing together. She and I are sitting in front of the radio. Often I put my arm around her shoulders as we wait for the news. There's fighting all along the frontier and everything's going badly. We listen to German broadcasts: they're announcing thousands of prisoners, tomorrow Hitler will be in Warsaw. "Poles," says the cheerful voice, "it's the Jews who are the cause of your troubles, the Jews who wanted the war, the Jews who are going to pay." Then the choirs, the songs. I turn the knob: Radio Warsaw is playing long pieces of mournful piano music. Then the bombers come back, at regular intervals; the cellar shakes. Incendiary bombs fall on the Jewish quarter, near us, and when we go upstairs again, the air is filled with dense smoke. "They're after the Jews," someone keeps saying.

My uncle comes to see us. He speaks to me.

"If the Germans enter Warsaw, it's the Jews they'll go for first. You know what they did in Germany. Your father doesn't trust them."

I nod as if I know. My mother is sitting near us and doesn't say a word. I nod uncomprehendingly: who are these German people whose language I know, why are they demolishing our lives, why do they hate the Jews? Then they begin to shell Warsaw, they're trying to hit a big insurance company building, and every day the silver bombers come back to the city; the fires are no sooner put out than they flame up again in the Muranow and Praga quarters, in the Smocza quarter and in Stare Miasto, the old town. I'm now constantly out in the streets: I want to see, know, understand, fight, defend. The streets are full of ragged soldiers without rifles, some lying down on the pavement, others shaking their fists in the middle of silent groups. They talk about thousands of tanks, dead horses rotting on the roads, raids on Grudziadz — where the entire Polish Army is, including my father. My mother has stopped even trying to make me stay in. Every morning I set out and stroll around the National Museum where the wounded are arriving, look at the grubby men lying on blood-stained stretchers, the women and children crying. In son   areas rubble strews the streets, clouds of white dust rise from the earth, families scrabble in the ruins.

All along Nowy Swiat (New World) Street, the shops are closed. I run along behind the red and yellow buses full of sol-

diers en route for Zoliborz. There, for several days, I and some
others dig holes and trenches. Because we are going to fight to the
end and the French and English will soon be on their way. When
I return, covered with dust and mud, my mother doesn't say a
word. One evening when I go to wash, I notice there isn't any
water.

"Ever since this morning," my mother says.

Then we run out of food. I stop going to the suburbs to dig
trenches. We have to live, we have to learn to struggle like beasts
to eat and drink. And the streets are full of beasts. I know men.
But the species seems to have vanished. I fight to keep my place
in a long line outside the local baker's. I push and shove women,
like the others. I'm strong. I watch, I want my share for myself
and my family, but I'm trying to understand. Maybe this struggle
for yourself, for your people, is natural? Everyone seems to have
stopped recognizing each other. Sometimes the soldiers hand out
their rations. In one of the Warsaw parks, near where we live, are
two of them with large greenish hats, who have opened their hav-
ersacks. Around them are women, children and one of those old,
bearded Jews, in a black skullcap. The women begin to shout,
"Not the Jew, Poles first! Don't give the Jew anything!"

The soldiers shrug and hand the Jew a chunk of gray bread,
but a woman rushes up, gives the Jew a shove and takes his bread.
She's screaming like a lunatic, "Not the Jew! Poles first!"

The Jew doesn't answer, but moves off. The soldiers go on
handing out food. I grit my teeth, don't say a word. I take a
chunk of bread. I don't look Jewish. The streets are full of hate,
now I know. You have to be on the alert, ready to spring, to run
away. I fight to keep my place by the well and bring home water.
I go to the Vistula where long lines are forming: drinking water
is being handed out. Two young Poles, hardly older than I, come
up and yell, "Jews to one side, Jews in another line!"

Then some Jews shuffle away and stand in line: sometimes for
fifty people served, only five Jews get water. I wait in line patiently, not moving, gritting my teeth. Yet neighbors become wild
beasts. And die fighting each other.

On the way back from the Vistula with a bucket of water, I

hear the bombers coming from the north, making for Zoliborz. Their noise makes the earth vibrate, immediately there are explosions, smoke filling the sky, people screaming; a façade ahead of me, at the end of the street, collapses all at once; there are flames. I plunge my head in my bucket of water, then run. The bombers have passed over. A *droshka* is on fire and the horse is just a lump, lying on its side, the driver alongside it, his body huge, swollen, an animal too. I run to another street, men are digging in the dust, I dig with them, and hands are stretching up from deep down under the rubble. Then I leave. In other streets, groups are looting shops with gutted fronts. Women are filling their aprons with canned foods, clasping their huge bellies and running away. Near Senatorska Street, I meet a neighbor's son. Tadek's older than I, we've never gone out together, but today, without even a word, we begin to walk along side by side. We roam the streets. I'm hungry and I sense that I'm the leader. Tadek follows me. We search. In Stawki Street a group of people are waving their arms wildly. We go closer: it's a pickle canning factory, the door has been smashed in. On the ground, on shelves all along the walls, are hundreds of cans. I don't hang back, I'm one of the first. I make a bag out of my shirt. I move swiftly, silently. Now and again, I glance to left and right. I've noticed a window. By now I know that you always have to work out an exit. Tadek follows suit. We leave hurriedly: in the factory women have started fighting, and we run to Senatorska Street. That night all of us eat our fill: large salt pickles, which we crunch between our teeth, which sting our gums. But we're not hungry anymore so my mother doesn't ask any questions. She eats the pickles too. We're all ill and vomit that night, but we're not hungry anymore. That's how life is now.

The next day, I set out again with Tadek. In the streets, among the retreating soldiers, heavy peasant carts are rumbling along. Refugees are sitting on the pavement with their canvas bags and blankets. I pass by, ignoring them: we have to eat, have to live. But the shops are empty, the counters bare. Some people come running by: "The station, there's a trainload of flour!" We begin to run too. On the platform they're unloading in silence: we're like ants, but it's each man for himself. I knock a sack off onto the track and grab it. It weighs about two hundred pounds. It's not flour but pumpkin seeds. We split them up and go off with a hundred pounds each on our backs. They're waiting for me at home now: I'm the breadwinner. When I come in with the bag on my back, my mother kisses me, my brothers are joyous and start dipping into the whitish seeds. You have to live. I sit down, I'm worn out, my hair's sticky with sweat, I've even stopped feeling hungry, but I'm at peace, feeding my family.

I carry on, day after day. Then suddenly, one afternoon, the streets empty out. Smoke from the fires still hangs over the city, I'm on the far side of the Vistula. I feel alone, I run. From time to time, I pass others who are running too. I call out to one of them:

"What is it?"

"The Germans, the Germans! We've surrendered!"

They'd won. They were coming.

2

The Strength That a Man Has in Him

I saw them. They were everywhere. They were marching in serried ranks along Jerusalem Avenue and the Third of May Avenue. They marched slowly, their heels ringing on the cobbles of the narrow streets. I was walking along the pavement, behind the rows of curious bystanders; I wanted to see them, to understand. They seemed tall, fair and invincible. Some had their helmets slung from their belts, as if they knew that they had nothing to fear. That we couldn't do anything now. Since the siege of Warsaw began I had got used to suffering, to unshaven and defeated Polish soldiers; but now here was this powerful army with its endless procession of trucks and tanks. Their planes were skimming the rooftops above Jerusalem Avenue. Patrols moved along the pavement: they didn't seem to notice the people, everyone drew aside. For a moment I followed three soldiers in ankle boots with long black bayonets. Yes, we were going to suffer. I remembered my father. We hadn't had any news of him for weeks.

But I hadn't time to think: you had to survive, you had to fight. At the street corner a large covered truck had halted: some Poles were waiting around it, their hands out. Two soldiers were standing there, surrounded by large round loaves, they were laughing and tossing the loaves. From an open car parked near the truck an officer was taking photos; another officer held a movie camera. But you had to eat. I forced my way into the group, quickly collected my two round loaves and ran off clutching them. The next day loudspeaker vans announced that the

Germans would be organizing the distribution of bread, so I went from center to center. The soldiers moved into a Jewish shop which had been cleared, near Sienna Street: there was already a long line of people from every area, talking in whispers, muttering that the Germans were handing out soup as well. Suddenly, a tall soldier appeared in the entrance. He was bareheaded, the sleeves of his jacket were rolled up, I can still see him, hands on hips, yelling, *"Juden, 'raus!"* Everyone in the line cowered, no one left the ranks. *"Juden, 'raus!"* he yelled again. Two women hurried off. One was a little old lady, with a black shawl over her head. The soldier walked up and down the line. He was scrutinizing us; then, at the end of the line, a man in a hat went over to him, and pointing to someone, called out, *"Jude."* Everyone turned around, and there was a small dark man, with a short curly beard, standing alone as everybody backed away from him. The soldier gestured and the man walked slowly forward. The man who'd denounced him smiled confidently. The soldier gripped the Jew's beard and began to jerk his head, then he kicked him and the man ran off. The whole line began to laugh with the soldier. And I laughed too, out of fear and anger.

I had my bread, I had my soup, so I went off to line up elsewhere. Everywhere, men were denouncing each other. I looked, I tried to burn into my brain the faces of these men and women who jostled men and women like themselves out of line, calling them *Juden.* But there were too many such faces, too many soldiers tugging at the hair and beards of old Jews. As I returned to Senatorska Street, a few minutes before curfew, I saw two soldiers shoving a man who was walking along very straight-backed. I thought: my father. I dashed over: it was just another Jew. They made him take off his shoes, and then kicked him and made him jump along, like a frog, on the road, for what seemed ages, and they laughed and passersby in the street laughed with them. The soldiers flung the Jew's shoes to a Pole who said thanks and took them, and they went off. At the end of the street stood the barefoot man who could have been my father.

My mother was waiting for me, the door was already open: she was afraid for me now, she often cried. In the daytime we went from office to office asking if anyone knew where my father was. Everywhere we went they threw us out. That evening, my uncle was waiting for me too. He'd been to the factory. A bomb had destroyed part of the outside and the stairs, but he'd managed to make his way up to the workrooms: the machines, hundreds of pairs of gloves were still there, no one had touched them. The looters and the Germans had assumed that the whole building had been gutted. The next day, very early, we set to work. It was cold, from time to time snow fell, a damp wind was blowing from across the Vistula. We all went to it: my uncle, my brothers and my mother. One of us kept watch, as we scrambled out of the ruins, carrying sackfuls of gloves. Having goods to sell might help keep us alive for a while. I made a final trip to the factory; all that remained were two sewing machines. I used to wander around there with my father, such a long time ago. I hoisted one of the machines onto my shoulder and set off. It was already curfew. There was a German truck at the corner of the street: I heard orders, guttural voices echoing in the deserted street, so I hid in a doorway. Soldiers came running, chasing stragglers and forcing them onto the truck. One of the stragglers tried to run away, there was a shot, a white and yellow flash close by me, and a single cry. Then the truck drove off with its lights on, leaving the man lying still in the middle of the road. I hoisted the machine and set off again. That's how it was, you just had to clench your teeth. I dashed across Senatorska Street. On the stairs I could breathe at last. I went up slowly, but the door wasn't ajar as it usually was when my mother was waiting for me. I knocked, two raps. My mother was smiling, she kissed me, she was still smiling, as before. I put the machine down in the hall, and she pushed me into the bedroom. On the bed, fully dressed, was my father, asleep, but he immediately opened his eyes and clasped me to him.

"It's all right, Martin, all right," he said.

He hugged me very tight. He made me sit down by him.

"I escaped," he began. "I'm leaving tomorrow morning."

I was all ears and eyes.

"The Germans, the Gestapo. They're sure to come here, sooner or later."

Calmly he proceeded to give me his best advice; he told me everything, sure of what he was talking about.

"Never get caught. But if they catch you, think of only one thing, escape. Even if you're scared stiff. Escape. You haven't a chance with them. If you escape, there's always hope. Never wait. The first chance is always the best."

He smiled.

"Do you remember, Martin, how you used to chase after the *droshkas?* How you could catch up with the horses? Well, if they catch up with you one day, take your feet in your hands and run."

It was an expression we both used and we began to laugh. Then he went on: he'd already been in Warsaw a few days but he wanted to check on the house before coming to see us. Now he was going to live under a false name, prepare for those — and there were lots of them — who wanted to cross the Bug and reach the Russian-occupied zone. From now on we might meet him in the streets, in the parks, at friends' houses, but never at home in Senatorska Street. In the morning, before leaving, he came and woke me: he was wearing a long leather overcoat and boots, he seemed enormous, yet I was almost as tall as he was. In the street I'd have taken him for a Nazi, or for one of the *Volksdeutscher,* Poles of German origin, that you saw arrogantly parading the streets with their swastika armbands.

"You look like a Nazi," I laughed.

"Copy me, outwit them, survive."

We never saw each other in Senatorska Street again.

He left us but we felt stronger. Survive. I kept repeating the word as I walked the streets. It was cold and I walked fast: the wind was stirring up ripples on the Vistula so that the river seemed to be flowing south. On the bridge, men, no doubt rounded up in the streets, were pushing German trucks which had collided. I hurried by, I had to get to the big market in the Praga quarter. In the square, in the small adjoining streets, in the courtyards of buildings, in the shelter of doorways, you could buy anything: some peasants had sacks of potatoes in front of them; one woman was selling boots, others cloth. In spite of the thickly falling snow you didn't move, a few steps to the left or right maybe, you held out your goods. I was selling gloves. I hung them in pairs around my neck, offered them to the passersby, went into the shops. Surely the Polish shopkeepers wouldn't cheat me. I held out a pair to a shopkeeper. He looked at them, studied me, tossed back his mane of black hair and put two zlotys on the counter. I yelled at him and started trying to take back my gloves.

"Shall I call the police, scum?" he said.

I took to my heels. I'd been treated as a thief so I held my tongue: I was a Jew. From the end of November, I was supposed to wear a white armband with a blue Star of David at least an inch in size, low down on my right arm. An armband which meant: this is a man you can rob, beat or kill. I didn't wear the armband but I was at everyone's mercy. I had to learn to protect myself from everyone. So I stopped going into shops, I kept on the alert, I chose my customers. I managed to wrest from them the zlotys which kept us alive at home. So long as we had zlotys we had bread.

Sometimes business was good: I'd go back to Senatorska Street before the end of the morning, stock up and set off again. I didn't say anything, just handed over the zlotys. I brought back bread and plunged out into the street again. In Targowa Street, the site of the Praga market, there was a group of soldiers. They were strolling idly in the middle of the road, looking for trouble. One of them, older than the rest, his face heavily lined all over, gold teeth in the center of his mouth, called out to me.

"What are you selling, Pole?"

It didn't do to understand: only Polish Jews knew German. I smiled, played the fool. The peaceful-looking old soldier came over, and before I had time to jump back, twisted my arm with one hand and searched me with the other, found the gloves under my thick jacket and threw them to his companions, and then offered me a few zlotys: an honest soldier. It was no good protesting: that's how it was.

They could do as they liked. Polish policemen, railwaymen in the black uniforms of the Todt organization, rapacious shopkeepers, crooks; any man with power could do whatever he wanted to me. I knew it; it was up to me to cope with life, all the same, in spite of them. I hid part of my money in my shoes, and the thugs who cornered me one day in Krasinski Gardens had only managed to take a pair of gloves off me.

Then a Polish policeman caught me by the sleeve.

"Where did you get those gloves?"

I hadn't heard him coming, I was bargaining with an old lady, my bad luck. I had to size up the uniformed man in a flash: one mistake and it could have been all over for me, for my family. His eyes, barely visible under his helmet, looked weary, distant. I tugged a little on my sleeve, he wasn't gripping me very tightly.

"I'm hungry, I'm hungry."

"Where did you get those gloves?"

"They're ours, my father had a factory, he's dead."

I spoke rapidly, staring him in the face.

"Are you a Jew?" he asked.

I shook my head. It could have meant yes if he'd wanted to take it that way. But he said nothing and let me go; I ran off.

Sometimes I had to submit. One time there were three policemen watching me. Possibly one of the shopkeepers had denounced me. They surrounded me, hit me and took me to the police station. In the passage about twenty people were waiting. Two had blood-smeared faces: they were wearing Jewish armbands. I was pushed over with the others, but I didn't even sit down. I was going to make a run for it, I sensed it, I knew it, I had to. The policemen left, I followed them without a word. The door was open. I kept a few feet behind them, then shot ahead and ran for it. Never wait, never get caught. The next day I returned to Praga wearing a hat and a long overcoat: it was a risk but you had to eat. I wasn't recognized and business went on.

At night I would fall asleep instantly. I always dreamed the same dream: we'd be going to see my father, as we actually did; we'd take every precaution, walking for hours along near-deserted streets, to make quite sure that we weren't being followed by members of the Gestapo, we'd keep walking, my mother out in front with my brothers, and I by myself, some distance behind. We'd arrive in a narrow street, a dead end, and my father would be standing at the end of it, standing against the wall; my mother and my brothers would run towards him and suddenly a heavy German truck would loom up, bear down on them, about to crush them against the wall, and I couldn't even cry out. That was my dream, every night. It would wake me up and I'd remember that morning — my eyes open, I'd have stopped dreaming, I could see the scene in Gesia Street again, a busy street: we were all wearing armbands, a Jewish street. The truck full of soldiers turned, presumably heading for Pawiak Prison, and entered Gesia Street at top speed: the people yelled, they made for the doorways, me with them, and the truck wove to and fro, clearing the road, mounting the pavement. The street was empty now, the truck had gone: against a wall, his arms still raised, was a man, crushed. We all went off and carried on with our lives, walking on the road, crowding the street, like a trail of ants.

I didn't go to Praga on Sundays. We stayed indoors, we tried to get a small fire going, sometimes my uncle would come and see us and talk with us: we'd count up our pairs of gloves, our only wealth. He'd tell me what he knew, talk to my mother about the *Lebensmittelkarten,* the ration cards they gave us when we went to sign on at the Jewish Community Council. They had a huge J on them. Like the armband: to point us out to thieves and murderers. There was also forced labor, the closing of Jewish schools, children whom you could see begging, barefoot, on the frosty roads, and young Poles yelling in the streets, "Long live a Jewless Poland! We want a Jewless Poland!" Armed with sticks, they roamed in gangs, breaking windows in Jewish shops and hitting Jews on the head. I would have liked to kill them. I was ready to kill.

The man came one Sunday. In his thirties, tall, strong, arrogant: black boots, a gray uniform rarely seen in Warsaw, and a swastika armband. A *Volksdeutscher.*

"My money," he said.

He laid some papers on the table.

"I'm the agent, I've taken over from the owner of the factory in Lodz, these are your debts. Pay up."

They were old invoices, from before the war, for goods bought by Father in Lodz.

"Pay up."

My mother answered meekly, "We've nothing left."

He repeated, "Pay up."

I was ready to kill him if he'd made so much as a move. But he merely yelled, threatened and hurled insults; slammed the door as if he'd break it. My mother sat down, called me over to her.

"I was scared, Martin, scared for you. They're stronger. Surviving is all that matters, you mustn't resort to anger in front of them. Later, Martin, later."

We were like ants. I went to see my father: he was waiting for me near the tall columns in Pilsudski Square, looking like a German or a *Volksdeutscher* in his big leather overcoat.

"They'll be back, Martin," he said. "They never give up. They're tenacious. But so are we. You'll have to move everything out, be ready for the worst."

I walked away, but I could hear his footsteps behind me, as though he were some passerby who didn't know me. And when he'd caught up with me, he said, without looking at me, "We'll have our revenge, Martin. We'll finish the stronger."

We emptied the apartment. The neighbors helped us: they hadn't turned into wolves. All that was left were our beds, a few chairs, a little crockery: our house was now a reflection of our life. It was cold, harsh and empty. I had loved the wide blue carpet, I had loved the bronze statue, I had loved the tall silver candlesticks. They were all gone. Our house was like the streets, with their gutted shops, children begging, men and women selling whatever they could because there wasn't any work and because prices were rising daily; our house resembled their emaciated faces, their hollow eyes. In our house as well as in the streets, *they* were the masters. And *they* did make a return visit. Members of the Gestapo in long overcoats as well as Poles.

"Where's your husband?"

My mother said that she hadn't heard anything since the war.

"Tell me everything," she went on. "Even if he's been killed. I want to know."

They fell silent. They looked at us. They went around the apartment. They opened the only cupboard that we'd kept. My brothers cried and whimpered. The Gestapo put on their hats, unsure whether to leave or not. We waited. We knew they'd come back. We waited for them every evening, we were ready. And they did come back. Others. They talked about the debts we had in Lodz.

"You're to pay up or we'll take everything."

My mother gestured at our few sticks of furniture.

"We'll make you get out your jewelry."

Then before they left: "You must tell us where your husband is."

They closed the door calmly; they left us, apprehensive, in our near-empty apartment. My mother began to comfort my brothers, I was counting pairs of gloves: one of the Gestapo kicked open the door. He stood in the doorway.

"You'll soon tell us where your husband is."

Then he left. There were times when I wanted to punch the walls: why couldn't we do anything, why were they so strong, why were they the bosses and we the slaves, why did everyone accept it? Why did the passersby laugh when they forced the Hassidim to dance like monkeys in the street? Why this hatred for us, why death everywhere, hanging over us? I went and saw my father. He talked to me slowly, as if to a friend. Snow was covering the walks in Ogrod Saski. My father helped me understand how the Nazis were setting the Poles against us; to understand the greed of many Poles, their desire to take our places; to understand also the help that we sometimes got, from our neighbors for instance. As we were talking, we heard shouts and laughter, and we saw a naked man crossing the park, chased by soldiers firing in the air. We moved away. Nalewki Street was full of street vendors and beggars.

"There'll be a ghetto," said my father. "We'll all be together, but it'll be terrible too. They won't leave us in peace."

I didn't answer. I felt old and wise like him.

"They've already started in Lodz. They'll do it here, too. We'll have to see each other less often because the Gestapo will be back."

We said goodbye on Tlomackie Square, opposite the big synagogue: I watched him leave, strong and upright. Each meeting could be our last. I put on my armband and entered the Jewish quarter, where we'd already been told that we'd have to live: I went along Gesia and Mila streets, Wolynska and Niska streets. I walked on. The streets were now my life; as I walked, I was thinking: I had to go and sell in Praga, go to the post office with my mother to change the dollars which my grandmother sent us from New York. I was thinking: life had changed so much in a few months. I was thinking, I was off my guard, I was in the rat-trap of Zamenhofa Street. Trucks were lined up along the pavement and the soldiers were rounding up all the men with kicks and rifle butts. An officer was pushing me. He was shoving me in the back, barely even looking at me.

"Fifteen," I said, "I'm only fifteen."

I hadn't much hope but I had to try it, a remote chance because you could only be recruited at sixteen. He stared at me, his eyes almost white, as if they hadn't any pupils.

"You're lying, Jew! You're lying, you scum!"

I repeated what I'd said. It was risky. They fired at the drop of a hat, they killed for a word too many.

"Get up!"

He kicked me and sent me sprawling on the snow, underneath the truck. I clambered on without a glance back. In the truck, beneath the canopy, everyone was silent. A soldier climbed in behind me and we drove off. All I could think of was jumping. Jumping, seizing any chance not to be cut down by a burst of fire in some wood beyond Zoliborz, near the Vistula, as had happened to scores of Jews, victims of these random street raids. But the soldier didn't stir. He smelled of wool and sweat, he had his boot against my foot and his gun across his knees, his finger on the trigger. Suddenly the truck stopped. Orders, or rather, yells: we were in the Zoliborz area with its well-spaced houses and gardens.

The Germans had driven out the Poles and settled in there. So we weren't going to die: we were handed shovels and we began to clear the avenues. The snow was fresh and it was blowing about like powder in the wind. The low, almost black clouds promised more snow. Our work was pointless. But we had to shovel the snow.

"Take off your gloves!"

It was the officer with the pale eyes.

"You're to work without gloves, you know that."

He struck me. I worked. My fingers were red, blue, clumsy. The officer moved away. I put my gloves back on. I didn't notice him come back.

"Scum!"

He didn't shout, he struck me. One blow on the neck, several on the face.

"Give me your gloves," he said.

I handed them to him and he flung them to another Jew with a laugh. That was their logic. They enjoyed being cruel. We worked all day, and when the snow began to fall again, we climbed back into the trucks. Night fell; maybe we were going to die now. Strange times, when anything could happen at any moment. The soldier was still sitting next to me, whistling, smoking, who'd ever guess such a quiet man could kill? More yells: we leaped down into a paved court. All around were buildings, barbed wire: it was an occupied barracks across the Vistula. A skinny youth with curly red hair told me not to worry, we were going to do the soldiers' chores, he'd been here before. We waited there motionless, the wind cutting through us. Two companies went by, bareheaded and singing, off on maneuvers; not one of the soldiers seemed to notice us: we were stones, objects, nothing. Soon we dashed into the yard with buckets and spades, washed the floorboards, cleared the snow. The red-haired boy motioned to me as we filed past the canteen: there was food on a wooden table. He went in, and then dashed out, slipping some herrings into his shirt, and went off with his buckets. We worked all night: now and then I managed to slip into a barracks and warm myself a bit. Dawn was gradually approaching: a clear, watery blue sky.

"They're going to take us back," said the red-haired boy.

They assembled us in the yard, we were lined up in two ranks. The officer with the pale eyes walked slowly forward. He stopped in front of me and I thought: he wants me dead.

"There's a thief here," he said quietly. "Whoever took the herrings must own up. He's got five minutes. Him or ten of you."

He immediately selected ten of us, myself the first. It was such a fine morning. My mother was waiting for me and I was going to die without a struggle. The officer walked up and down in front of us, rubbing his hands with relish.

"It was me."

The red-haired boy stepped forward, walked up to the officer and stood in front of him.

"It was me," he repeated.

Probably everyone in the ranks felt, like me, that his heart was going to burst. The officer with the pale eyes paused, then kicked the red-haired boy in the groin, making him double up soundlessly. The officer took a spade and began to hit him all over the body, and my friend, whose name I didn't know, collapsed in the snow, clasping his head, still without a sound. The officer drew his revolver and fired. We went back to work under a volley of insults. We were swine and scum, yelled the soldiers. Shortly after midday they took us back to Warsaw; not far from Zamenhofa Street, the trucks stopped and we scattered at the double. My mother and brothers were waiting for me. I didn't say anything, that was life, it hung on a word, it wasn't even worth a few herrings. We knew that. Why go on about it?

It took me several days to forget the officer with the pale eyes: I could see him everywhere, pursuing me with his incomprehensible hatred; I seemed to recognize him in every uniformed figure glimpsed at a distance in the street: I would run away, dash into the yards of buildings, climb the stairs and wait ages, huddled on a step, shivering. I was afraid, for the first time in the war. I'd encountered hatred which kills irrationally. I'd never met that officer before yet he wanted me dead; he'd killed a man by hitting him with a spade but it was me he was looking at: it was me he was killing. I should have reasoned with myself, to cure myself of that fever, the panic which stemmed from fears that had accumulated deep down inside over a period of weeks. I didn't talk to anyone about it, I controlled my sickness by myself, forcing myself to walk slowly in the streets, courting the worst. Then one day I realized that I had triumphed. I was able to go back to Praga market, I was able to whistle again. I gave myself a break: I ran, then walked slowly, making a long detour along the river. I'd discovered the strength that a man has in him. If he wants to, he can triumph; if he wants to, he can die without a murmur; if he wants to, he can survive. Thanks, my red-haired friend, whose name I never knew and who died for us without a murmur. I was no longer afraid.

The days passed. Selling became difficult in Praga. The police and the Germans appeared more often, blocking the exits, overturning the stalls, arresting men. About ten o'clock one morning, while I was standing to one side, my goods under my arm, keeping an eye on the square, trying to gauge the atmosphere, to guess if *they* would be coming, they arrived. They were Poles. They dashed up, arrested men and shoved them into their wagons. Some Germans, off duty, were taking it all in. I went into a shop, and without a word put down my pairs of gloves behind the door, and left before anyone could call me back. I went around the square and lay flat on the ground, grimacing. People were running, I was calm, the cold was gripping me, the snow was melting under me, soaking my clothes, but I didn't stir. I soon realized that I was alone and that the policemen were advancing methodically towards me. I'd scarcely realized it when they were there; one of them kicked me in the ribs. I could hear the yells of those who'd run away and discovered that they were cut off at the far end of the square, and that the narrow streets which led to the Vistula were sealed by roadblocks.

"What's the matter with him?" someone asked above me.

They gave me another kick. I didn't stir. So they went away, leaving me in the snow, motionless, freezing, but free. Time passed slowly: the market traders filed into the police wagons. They were Poles, all they risked was a fine. Death was always sure to stare me in the face, I had to come to terms with it. Then the square fell silent. Tearful women came and set up their stalls again. I waited a bit longer. Some of them gathered around me.

"They've killed him," they said.

I waited a bit longer still, then I leaped up and ran to the shop: my gloves were on the counter. The owner was talking, holding forth. When he saw me rush in, he shouted, "Who said you could . . . ?"

I took the parcel and left, still running.

"Swine!"

I could hear him yelling. So what: it was every man for himself. I was alive and I had the goods: I wasn't even aware of my frozen shirt sticking to my skin.

But you couldn't rest on your luck. Life had become an obstacle race: you jumped the first hurdle, there was another one just beyond it, higher, and then another beyond that, closer and even more difficult. You got no time to recover your breath. We were weighed down with bad news, the Germans were in the ascendancy everywhere; regulations became harsher, raids more frequent. Only the weather became milder. The snow melted. At last grass reappeared on the banks of the Vistula and in the gardens: I wanted to run among the trees, wander in the forest, as my father and I used to for hours and hours. But the days of walks were over: so I left very early in the morning to look at the river and the colors of the water. It was dawn and the city seemed calm, peaceful, the streets weren't busy yet, the beggars were just invisible black lumps. I took deep gulps of air, it was icy, it took away my breath, and I felt free. I'd found a cat on the bank: a large creature with short gray hair that it had taken me hours to approach. Every morning I spoke to it gently. It watched me, ready to run away, eyes half-closed, paws curled. I'd christened him Laidak. I talked to him, I could have spoken to him forever. I was making plans, laughing. I told Laidak how glad I was to have escaped the raid on the market square.

"Are you a Jew, Laidak?"

I laughed till I thought I'd never stop. Sometimes I tossed him a little food, and he gobbled it down, still watching me; if I made a move he'd disappear. Laidak was cautious, I'd only managed to touch him a couple of times. He must have been through a war too, and I was a sort of cat. I knew that even if the mornings were quiet, the evenings were dangerous, so I didn't loiter in the streets.

Each night I went home to Senatorska Street and we waited till the morning, hoping they wouldn't come that night. For weeks they left us alone, but in a constant state of apprehension. Then they smashed in the door, new faces, five of them, hats down over their eyes. Only one spoke Polish, but all of them kept shouting.

"Go get your husband."

My mother began her explanations again: she hadn't heard anything since the war, maybe they could tell her, as members of the police. But I sensed that everything would be different that evening. The man who spoke Polish was interpreting. One of the men went up to my mother and slapped her full in the face. Her bun came undone and an angry cry welled up in my throat but I didn't move. The man carried on, then he spoke in German and the other translated.

"Madam, you're to tell us where your husband is."

Madam. I repeated the word to myself. The man had struck my mother yet called her madam.

"Madam, we're going to take this young man, we'll leave you our address. We're giving you twenty-four hours to find your husband and bring him to us."

He gave me a withering look. The others searched the house, tossing whatever they found to the floor.

"Whatever happens, you'll get this young man back. Alive or dead."

My mother started whimpering, she clung to me: I was like a block of wood, she was asking for mercy, she kept saying, "Leave him here."

Suddenly she fell silent.

"Arrest me," she said. "Leave the children."

One of the men was writing.

"Here's the address, madam. Give it to your husband. And come get your son within twenty-four hours."

They bundled me onto the stairs, my mother rushed after me

and clasped me to her: "Run, Martin, run away." They tore her from me, flung her to the ground, and took me down. At the foot of the stairs, the one who'd kept silent kneed me in the stomach and drew a revolver.

"Take us to your father," he said in German.

I didn't move. I'd understood but I didn't reply until the words had been translated into Polish. Then I started talking: I didn't know anything, I'd have been only too glad to take them to my father but I hadn't seen him since he went away. They exchanged looks, they were doubtful, maybe I'd gotten away with it. But I hadn't.

"You'll remember everything in Szucha Alley."

The Gestapo had its headquarters in Szucha Alley. In the street they bundled me into a van: inside was a soldier, unconcerned. They got into a car and we drove off. We tore along. I began to speak to the soldier but he struck me with his rifle butt and sent me staggering to the other end of the van. Laidak's been caught, I thought, but Laidak's going to hold his tongue and run away. That gave me courage. We stopped several times but the soldier never took his eyes off me. Finally we came to Szucha Alley, the huge, well-lit building that housed the Gestapo: we went in. Doors, corridors, more doors and more corridors. Standing in a line against a wall, men and women were waiting: there was fear in their eyes. All I could see was a window and the night outside. One of the men came up to me, the one who'd slapped my mother, and struck me across the mouth.

"Your father's a coward," he said in clumsy Polish. "He's going to walk out on you."

He removed his hat. He had a bullethead and close-cropped hair.

"The Jews are all cowards," he went on.

Then he went out into the corridor, ignoring me and leaving the door open. I could see a woman standing there, her arms in the air. I made a dash for the window. Outside it was night, I gripped the handle, the air was keen, I turned around: the woman was gaping in terror and astonishment. I jumped. I thought: I'm going to kill myself, but there I was, running across a yard, towards a wall. I scaled it. I found myself in another yard, I ran, clambered over an iron gate: I was in the street. I ran on. I had to make it before they did. I went upstairs, pushed open the door and yelled:

"Mother, brothers, leave everything! Come on!"

We scrambled downstairs, one of my brothers barefoot, we ran, and kept running through deserted Warsaw, dodging the patrols, through dark, empty squares. My uncle lived in Freta Street. He took us in for the night: he listened to me in silence, my mother was kissing me.

"I knew it," she said. "You're like your father."

I felt proud. The next day, curfew over, we scattered: friends took us in. I didn't go out for two or three days. I was staying with a friend of my mother's who lived in a large gloomy apartment at the end of Sienna Street. Her husband, a doctor, had left Poland on the eve of the war and hadn't returned. She hugged me and took my breath away, she got me talking, and I talked my head off, but at night I locked my bedroom door and there, in that strange room that smelled of dust, the vague excitement that she'd aroused in me during the day soon died away. We didn't have a home anymore, we'd never go back to Senatorska Street, and we were split up, one brother in one part of Warsaw, my mother and my other brother somewhere else, and my father changing his address every day. Soon — my father had gotten word to us — we'd have false papers, another name. Not even that much would remain of our past. A family's a funny thing — never had I realized what it meant to me as I did then. The Gestapo could have tortured me, I wouldn't have given my father away, and when the man struck my mother, even though I didn't stir, I felt as if I were shrieking, going mad. A family was the whole world; and now, because of *them,* that world was in little bits. In the nights, I thought about how one day I'd rebuild a world of my own, a family.

But that day seemed as distant as the coming of peace. I spent a good deal of every night on the alert, listening for the footsteps of the patrols, jumping when a car braked. After two or three days' wait, I couldn't go on living in that apartment, with that woman sighing against me, crazed with fear, starting to talk about how she and I would go away together, many miles from Warsaw. I took advantage of one of her outings to run away and return to the streets and the sunshine: I felt willing even to be caught as long as it was under the open blue sky. My father had been informed and was to meet me in the old town, the Stare Miasto, where the narrow streets and dark courtyards meant that you could slip away easily. He looked worried, grave.

"You really are a man," he said. "You escaped from them. And I know you didn't talk."

I liked life, I felt strong now. How was it my father could fill me with joy with a word; would I be able to give such strength to others too? To the children I'd have one day?

"What do you want to do?"

He was questioning me. I explained that I had to go back to Praga market and recover the goods we'd left stored with friends and relatives. Mother did her best to sell instead of me; but it wasn't her proper role, because I was there and anyway she didn't know how to cope. They'd rob her.

"Don't hang around in Senatorska Street or Szucha Alley," he laughed.

Then he embraced me, which was something he had never done. Once again I went out in the streets on my own trying to sell some object that would enable us to survive. Everywhere I saw fear in people's eyes and I recognized the sickness which had affected me too, when I'd seen my young red-haired friend die. I kept my ears open, I found out that they were building a brick wall up in Dzika Street and in some of the other streets too. I went to have a look. There were some workers there, Jews with armbands. They were laying long bricks and the gray cement was flowing, but they couldn't keep it level: they were casual laborers, no doubt glad to have found work. The wall was already six feet high, and one of them, up a ladder, was still adding on bricks. The whole street was going to be sealed off: we'd soon be penned in like beasts. People were saying that they'd already sealed off the ghetto in Lodz.

For a moment I felt like running away: I'd leave Warsaw, I'd

go and work for the Polish peasants, I'd speak the language without a Jewish accent, I'd fill my belly, and I'd come back when the
war was over. I'd escape from the mob, from the fear and from
the ghetto-to-be. I was walking in Nalewki Street, dreaming away,
when the trucks stopped and I had to go down on all fours like
all the rest, I'd have to jump like a frog, and do it well, but even
that wouldn't prevent my getting struck on the back, the soldiers
would laugh and belt me. Old men who didn't move fast enough
were knocked down. I glanced up, the whole street was on all
fours and the soldiers were firing head-high. Other shots could be
heard from neighboring streets. It must have been a big raid, a
day of sport and terror. Not more than a few yards ahead of me, a
woman, standing with her feet apart in the middle of the road,
was resisting, trying to hold onto a baby, and two huge soldiers
were wresting it from her. I could see her staring eyes, all I could
see were her panic-stricken eyes. They grabbed the child, played
catch with it; there she was, holding out her arms, not knowing
whom to approach, trying to seize the child which wasn't even
crying. Then one of the soldiers dropped it.

The trucks moved off again, we got up, and I went on walking.
I didn't even know what I'd been dreaming about when the
trucks had stopped in Nalewki Street — maybe about the countryside, running away. But can you run away, desert your family if
you're a man? The next few days I went back to Praga market;
but we'd almost run out of goods, and who'd buy gloves with
summer coming anyway?

All anyone could talk about was the massacre which had taken
place in the streets of Warsaw. Hundreds of Jews had been killed,
others taken away to the forest. I'd been lucky to escape with a
few jumps and a few blows in Nalewki Street. Since then some
had gone into hiding. My mother, whom I met every two or
three days, begged me to stop going out, but I wanted to see. It
wasn't so much the need to sell which drove me out into the
streets, as the need to look, take it all in, find out. Events had become like strong drink to me. I had to know, record this cruel
world with my eyes, in my mind, relate one day all that I'd seen,
all that we suffered. But the cost could be high.

It was I who wanted to stay and watch that day in Sienna Street. I was with Stasiek Borowski. I liked him; we often used to roam about together and, in spite of his weight, he could run as fast as I could, and we'd already managed to get away on several occasions, in the nick of time: he was as round as a knot of muscles. He wanted to leave Sienna Street, but I felt immobilized, riveted. Some Jews had been assembled in the middle of the road, in that middle-class street where lots of Poles lived, and the Germans were making them dance, leap about, take off their clothes and sing. The others had to clap time, and the soldiers were egging them on with blows and yells. In the middle of the group, an old Jew, almost naked, was imitating a bear, balancing on one foot, looking up, and begging its master. Stasiek and I were in the crowd of laughing spectators and all I could see were those smug, grinning faces. Stasiek tugged at my sleeve, I pulled away: we weren't wearing our armbands, though I had on a fixed grin which should have done the trick. As Jews we weren't exactly used to playing with fire: for a long time we'd known that you had to run. But I wanted to hear the laughter, watch that bald man, in his waistcoat, doubled up, roaring his head off. It wasn't the butchers and their victims who fascinated me but their audience. Stasiek nudged me again but it was too late. The street was sealed off. The soldiers closed in, shoulder to shoulder, and all of a sudden there was silence: the bald man stopped laughing, and looked from left to right in alarm. We were bundled over to the trucks and the Jews stayed in the middle of the road, not moving; then as the truck moved off, I saw the almost naked Jew slowly getting dressed again. He'd acted as bait. That day the Nazis were after Polish cattle.

That day, for the first time, I entered Pawiak, the huge gray prison which was the talk of Warsaw; it was my first arrest and fate had decreed that I should be captured as a Pole. Stasiek Borowski had recovered his good humor.

"Maybe if we get out our Jewish armbands, they'll let us go. Will you have a try, Martin? You always want to see, and know, this is a great opportunity."

I held my tongue. There were hundreds of us in the yard. We

were split up into small groups and driven with kicks and yells through the damp corridors. Stasiek and I tried to stick together and we were shoved in turn into an overcrowded cell. We could scarcely move, men were whimpering, some were asking for cigarettes, others were questioning themselves out loud, more still were cursing the Jews, who had to be responsible for everything. I took a look at the skylight and tried to move closer to it. From the far end of the cell a voice called out, "Shut up, you idiots!"

The voice ordered us to settle down, everyone gradually obeyed, and we finally managed to sit down. The man who'd spoken was a prisoner in his thirties, with a long scar on his cheek; from his accent you could tell that he was a Warsaw tough, with dirty gray curls that almost concealed his eyes. I got talking with him: when I mentioned the word escape, he started to laugh uncontrollably, then fell asleep, but I stayed beside him. In a prison, the old thugs are the ones who know the answers, and I wasn't going to seek advice from the bald bourgeois Pole who was there too, sniffling away, his waistcoat over his head to ward off the cold. Later on, Siwy, the hood, began to talk: he'd been in prison three months; he'd been drinking, he'd assaulted a cop, and he'd wound up in his beloved Pawiak. He talked about the prison as if it were a woman.

"You can't leave Pawiak," he said. "She turns you out, and yet you're fond of her and she's fond of you, she won't forget you. You always wind up in Pawiak. Always."

The next day we were assembled in the yard. I was near Siwy.

"You're here to work," yelled someone I couldn't see. "Poland has waged war on the Reich, killing our German comrades. The Poles must pay with work."

Stasiek and I were waiting, not moving, wary, trying to guess what was in store for us because we were Jews, twice guilty, earmarked for death. When we saw the Polish guards setting up tables by the wall and bringing typewriters, we understood.

"Armband," said Stasiek. "In case we're searched."

I clutched the piece of cloth in my pocket on which our lives depended. I began to rip it apart with my nails and raised it to my mouth. Stasiek followed suit and we began to chew away, slipping towards the end of the line of prisoners building up in the yard. Near the tables a soldier was shouting.

"Call out your names, empty your pockets! If you keep anything, *kaput!*"

I laid my money on the table, I'd nothing left on me, nor had Stasiek, but once again we'd saved our lives, once again.

We waited for hours in silence. I gazed at the sky, trying not to notice the walls or roofs, only the sky. Suddenly we saw the SS men come on the scene. We were used to the black-uniformed soldiers: it was one of them who'd snatched the baby from its mother, one of them who'd let go of it. We knew all about the SS. Without a word, they lined us up: the Polish guards and the German soldiers rushed about, like dogs around their masters. The SS men kept to the shadows of the walls. Then they moved forward and a group of black-uniformed officers came out of the main building. Stasiek muttered, "It's Himmler." The officers chatted together, looked at us, laughed, walked up and down the ranks, pausing in front of some of us. In my row was a very tall, thin man, with a long black beard. He looked as if he were a professor or a doctor. The group of officers halted in front of him. I could hear occasional words.

"Why were you arrested?"

"I'd very much like to know, Herr Reichsminister."

He had a professor's voice, very deliberate, which echoed through the yard, finally reaching the SS officer.

"Traitors must be punished, Professor Bursche."

"I'm not a traitor to my honor."

"You've betrayed your native land."

"I'll never betray my native land."

There was laughter and the group moved off. Could that plump little man, tightly buttoned up in his black uniform, be the Herr Reichsminister Himmler, Reichsführer SS, king of the butchers?

Some trucks drew up: it was the SS men who bundled us on. I followed Siwy, and Stasiek Borowski followed me. Behind each truck was a carload of SS men.

"We must run away, Siwy," I said.

"Goodbye, Pawiak," he kept saying. "Goodbye, Pawiak."

I started to tell him about the camps, the executions in the woods. He listened to me, flicking back his mane of gray hair.

I recognized Sczesliwice Station. At that point the SS men began to yell. They set to with their rifle butts, fired twice in the air, and like a flock of sheep we poured out onto the platform. I stayed with Siwy.

"They're going to shoot us, Siwy."

We were packed into cattle cars and I stayed near the door, testing the wood with my hands, worming my way as best I could to the side of the car. Night had fallen; some men had fainted, then the train began moving and we got a little air.

"I've got a knife," said Siwy. "There's a grating at the end of the car on your side. Shove!"

We inched our way forward, and finally I felt fresh air on my legs. We had to stoop. Stasiek thrust back the others' bodies. Some were dozing shoulder to shoulder. Siwy went to work.

"I'm going to jump," he said. "I'll use you to push against. You shove me out. When you jump, roll over with your arms around your head and then lie still."

I explained to Stasiek. We crouched down. Siwy doubled himself up, his head out, and I gave him a shove. Then nothing, just the train and one more place in the car.

"You first," said Stasiek Borowski.

He shoved me. Gravel ripped at my hands, but it was soil, firm, unyielding, hard. After a few seconds there were shots and the train slowed down, but by then it was a long way off. Maybe Stasiek had jumped too. I ran through the countryside, the grass was sodden, branches caught at my clothes. In a clearing, surrounded by a wooden fence, was a farm: the peasants helped me. The men didn't ask any questions but gave me bread and money. I ran into the woods in the direction of Warsaw which they'd indicated to me. In the morning, when the mist had lifted, I saw Zyrardow Station, surrounded by fields. I took the first train. The car was full of peasant women with white scarves around their plump red faces: out in the country life was going on, peacefully. All went well at Warsaw Station. I was back in my streets, with their beggars and ragged children.

Two days later, I met my father.

"I've been to Pawiak," I said.

I had to tell him about my first big escape.

"You were careless, Martin. You won't always have luck on your side."

But he'd barely time to lecture me. He'd just taken part in the first underground operation: he and his group had killed a German policeman in a restaurant in the suburbs of Warsaw. A well-known butcher among butchers. There had been reprisals against Warsaw: a little more terror hung over the city. The cost of every operation kept rising.

That was the last I saw of Siwy, the old thug of Pawiak, and of my friend Stasiek Borowski, who helped me jump in the night.

3

The Game of Life and Death

WHEN we walked in the forest, back when I didn't know anything, before my real birth, before the war, my father didn't like me meddling with ants. They were huge, reddish in color, disciplined: their trails crisscrossed the paths. I used to follow them to their ant hill, and with a branch, prod one of the holes into which they had vanished. I couldn't bear to leave the swarming mass, the stampede I'd caused. There were thousands of them, rushing in and out, and in a second, panic would spread to the farthest trails. My father would call me to no avail, he'd come for me.

"Ants again!" he'd say.

Then he'd talk about the ants' work, the natural order which you mustn't disturb. I'd barely listen to him. I was watching.

Ever since the beginning of October we'd been like panic-stricken ants. In the streets groups of men harangued and gesticulated; people came and went from door to door. Furniture would pile up on the pavement, then people would carry it upstairs, then it would be hurled out of the windows. Poles argued over pictures a Jew was auctioning off. I went back into our courtyard: an old lady was sitting in the entrance, crying. She buttonholed me as I passed by, calling out, "Thirty-seven years I've been here, all my life, now I've got to leave everything."

I hadn't the heart to stay, so I went. Families had stacked their beds and all their luggage on carts and boldly driven off: ants. At regular intervals, the loudspeaker truck announced the bound-

MAP AND LOCATION OF THE WARSAW GHETTO

The ghetto as it was marked out by the Germans in 1940 comprised the "traditional" ghetto and part of the "Aryan" city.

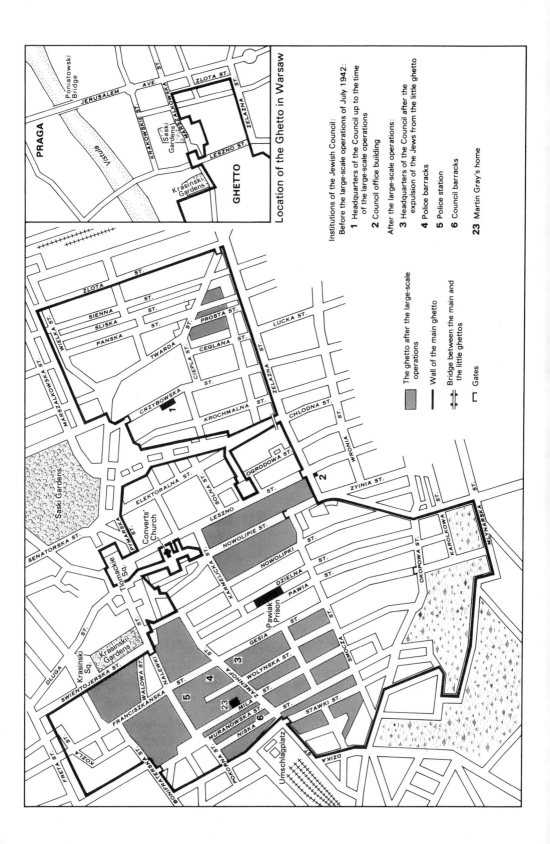

Location of the Ghetto in Warsaw

PRAGA

Poniatowski Bridge

JERUSALEM AVE.

Saski Gardens

Krasinski Gardens

GHETTO

Vistula

KRAKOWSKIE ST.
KARSZALKOWSKA ST.
ZLOTA ST.
ZELAZNA ST.
LESZNO ST.

Institutions of the Jewish Council:

Before the large-scale operations of July 1942:

1 Headquarters of the Council up to the time of the large-scale operations

2 Council office building

After the large-scale operations:

3 Headquarters of the Council after the expulsion of the Jews from the little ghetto

4 Police barracks

5 Police station

6 Council barracks

23 Martin Gray's home

The ghetto after the large-scale operations

Wall of the main ghetto

Bridge between the main and the little ghettos

Gates

ZLOTA ST.
SIENNA ST.
SLISKA ST.
PANSKA ST.
PROSTA ST.
LUCKA ST.
CEGLANA ST.
TWARDA ST.
CIEPLA ST.
CRZYBOWSKA ST.
KROCHMALNA ST.
CHLODNA ST.
WRONIA ST.
ZELAZNA ST.
ZYINIA ST.
WIELKA ST.
MARSZALKOWSKA ST.
Saski Gardens
SENATORSKA ST.
ELEKTORALNA ST.
SOLNA ST.
OGRODOWA ST.
LESZNO ST.
NOWOLIPIE ST.
NOWOLIPKI ST.
DZIELNA ST.
PAWIA ST.
KARMELICKA ST.
'Converts' Church
Tlomackie Sq.
PRZMARSKA ST.
DLUGA ST.
Krasinski Gardens
Krasinski Sq.
SWIENTOJERSKA ST.
FRANCISZKANSKA ST.
NALEWKI ST.
ZAMENHOFA ST.
Pawiak Prison
GESIA ST.
WOLYNSKA ST.
MILA ST.
MURANOWSKA ST.
NISKA ST.
STAWKI ST.
SMOCZA ST.
DZIKA ST.
Umschlagplatz
OKOPOWA ST.
KAROLKOWA ST.
MLYNARSKA ST.
FRETA ST.
KOZLA ST.
BONIFRATERSKA ST.
POKORNA ST.
 zamenhofa st.

aries of the Jewish quarter, prohibitions, probable deadlines for relocation: first, October 31, then November 15. I looked and listened. My father came over several times.

"It's the ghetto," he said. "They're going to really hurt us. But we'll be with our own people. For a while, it may be simpler. Only for a while."

We knew where we had to go, to a building on Mila Street, No. 23, one of my father's secret apartments. But we were waiting for the final boundary to be set, to make sure that there wouldn't be any further delays or fresh regulations. But what can you ever be sure of? I was learning, still learning, every second, that at such a time, laws, words, life were all uncertain. All of us, Poles and Jews alike, had become creatures subject to fate, to chance. At 31 Dzielna Street, I saw a huge bald-headed stevedore laughing as he tossed furniture out of the windows. In Wronia Street, I heard a Jewish child, bright-eyed, shouting, "I'm German, I'm German!"

His shrill voice pierced my ears. An old man tried to reason with him, stroking his hair, but the child kept on shouting. My father was forever saying, "You mustn't lose your head, keep on your guard."

My mother wanted to leave at once. I hugged her to me, talked to her gently, kept saying, like my father, that we must hang on, not go out. The previous day, in Ciepla Street, I'd met a group of SS men: one of them, who seemed to be in charge, was nodding to left and right, and the others were standing around him laughing. I followed them at a safe distance, creeping from one doorway to the next. They were advancing along the middle of the road, the street emptying in front of them. They went into a shop and I heard cries, more cries and still more cries: two women came running out, naked, clutching their clothes. Further along, the same day, in Muranowska Street, against the wall, about twenty Jews, arms in the air, were waiting. I passed by and slipped away. The streets were full of frantic people, pushing and shoving, you could hardly walk: in Leszno Street and Grzybowska Street, the crowd was so dense that I had to elbow my way through. My father was worried.

"You shouldn't be outside," he said. "They're making raids. They're killing people."

My mother pleaded with me, wept, asked my father to put his foot down.

"I've got to know."

It was the only answer I could give. I wanted to know. I wanted to see that brick wall going up, getting larger and sealing us off. Near Parysowski Square it looked like a prison wall, and the whole of our quarter (because we weren't even entitled, according to the loudspeakers, to call it the ghetto) would be a prison, the Warsaw Jews' Pawiak. I wanted to know because I didn't want to get shut in. I walked among the crowds and kept repeating to myself, "Don't get caught." I was almost happy. It was cold: around me people were beginning to huddle, to shiver. I didn't feel cold, I felt ready. I was Laidak, the cat on the banks of the Vistula, who never let himself get shut in.

Saturday, November 16: the ghetto. Yesterday, my father moved us to 23 Mila Street. Passing Nowolipki Street, near the church, we saw some priests trying to collect signatures for a petition asking for the street to be excluded from the ghetto. Everyone was trying to protect his property as best he could, clinging to the past for a few hours, to what made up his life. Some had already lost everything: the Praga Jews had been brought by truck to the ghetto. They had nothing left, only a few suitcases. They hung about on the stairs, outside the doors, sheltering themselves from the cold. My father kept saying, "Everything now is a question of solidarity. We've got to show them!"

I didn't even bother to look around the four rooms in our apartment. I was happy for my mother and my brothers, we'd found a house, a world for ourselves. But I couldn't stay. I wanted to see things. My father had already left us: he was working to organize a reception center for the refugees. He had his job. My mother pleaded with me, I kissed her, hugged her to me: she was so sweet to me. My brothers clung to me. I laughed, cracked jokes, but it was no good: for their sake, for mine, I had to be out in the streets, amidst the violence, the lives and deaths of others. My people, mine.

On that Saturday, November 16, there were patrols on the corner of every street. Helmeted Germans, a few yards away from the Polish policemen in their blue uniforms, known as the Blues, and

further on, with their yellow armbands, and their white armbands with the Star of David, their belts and boots, were the
Jewish police of the *Jüdischer Ordnungsdienst,* the Jewish
disciplinary corps. They were the ones I wanted to check up on,
the ones who were going to maintain order in the ghetto. For us
or against us? They were controlling the passersby, supervising
the long lines that had formed in front of the shops. The crowd
was everywhere, then suddenly I came upon a wide-open space:
they were there. I edged forward: three elderly Jews, arms out,
were doing exercises. One of them stumbled and fell in the mud.
He lay there, not moving, and a soldier walked slowly over his
body. Further on, in Leszno Street, some SS men were making the
Jewish police hop along on one foot, keeping time. Them too,
like us. In Ogrodowa Street, a woman was kissing the pavement
while *they* laughed. We were enclosed and helpless! The crowd
was massed along the wall, silent, hypnotized. The broken glass
and barbed wire on top of the wall were clearly visible. The people took a look, then moved off. You'd have to scale the walls
with ladders and planks of wood. You could also go into one of
the houses that gave onto the Aryan side, with their doors
bricked up. But a wall can be breached, crossed.

I skirted the ghetto wall. All I could see was the wall, one sentence was reechoing in my mind: they won't shut me in. I'd
reached one of the gates to the ghetto: a barbed-wire barricade
had been erected in the middle of the street and two sentry boxes
placed on each side of a narrow passageway. There were Germans
there, chatting, manning the passageway, helmeted, armed. I felt
like going up to them, dashing into the thick of them and running away. But the street was too narrow and I was sure to get
killed. I had to pass through and survive. I waited, fascinated by
the narrow passageway: our freedom, the door to the cage.

A column of Jews from the Aryan sectors, with canvas bags and
suitcases, arrived in front of the entrance escorted by Polish police. The Germans drew aside: the Jews were tired, dirty, the children dragging their feet; where were they from? Maybe from
Praga. The men bared their heads to the Germans. One of the
Jews, a youngish man, kept his hat on. They saw him; an order

was given. The column halted, he was bundled out. No one in the column looked at him. His hat was knocked off with a rifle butt. In front of the sentry box, a German officer, his arms folded, was observing the scene. The Polish policemen beat the man until he fell on the road, then they called in the Jewish police. The German officer stepped forward and gave an order and the soldiers guffawed. Before long the Jewish police were urinating on the wounded man. Shortly afterwards, the column moved off again and the soldiers started chatting again in the middle of the road.

I felt sick. I sat down on the curb. People walked past me. They were shutting us in, beating us, killing us, humiliating us. What of Stasiek Borowski, my friend in the cattle car? And what had become of the woman with her hands in the air who had looked at me at the Gestapo headquarters in Szucha Alley? And how about the child they'd dropped on the pavement, and my red-haired friend? My life, my short life, was full of dead people. They'd killed people around me unceasingly. I got up and walked towards Mila Street.

In Nalewki Street I saw the streetcars: two cars that had just passed the gate to the ghetto and were coming from over there, Aryan Warsaw, and from over there, Krasinski Gardens. On the platform of the first car was a group of German soldiers. They were laughing, staring at the crowd, visiting the ghetto as they would a zoo. On the platform of the second car, a Polish policeman, a Blue, was making sure that no one got on as they passed through the ghetto. The Poles in the streetcar were crossing the ghetto to get from one area to another. On the corner of Nalewki and Gesia streets, while the first streetcar was still in Nalewki Street, a man jumped off and vanished in the crowd. I ran behind the streetcar. It was tearing down the length of Zamenhofa Street, straight ahead, and reached Dzika Street, where, after slowing down at the gate, it crossed the wall and passed on. I ran back down Zamenhofa Street, Gesia Street and Nalewki Street. Again I followed the two streetcars. There was no doubt about it: a streetcar was crossing the ghetto, from gate to gate, from the Nalewki gate to the Dzika gate; a Blue was stopping passengers from getting off or on as they passed through. But if you could get on or jump off, you could move in or out of the ghetto.

I didn't sleep much that night. Next morning I was already on guard near the Nalewki gate. I kept watch. I let several streetcars go past. It was early. There were no Germans on the front platform: it wasn't yet time to visit the zoo. They were sleeping with the whores of Warsaw. I took up position on the corner of Gesia Street. The streetcar came rattling along. I didn't even have to look at it anymore: every one of its sounds was already familiar. It was about to brake as it took the corner and I could soon see the first car entering Gesia Street.

There it was: the platform was in front of me. I leaped. The streetcar kept moving, I was on the platform: the Poles didn't seem to be looking at me, they were looking away. Zamenhofa Street already, the crowd on the pavement overflowing into the roadway, the somber, tragic crowd. We crossed Mila Street, the air was brisk, I wanted to yell, flout their laws, escape from fear, escape from prison, live; my life was flowing back into me as the streetcar trolleys grated on the wires. I hadn't left the ghetto, not yet, but I knew that I'd make it. At the end of Zamenhofa Street, the streetcar slowed down: we were nearing the Dzika gate. I hunched on the platform. The streetcar stopped and I saw the figure of a German; but it wasn't an SS man. He walked up to the platform and saw me, too. How can I forget that thin, aging face, those bushy gray eyebrows? We looked at each other for what seemed a long time. Then he winked at me. The streetcar set off again. I was outside the ghetto. I'd met a man.

My armband was in my pocket, the streetcar was heading for the west of Warsaw; naturally I was in danger of my life, but I was free because I'd broken their rules. If they killed me, they'd kill me free and that changed everything. I leaped down from the streetcar just beyond the cemetery: the streets seemed empty simply because people weren't pushing and shoving, as they did in that overpopulated ant hill of a ghetto with its half-million inhabitants, both Warsaw and provincial Jews crammed into it—"in order to starve to death there," as my father said. In gentle, spacious Aryan Warsaw, the passersby seemed relaxed, calm, elegant: I was forgetting those eyes transfixed with fear and hunger. The cafés of Nowy Swiat were full: Germans were strolling there with giggling women, almost like peacetime, if I hadn't occasionally noticed groups of children begging and suddenly dashing away, probably Jews who'd already managed, like myself, to cross the wall. But I wasn't there to beg. I was fighting the prison by escaping, I was stronger than the butchers. I could do as I pleased, in spite of them, in defiance of them. I wanted to gather my strength here, in the gardens, here on the banks of the Vistula. Because the ghetto was also a world of concrete and asphalt, with no trees. We weren't entitled to gardens. So I walked through Krasinski Gardens, and beyond Swientojerska Street I could see the wall and the German soldiers mounting guard. It's good to be aware of your strength, your muscles, your ideas coming and going clearly and precisely. I felt like running. I was outside; now I wanted to go in and come out again, and then I'd feel alive.

I went back down the long, straight run of Dluga Street. In it was a cake shop where we used to go with my father. I recognized it by its white façade: Gogolewski's cake shop. There was no one lining up there. I bought, at a price, some bread; I ate it hungrily. Then I bought some cheesecake, some *sernik,* then some other treats like those my father used to bring us back, some *bayaderki.* Then I waited for the streetcar at the stop before Teatralny Square. Above the wall was the roof of the great Tlomackie synagogue: I was going back, willingly, and full of vigor, air and white bread. At the last stop before the ghetto, the Blue jumped onto the platform of the second car. I was there, close by him. He was a plump man, he took no notice of me. I barely glanced at him but I stayed by him: I still had some money. It was a gamble. He tugged at the leather bell pull: the streetcar moved off again. It was a gamble. I touched his hand and without a word slipped him some notes. He crumpled them up and pocketed them, without looking around.

At the Nalewki gate, the Blue made a sign, and the streetcar, which had slowed down, gathered speed. I'd won. I was back in the ghetto and I jumped off at the corner of Gesia Street; the first car was barely out of sight. I slipped my armband back on: around me once again were the crowd, the fixed looks, men and women talking incessantly, beggars. They were all my people, my brothers, possibly not young enough to risk their lives, possibly not strong enough. But I was strong enough for them and I was on their side. I went down Gesia Street, clutching my bread, holding my cakes. People were looking at me.

"How much?"

The man placed his hand on my sleeve. He was elderly, wearing a smart hat and coat.

"Don't stay here, come with me."

He nudged me into a porch. I was on my guard; a few stairs to the right, up which I could escape, reassured me.

"I'm buying," he said. "How much?"

"I'm only selling the bread."

"How much?"

I named a figure which seemed enormous.

"They each weigh two pounds."

He wasn't even listening, he pulled out his wallet. Outside was the grayish-black crowd, outside was the sound of footsteps and voices.

"I'm a buyer," he said. "Every day, if you can. Here's my address."

He held out the notes and a piece of paper, and slipped the two loaves under his coat. I watched him go, tall, his hat high above the crowd, but soon hidden by the streetcar, passing by with its Blue and its German soldiers on the platforms. I went back into the porch to avoid the crowd, and to piece together the bits of the day, my great day, my glorious experience. I sat down on the first step of the stairs up which I'd planned to run away. But the man, that well-to-do, respectable óld gentleman was only after my bread. I looked in my hand: it was full of his zlotys, my zlotys. I'd gambled on the streetcar, gambled on the German, gambled on the Blue, gambled with my life, and I'd won; here were my winnings. I laughed: the notes were there all right. I could almost feel the fleshy arm of the Polish policeman who not so long ago had accepted my money, money from a Jewish kid on the run who'd managed to leave the ghetto and had returned of his own free will. I'd gambled with my life, and my new trove of zlotys were nothing, the least part of my winnings: I'd won a conspiratorial wink from a German soldier and I'd won my freedom.

In the old days, my father — it was a game of ours — often used to hand me his cigar; I'd take a deep breath, I'd be wreathed in smoke, and he'd laugh because I'd have to sit down on the blue carpet. My head would spin, and my head was spinning now too. With happiness and fear and faith, all rolled together. I had to deal with each of my thoughts in turn, calmly.

I'd gambled and I'd won: by discovering, if only once, a man inside the uniform of the butchers; and that it was possible to bribe a man who loathes you. I'd won by discovering that men were like the clay on the banks of the Vistula, which I used to mold as I pleased.

For a long time I sat on the step, not moving. Outside, the crowd was becoming grayer and less dense. It would soon be curfew. But I had time: I wasn't like the others hurrying along that street. I'd crossed the wall, I'd cheated the butchers. Those men and women, my brothers, with their white armbands low down on their sleeves were, unless they rebelled, doomed beasts, earmarked for death. They were my brothers and yet I felt different: I wanted to yell out to them, "Be like me, everything is possible!" But could they? I was young, that was my good luck. I could walk about and make plans, work out how many loaves to buy next day, and how much I was going to sell them for. I could organize, think things up. Ideas came to me, one by one. Nothing would be left to chance; I would remember zlotys for the Blue, I must find a way of not entrusting my life to a German: they were seldom understanding. At each step, my plan matured: that was my freedom, the proof that I was stronger than they, the butchers, the guards, the murderers. I was going to live.

At the corner of Wolynska Street and Zamenhofa Street, a family of Jews, surrounded by a few suitcases, was sitting on the curb. Probably Jews from Praga dumped there by a truck, with nothing to call their own. A small girl in pigtails was staring in front of her: I crossed the street, put two cakes in her lap. It was nothing, but since I'd decided to live, to be free, I had to help others live a little. What was the point of living for yourself?

My father was waiting for me outside the door. There was a man with him.

"You're late getting back," he said. "Too late."

He was looking away from me, as if he were afraid to learn everything at once.

"This is Dr. Celmajster," he went on, "our second-floor neighbor. We're organizing a house committee for the destitute."

I was barely listening to him. He was like me, he wanted to survive, to fight, to help. I had to explain to him. Everything between us had to be crystal clear.

"I went across to the other side, Father."

They stared at me in silence. I showed them the package of cakes.

"Gogolewski's cake shop, Dluga Street," said Dr. Celmajster.

My father listened to me, his face tense. I told him the whole story, the soldier, the Blue and the bread. He fell silent.

"You said they wanted to starve us out, strangle us."

I said it again, my voice rising, sensing his anger.

"And you think you can do it alone, a kid of fifteen?"

It was the first time that I'd defied him, and it was anguish.

"I'm not going to let myself be strangled, Father. I'll get bread. Surely we're not going to let ourselves die of hunger."

I closed in on them.

"Surely we're not going to let all these people die!"

Celmajster muttered, "You could be arrested."

"I'd rather."

They fell silent. Mila Street was empty: we went upstairs, not saying a word.

"We must trust him," said the doctor, as he left for home.

When we were alone on the stairs, my father began talking to me. I was two steps above him, and he was looking up at me: I was both happy and embarrassed. Every time he spoke, every time he went on the defensive, I wanted to take his face in my hands and say gently, "You can trust me, Father." I felt that I was going to save them all, him, all my people, the whole ghetto.

"You know that they're killing people," he said, "that they want to exterminate the lot of us, starve us to death, work us to death. Please understand, Martin."

He explained further: to beat them, we had to endure, fight, not give in, but know how to cheat if necessary. I was listening. Those were my plans, my schemes.

"But, Father, to survive we first have to eat. I'll see to that."

He began to laugh.

"You've got a nerve," he said.

He gave me a push upstairs.

"Go on then, smuggler," he said.

My father had hit the nail on the head. I became a smuggler, day after day. Hopping on and off streetcars, hiding my armband in my shirt, sometimes slipping it onto my arm, knowing the police who would "cooperate" — the ones you could take a chance on because they could be bribed — discovering goods, selling them, working out profits and expenses: that was now my life.

I used to leave as curfew ended, in the still icy night. I'd check on the streetcars: which Blue was on duty that morning. Sometimes I'd have to wait, sometimes I'd take a chance, sometimes I'd back a certainty. But I gambled. I'd cross the wall and back several times a day: I'd gamble on my life several times a day. But I was alive, free. With each journey, my system grew more perfect, new plans emerged. When you're in danger of your life, your brain moves fast. I now had contacts, business connections, regulars, official suppliers in Aryan Warsaw. False papers, too: a travel-pass which had already saved me a couple of times. It certified that I was living on the Aryan side and that I was a young Pole of pure race. Though it was cold, I wore an open-necked shirt: this revealed a thin gold chain and a small medallion of the Virgin Mary. In the evenings I learned the Mass in Latin and the main prayers: my life could hang on a few words.

My profits were huge because the ghetto was hungry, the ghetto was cold. A few days before Christmas, the temperature went down to zero. In Karmelicka Street, I saw groups of ragged children huddled together, holding out their hands; the whole ghetto was swarming with famished orphans, begging. They used to hang about the soup kitchens. I gave what I could. A little girl, with skinny legs, red with the cold, had gotten into the habit of watching for me in the evenings at the corner of Mila Street: she didn't move, she merely looked at me. Then she disappeared.

"Leeches, sucking our blood," in the words of the ghetto song. I kept saying it over to myself, gritting my teeth. Because they wanted to exterminate us. Through starvation, cold and work; and through cruelty.

At the gate in Leszno Street, a street I didn't like, a dangerous street where there were raids, I'd seen a group of Jewish laborers on their way home. They were employed on the Aryan side. German guards sprang at them like wolves, setting to with rifle butts, hurling insults, forcing the weary, hollow-cheeked men to their knees. Then they searched them, and hunks of bread, potatoes and a small sack of flour were piled up on the road. The guards forced the workers to throw their goods over the other side of the wall. Some tried to tear off a mouthful of bread: they were beaten.

They wanted us dead. Sometimes I felt ashamed of filling my belly, ashamed of selling, ashamed of watching corpselike children clutching at passersby, dying beggars, a heavily made-up woman extending her hand and trying to smile. Ashamed at not being able to stop it. Sometimes, I felt that I too ought to lie on the pavement, dying of cold and hunger.

But my shame didn't last. They wanted us all dead: but they wouldn't have me and a few more with me. Father told me about Dr. Janusz Korczak's orphanage: thanks to him, hundreds of children were avoiding starvation. When I could, I brought money and grain. My mother and Mrs. Celmajster were organizing the distribution of food. I gave. But what I gave amounted to almost nothing. Our ghetto was an inferno of misery, a sick creature with half a million wounds, each one crying out in hunger, cold and desperation. We were all like frenzied ants trying to survive, to get away. While *they,* the Polish guards and the Germans, the soldiers of death, were watching us rot and die behind the walls within which they had enclosed us. And when we tried to leave, to pass through the gates of their prison, they'd kill us.

One day in Leszno Street I heard screams. From a distance I saw a man crawling from the ruins of the post office: they were stabbing him with a bayonet. It was explained to me that the man had been caught coming out of a cellar. Probably he'd found a tunnel under the wall. He'd returned with some bread, now he was to die. They were killing, beating people up: women escaping with hunks of bread, children managing to beg a few copper coins on the Aryan side. Sometimes the soldiers did turn a blind eye, sometimes they even handed out confiscated goods, sometimes they looked sorry and didn't search, let the children through.

But what did those few exceptions matter? A wink or two between men didn't make any difference. They wanted us dead. I was, in my own way, struggling to prevent their succeeding. If the ghetto kept going, day after day, it was because I wasn't the only one to cross the wall: there were smugglers everywhere. Aryans were entering the ghetto, selling their goods and leaving, having been paid in "hard" money (gold) or "soft" money (paper). In Kozla Street, contact with the Aryan side could be made through an attic. It was not easy, even for the butchers, to keep track of half a million people, to kill them all off at one stroke. Yet the butchers were zealous: they'd opened shops and factories, and were making us work like slaves; we were turning out uniforms, helmets and belts for the great army of butchers.

They were shrewd. As they couldn't slaughter us all in one day, they let a few of us organize our lives. At 13 Leszno Street, with the approval of the Gestapo, Ganzweich and Sternfeld established an economic police force, a looting and smuggling firm, a mafia which *they* supervised. But "the Thirteen," as they were known, also helped us to live: they gave to the poor. They stole and gave alms. It was the same with Kohn and Heller, two shopkeepers, officially tolerated ghetto smugglers: their horse-drawn rattletraps were our "streetcars," filthy and smelly but useful; cars drove slowly through the rickshaws, bicycle-taxis which plowed into the throng: fat, well-dressed men drawn by starving men through a sad and hungry crowd.

Yes, they might well film this scene, they often did; yes, everything in the ghetto was extreme, both wealth and poverty. I know: there were nightclubs and yet children died of hunger at their doors. Yes, corruption and devotion went hand in hand. I sold my goods at exorbitant prices, ate cakes from Gogolewski's cake shop, and dispensed charity. Was it unfair? I lived as best I could in the hell which *they* had created. I was holding my own, all of us were trying to hold our own.

It was true that I'd grown selfish, it was true that I could see a dying man and pass him by without stopping. Because I'd realized that in order to have my revenge I had to live, at all costs. And to live I had to be able not to stop, to be able to watch him dying.

Selfishness was the weapon they'd given me, and I had seized it to use on them. For those I loved.

Each day I fought better. I'd hop onto the platform with a sack; the Polish policeman, the Blue on duty, was in the know; sometimes, because of me, the streetcar would slow down at the corner of Gesia Street. I'd run to the shops and apartments where I was awaited. A few words, a few gestures: the sack empty, I'd have my zlotys, then I'd run back to Nalewki Street for another trip, my folding money ready for the Blue.

"*Mouès, mouès,* the best thing in the world." I'd whistle the song. *Mouès* was money. I was bribing the butchers: the men I had to pay were worthless. I'd never betray my people for a few soiled, crumpled bank notes. I'd return happily to Mila Street, tired and elated, I'd bring back some sweets, sometimes an orange. Father had long ceased to say anything, but I could sense both his concern and his respect for me. One day, I brought some money across for him: sums he was owed from the Aryan side. He thanked me, but did he realize the joy he was giving me? I was a man, fighting, living: several times a day I cheated the butchers and their laws.

But I had bitten off more than I could chew. At 23 Mila Street, I ran into Pavel, our neighbor's son.

"Pavel, listen to me, we've got to beat them. Help me do what they tell us not to."

In our yard, I explained to him what I was doing. He was a typical Jewish intellectual: glasses, curly hair, and a member of *Hashomer Hatzair,* the Zionist organization for the betterment of man. He shook his head. He was unsure. I reassured him.

"You won't have to cross the wall, you couldn't. You look too Jewish."

He laughed. He was still unsure.

"Selling," he said with a hint of contempt.

"Living."

I explained further, at some length.

"Well?"

Finally he agreed. I was laughing inside: I was getting to know men, I was seeing so much of them. I knew how to talk to them: neither their age nor their uniforms impressed me. All you had to do was find their soft spot, and they did what you expected of them. All you had to do was to think quicker than them, make up your mind before them, for them.

Pavel and I were now a team. I didn't have to jump off street-cars: I'd throw my sack off and he'd hand me an empty one with money inside. All I had to do was go over to the Aryan side and buy more goods; Pavel would be there with his empty sack and the money. In the evening, we worked out our profits. There was a separate pile, always the first one, for other people. Pavel under-took to give to those in need: the Korczak orphanage or the beg-gars, or the public soup kitchens that were opening up in the ghetto. Every bank note was a victory.

Pavel felt that I took too many risks: one or two trips a day were enough. Why "tear about" so fast, why not pick out one or two policemen that you felt sure would agree to be accomplices, regu-lar *graieks,* and "cooperate" only with them? Pavel couldn't un-derstand my spirit, my enthusiasm.

In the evenings, in his room, he'd try to reason with me. We smoked quietly. I barely listened to him, tired and happy, impa-tient for the next day. Then when Pola, Pavel's sister, came in, I'd begin to sound off. I'd strut about, puffing away like some big shot. For hours Pola wouldn't say a word. She'd look at me. Then, one evening, she spoke up.

"For Martin, it's a passion," she said.

She understood me. Pavel shrugged.

"I'm not the one who crosses over," he said. "You say you want to survive, but you take too many chances."

The bank notes were still on the table. I took the pile for "the others."

"There's more than yesterday, Pavel."

"And if you lose, there'll be nothing tomorrow."

I went down into the courtyard with Pola: our private retreat between the walls. It was freezing cold and pitch dark.

"Pavel's worried about you. He feels guilty about not crossing over with you."

There was a burst of gunfire. Bitter cold. We went in and climbed upstairs in the dark to the attic: my father and I had begun to make a hideout. "You never know," he'd said. "They won't leave us in peace, even here in the ghetto." Pola and I lay against each other for a long while, not speaking, almost without moving. Then we came down again.

"Don't get caught, Martin."

It wasn't the soldiers who caught me. One morning when I jumped off the streetcar, just beyond the cemetery as usual, I thought I was safe and sound: we'd passed through the gate without any trouble. I walked quickly, already working out the price I was going to offer my grain merchant. Too late I heard them running. There were four of them, with real hoods' faces: one of them, pockmarked, had a stupid smile.

"Oh, what a nice little cat," he said. "Meow, meow."

They grabbed me by the arms and bundled me into a yard.

"A big, fat Bedouin who's been looking after himself."

He reeked of vodka. He was breathing in my face.

"Cat," "Bedouin," I knew the words, they meant Jew, a Jew in disguise, fair game for crooks to pursue and rob.

"Let's have it, Jew."

They surrounded me and jostled me. I tried to dash away, but they hit me, knocked me down, sat on me and searched me. They found the zlotys. The six-footer whistled as he counted the notes.

"What a nice little cat," he repeated.

They took off my shoes: one of them tried them on. They slapped me, searched me again and went off.

"See you," said the one who stank of vodka.

It was raining. I sat in the deserted yard, with no shoes, robbed, crying with rage, fury and humiliation. As if the butchers weren't enough. There had to be jackals on the scent, too. And they'd inflicted my first defeat on me. I'd managed to persuade my dealers to lend me some money for the return journey: I needed it to pay the Blue. So I started again, warily, jumping off later, trying to avoid them. But those *Schmaltzowniki* hadn't forgotten me. They were thriving on our misfortunes. On one occasion I sprinted away and managed to escape them, but I was taking other risks: I could have been arrested. It was an unequal battle, I was losing all the way. They robbed me three times again, within a few days. I couldn't yell or protect myself because I couldn't afford to have any marks on my face: a man who'd been beaten up was suspect. When they cornered me after a chase, they had a good laugh about it.

I was a good prize and I'd even stopped putting up a struggle. They searched me from head to foot and beat me up.

"A stubborn little Bedouin."

I was getting to know the one with the pitted face and the red-haired one they called Rudy. I tried to talk to them, but they were counting their money, dividing it, arguing and ignoring me.

"Come back and see us soon," they said.

One evening, it was I who followed them, out of curiosity. They'd walk along, swinging their shoulders, pushing and shoving, jostling the passersby. I watched them chase a young Jew, flailing his arms, whom they beat and left half-conscious in an alleyway. But I couldn't stop to tend to him. Eventually they went into a café-restaurant at the end of Dluga Street and started drinking. I stared at the men in fascination: they were laughing together, drinking. That was my money there on the table, that was my life flowing into their glasses, and the lives of other men who were starving to death five hundred yards away. With that money, I could have staved off some of their deaths for a few days.

The bullies were drinking. I had to tear myself away from the sidewalk where I was watching them order bottle after bottle. I had to arrange my return, find money and risk my life. All for nothing? I had to explain to my father, Pavel and Pola.

Pavel kept saying, "The bastards, the swine! What cowards!"

I listened to him: it was as if I were hearing my own voice. I'd been saying the same words to myself for hours.

"What can you do? That's how they are," I said.

"They're another wall. We've got to cross it like the first one. And it's obviously going to be more difficult."

All the next day I walked the ghetto. It was a long time since I'd taken a chance in those overcrowded streets. Children were rummaging in rubbish bins, a woman with her dead baby in her arms was begging at the corner of Nowolipki Street and Smocza Street; a smart couple, the man dignified, arms folded, the woman heavily made-up, were singing in the middle of the road. There was a man selling books by the basket, another was lying unconscious, probably through cold and hunger. Everything was going to hell: death was in the air, a creeping, gnawing death. At the end of Stawki Street, huts were being built, railway tracks and platforms being made ready to collect and transport people who'd been rounded up. Sometimes the soldiers would fan out and round people up, for no reason, without even an excuse. They were rounding people up for the fun of it and because they were both might and right. My mother was scared: she stopped going out. A few hundred yards and everything was changed; at 12 Rymarska Street the Melody Palace nightclub was featuring "Diana Blumenfeld singing the songs of the ghetto."

A crowd had gathered at the door, so I went up to it: Rubinstein the Clown was there, pulling faces, waving his arms, wriggling and yelling, "We're all equal. Lie down on your sides, leave room for your neighbors."

I liked him. I watched him run over to the soldiers, defy them, poke fun at them, make them laugh, gamble with his life. He was fighting too, in his own way.

I'd forgotten the horror and misery of the streets. On my streetcar, with my *graieks,* slipping zlotys to my cooperative Blues, momentarily entrusting my life to them, I wasn't as unhappy as I was here. I had to go out again, and cross that wall of bullies, simple, grasping *Schmaltzowniki:* I walked, slept badly. They stole so as to drink. All right, they'd get something to drink!

I left the ghetto the next day on the first streetcar. It was snowing heavily and the city, beyond the wall, seemed empty, still silent. I had little money on me, a few zlotys folded into my shoes: my worst pair, with holes in the soles, the wet and cold freezing my feet. In Wronia Street, I bought two bottles of vodka, and then posted myself in front of their haunt, the café-restaurant in Dluga Street. The snow was still falling: the wind blew down Dluga Street, whipping up drifts. All I had for shelter was the corner of a doorway. I cursed the bullies and had visions of hurling a grenade into that damned café, of purging Warsaw of its jackals.

First to arrive was the redheaded Rudy, his collar up, then two others came in, slapping each other's backs. Later, the oldest, the one with the pockmarked face, arrived with a girl bundled up in a long fur coat. In spite of my impatience, I waited, telling myself I had to learn how to wait, remembering Laidak who could pause for minutes in front of the bit of meat that I threw him before he snatched it in one lunge. I had to let them drink, catch them when the alcohol began to mellow them. Then luck was on my side: because of the snow, they hadn't hunted the "Bedouins" down, and so their thirst would be tremendous.

I slipped across the street, through the door; suddenly I was immersed in a stench of cabbage, gray smoke, and an atmosphere like a Turkish bath. Someone yelled, "Shut the door!"

I'd forgotten it. I was sweating. I could see them at their table, slumped against the wall, around a bottle. The girl was there, sitting upright, fair hair hanging down. They hadn't noticed me. I sat at the end of their table and I put the two bottles of vodka, two large bottles with red labels, in front of me.

"I'm Martin," I said. "Sometimes known as Mietek."

They looked at me, and at the bottles. The girl glanced at them inquiringly.

"It's a Bedouin," said Rudy.

"I'm Martin."

I opened the first bottle and they shoved over their glasses. Then I began to talk:

"I've nothing on me today, not even good shoes. I've come to talk business."

The pockmarked man gave a quiet laugh. He held out his glass.

"Goddamned stubborn little Bedouin! You beat him up, and then back he comes on business. You're all the same, you Bedouins."

"Who are you?"

"Stefan, Stefan Dziobak. Dziobak the Pox."

He laughed softly again. One by one they gave their names. There was Mietek Skover, known as Mietek the Giant: a round, pallid baby-face, almost beardless, six feet tall, with small, bright eyes, piercing, vicious eyes. The last, the least talkative, was named Mokotow, after a Warsaw prison; and the blonde was his sister, Marie. I talked, explained, they drank. I didn't mention the ghetto and the people starving to death, what was the point? I talked about vodka, daily returns, lavish meals, guaranteed profits and minimal risks.

"I want to form a partnership," I said. "And we all stand to gain."

They fell silent. They drank.

"You're just a Jew," said Dziobak the Pox. "And a Jew's a Jew."

Marie said something under her breath, but they all heard her, including me:

"Zlotys are zlotys. And if the Bedouins are smarter than us . . . ."

"How do you mean?"

Mokotow talked seriously and drank the least. I opened the second bottle, joy slowly welling up inside me, the joy of victory: I was about to cross the new wall. I was nothing, just a young Jew on the run, and here were these men of the underworld, these jackals, these thugs, listening to me. Maybe because I didn't even seem to resent the fact that they'd robbed me, maybe because they felt that I was after a genuine partnership, frank and lasting. I

asked if I could trust them: Dziobak the Pox began to laugh. He
pointed to Mokotow:

"He's known as Mokotow the Tomb. So, my little Bedouin . . ."

He pulled out a switch-blade knife and laid it on the table.

"If we didn't quite like you, don't you suppose we'd already
have cut off your tongue? Or your little tail?"

They all started laughing.

"But his little tail's already been cut off," said Mietek the
Giant.

They banged the table delightedly and I joined in their laughter. Only Marie remained aloof, not sharing our hilarity.

"We've already got Mietek the Giant," said Dziobak. "You can
be Mietek the Snip."

We roared with laughter and I drank with them: I felt good.
They were simple men, I had to become their leader and friend,
and it wasn't out of the question. I outlined my plan: they would
protect me and, in return, I would pay them regularly, every day.
They'd pass through the ghetto with me: as Poles they could take
the streetcar without danger, I'd see to the rest. They'd stay
around me and use their fists because there were other gangs on
the lookout for Bedouins. In return, zlotys, vodka, and good food.

"There'll be fewer and fewer Bedouins crossing the wall. With
me, every day . . ."

I ordered another bottle of vodka.

"Wait, Yadia."

Mietek the Giant gripped the waitress by the arm. She was a
fair-haired girl, with a healthy, glowing face, full of life; a girl
fresh and juicy as an orange.

Probably thanks to the vodka, I said, "Yadia's beautiful!"

She began to laugh, her hair bobbing up and down.

"What do you think of Mietek the Snip here?" asked Dziobak.

She laughed even louder, looking me in the eyes, and I felt really good. I wanted to laugh, and for the first time in my life I
wanted to plunge my face between a woman's breasts. I looked her
in the eyes and, laughing, told her so.

"When do we start?" said Mokotow.

Mietek pushed Yadia away and I quickly sobered up. I'd won.

Mokotow the Tomb was their leader. I could tell it from the others' silence when he was speaking: Rudy would clean his nails or scratch his head, constantly switching from one to the other; Mietek the Giant closed his eyes and relaxed, he didn't seem to be listening but in fact he was tense, didn't miss a thing; Dziobak the Pox nearly always wore that ominous, quiet smile which he'd had since the start of our conversation. Strange fellows, thugs, but I eventually felt at ease with them in the café, not only because I'd talked them into working with me. But because they didn't have masks: they didn't have uniforms, they didn't stand for law and order. They were the scum of Warsaw. They'd take my money, they'd shake down Bedouins, but they hadn't built the ghetto wall. They hadn't yelled "Juden 'raus!" when the Germans were handing out bread and soup, towards the end of September 1939. At that time I'd seen middle-class businessmen in hats step out of the crowds and denounce others. And I'd seen an officer beat my red-haired friend to death; I'd seen policemen — law and order — strike women and children, and rob them. Several times each day I'd slip money to a Blue, a respected policeman who was selling himself for zlotys. Rudy, Mietek the Giant, Dziobak the Pox and Mokotow the Tomb were crooks, hoodlums, thieves, bullies, jackals, but they didn't cheat, they didn't pretend. They liked food and drink. They stole: they were honest-to-goodness scoundrels.

"We'll start tomorrow." I said.

I had to get a hold on them immediately, show them that our partnership would pay off at once. Even though I wasn't yet quite sure how to work things, even though I was terrified of failing, I couldn't turn back. We arranged a meeting place near the cemetery, where they'd jumped me the first time. Mokotow heard me out. Then he filled our two glasses, it was the end of the bottle: we clinked glasses and emptied them at a gulp, banging them down simultaneously on the table.

Mokotow came out with me: the snow was still falling but the wind had dropped. He took a few steps.

"You can trust us," he said.

Then he turned away.

I went back to the ghetto: the Blue took his zlotys, the streetcar slowed down, I jumped off, and there was the crowd in the snow, children begging and a half-naked body on the pavement, covered with sheets of paper where the snow was banking up. The daily round, risks and hell. The next few hours were decisive: I had to sort things out and make a go of it. I was moving from a craft to an industry, from amateur to professional standing: I now had a paid staff, and if I wanted to keep them I had to pay them, and so step up my trade. The gears were starting to mesh: I had to grow or die. I told Pavel and Pola: their mother had a few savings, I'd need them the next day.

Then I went and talked with my father. I knew where to find him: every day he was busy receiving Jews whom the Germans sent us from all over Europe, from the Reich or from Austria, arriving with their suitcases, cardboard boxes, and all the arrogance and prejudices of cultivated Western Jews, brought abruptly face to face with our prison, the Polish ghetto where you died for a look or a word, where you perished of cold or starved to death, where typhoid hounded you. Father was there, at the 14 Prosta Street reception center, meeting deportees from Danzig. As I entered, one of them, with a pommel on his walking stick, was yelling that he was a Catholic, that even his father had been converted, that he hated Jews, that he wanted to know if there was a church. I wanted to punch him in the face, but my father calmly answered, "You'll find the Converts' Church in Grzybowska Street."

He saw me and came over to me, suddenly all smiles.

"Father, this is important."

He shook his head as he listened to me, and looked at me disapprovingly, pursing his lips. But he'd stopped even trying to disagree with me, and when I finished he merely asked me, "What do you want?"

I wanted him to introduce me to the boss of the porters, that closed fraternity of tough, violent men who ran the ghetto transport system, many of whom had become smugglers. They sometimes gave to the poor too, and I knew that my father knew them.

"Martin," he said, "they're the worst of the ghetto."

I shrugged; did it matter what they were? I needed them, we

all needed them: my father, the children in Dr. Korczak's orphanage, and the people in the streets, the Hassidim who were praying, and the intellectuals who were printing the small underground newspapers which Pavel had shown me and which Pola handed out.

It was so dark that passersby were bumping into each other. The Germans had ordered a complete blackout and there was talk of war with Russia. My father and I were standing opposite a low building in Kozla Street.

"I'm going in," my father said. "Wait. I'll put in a word for you, but don't expect more than that. After that, I'll go."

I thanked him: it was my business and it was up to me to make the next move. I paused briefly in the yard, gripped by the icy wind, which had blown up again, and was whistling around the walls. My father called me.

"They're waiting for you."

He gave me a pat on the shoulder which meant, "Go on, my boy, go on, pull it off, go on, since you think you're doing right, go on."

In an almost empty apartment there were four of them, bull-necked and broad-shouldered, one with a large scar across one cheek, all four watching me as I came in. It was my day for the underworld all right, Jewish and Aryan.

"So you've come hunting on our ground, eh, kid?"

I didn't answer. I leaned against the wall and spoke: no high-sounding words here either, just zlotys, so many for each sack carried from the streetcar to my customers in the ghetto. They would have nothing to worry about: they just had to be there when the streetcar slowed down. I'd throw the bags to them. It was up to them to grab them quickly and clear out. It was their job. Later, I got to know their names; but Trisk the Cart, Yankle the Blind, Kive the Long and Chaim the Monkey didn't introduce themselves that evening. They listened to me, then discussed my prices and nodded agreement.

"You'll have your porters tomorrow," said Yankle the Blind. "But just for one day, to see how it goes. After that, it depends."

That was all I wanted: the wheels now merely had to turn. I went to see Pavel and Pola: they had the money. Everything was ready: Pavel would post himself on Zamenhofa Street, between Wolynska and Muranowska streets, and do the unloading in a straight line, but we'd move fast, the porters would only have to remove the sacks. I'd arrange with the driver to slow down.

I lay down on my bed without bothering to get undressed. I was exhausted, I felt sick; I'd smoked and drunk more than ever before, and on top of that I'd met a kind of men I couldn't even have imagined a few months earlier: Dziobak the Pox, Yankle the Blind, Mokotow the Tomb. I'd done business with them, clinked glasses of vodka with them. I dreamed of Yadia, clasping me to her breasts which must surely be round and full beneath her embroidered blouse. I was living in strange times: everything was possible. You could age ten years in an hour; a second's inattention and death would devour you. At the whim of an SS man fate placed in your way, you could be kicked to death. The words "possible" and "impossible" no longer had any meaning in Warsaw. I had to trust men named after prisons, I had to defy policemen embodying the law. Here I was, the son of a decent family from Senatorska Street, a smuggler, recruiting Rudy the Redhead and Mietek the Giant; I, Martin, whose mother, only a year earlier, was wiping his tears, I had become Mietek the Snip.

They were there at the agreed place. I recognized Mietek the Giant and Mokotow the Tomb, sitting in a doorway. Rudy was propped up against the wall a few yards further on, and Dziobak the Pox was on his own, smoking, smiling as usual.

"No wall for you," he said. "You keep moving."

I merely nodded by way of reply: I had to establish my hold on them that morning, the time for drinks and jokes was over. Now we were working. They gathered around me and I explained: the German police changed over every two hours, the Polish Blues every four hours, and the Jewish police every seven hours. They had to get to know which were the *graieks,* the "cooperators," the ones I could bribe. I'd deal with that, but they had to know about it. We set off under low, heavy clouds which threatened snow, Dziobak got out of breath, because I was setting a brisk pace.

"It's not a race, Bedouin," he said. "You'll kill us."

"You'll lose weight. You'll enjoy your drink more."

I went into more detail: I had some sacks. There were four waiting for me because I was late. We picked out the right streetcar. The Blue who jumped on the platform was "cooperating."

They then stood in front of the sacks, a wall.

I spoke a few words about the ghetto: they'd see. I'd throw off the sacks in Zamenhofa Street. If there were any Germans or policemen who refused to cooperate, nobody would be any the wiser. We wouldn't get off the streetcar.

"You're good little Poles, so death to the Bedouins!"

They laughed. I'd got them on my side, I knew what I wanted. That was my strength.

So we began, one trip, two trips, soon an entire routine. A routine in which you risked your life ten times a day, but it was still a routine. Sometimes we loaded a dozen sacks onto the platform, a ton of goods, an almost incredible volume. They formed a barrier of violence with their tough purposeful faces. The money came in: three times, four times the money I'd made before. I was paying the police, paying the porters, paying the driver, paying the conductor, I was even paying the Germans and I was paying Mietek and Mokotow, Rudy and Dziobak. It was always I who actually handed over the sacks in Zamenhofa Street. I watched Pavel directing the porters. Holding the sacks of grain, hoisting them with a jerk of the hips, feeling the soft warm grain, flour or sugar through the sacking: who could have guessed my joy, my pride? Because those sacks meant life for my people, for the ghetto. My men stood guard around me when I unloaded. It took no more than a few minutes. They were my troops, well paid; they drank, they stuffed themselves more than ever. Then they discovered the ghetto. They didn't say anything but I saw Mokotow give money to some beggars who approached the platform. They stopped talking about Bedouins.

Several times we had to fight other gangs. Mietek the Giant cracked skulls, and not only to fulfill his contract. Dziobak wanted to kill. Mokotow and I intervened.

"We must negotiate," I told Mokotow. "Brawls attract attention."

Dziobak the Pox stuck his knife in the table.

"They'll understand," he said.

I explained my concern and my plan: we had to associate with the best of the other gangs; if not, someone would denounce us to the Gestapo. If they refused, then possibly . . . I pointed to the knife. Mokotow went on a tour of the slums of Warsaw, and we gradually won over Zamek the Wise, a massive boxer with hammer fists, and his brother-in-law, Wacek the Peasant. Priceless Wacek: he was a genuine peasant who had turned up one day at Zamek's in Warsaw and who became a crook without even realizing it: to him, jobs in the city meant various kinds of robbery. Wacek the Peasant may have been a yokel but thanks to him we were able to buy our grain direct from the country. Sometimes we went and waited for him at the East Station in Praga, with a flat wagon drawn by two horses, and he'd turn up with some country lads: in a few minutes, in full view of the police, we'd load our sacks and take off. Then I had to take on Ptaszek the Bird, with the weak, sensitive face. It was better to have him with me than against me. He was a born informer. He'd gaze at me with his dewy eyes, talk in his syrupy voice, and I knew from Mietek the Giant that he was continually saying, "We don't need the Bedouins, we could do the same without the little Jew."

Mokotow beat him up several times but Ptaszek didn't even try to cover up or pretend that he was joking. I gave Rudy the Red the job of keeping an eye on him, but I often contemplated Dziobak the Pox's switch-blade knife.

I could only hold the loyalty of these men by what I gave them and by the respect they had for me, not through any fear I inspired. I was nothing. It was what I did, and I existed by what I obtained: they were well aware that a word would be enough for the Gestapo or the guards or the Poles, to seize me. One word and I'd disappear. I was careful not to play tough with my giants and crooks, who weren't averse to using their fists or knives. I had to control the gang through ingenuity, self-interest and friendship, not fear. I was the one who felt scared. Sometimes, when I dropped my act, reverted to my "old" manner, that gang sitting around me resembled a nightmare. I could barely look at Pila the

Saw. With low forehead, close-set eyes and weak chin, he had the typical criminal's face. He'd escaped from every prison in Poland. In his boot he carried a filed-down screwdriver, a narrow steel blade with a wooden handle. When Pila the Saw stood on the platform, arms folded, other passengers passed him and sat quietly inside the streetcar. Because of Mietek, Mokotow, Rudy, Dziobak, Wacek and Zamek, as well as Pila, there were never any troublemakers. If curious passersby began hanging around, Mokotow or Mietek would come up and gradually ease them inside, saying not a word.

I'd move in quietly among the passengers, "read" the paper, and observe what was happening on the platforms: would the Blue take money? Would the Germans get on? I gambled my life on every trip. But on every trip I tried to add to my trumps. I now looked like a real Polish tough, I wore the same clothes: the small white hat with the upturned brim and the long boots or *saperki*. My gold chain and Virgin Mary were visible through my open-necked shirt. I looked harmless behind my newspaper, harmless as any flashy kid. I cashed in on my youth. Once past the gate, as the surrounding ghetto began to reveal its open sores, I'd grow tense. Soon we'd be at the corner of Nalewki and Gesia streets, then the one at Gesia and Zamenhofa, then came the straightaway, the driver, a well-paid *graiek,* already slowing down. I'd lower my newspaper, see the corner of Wolynska Street: that was the moment. If I lost, my life was gone. I'd dash towards the platform. By now Mietek the Giant would have shoved off one sack: a heave, a porter in position, then another, another sack. Human lives were measured in seconds. Not a word: astonished bystanders looked on. One sack to go, Pavel would hand me the bags containing the money. The porters would disperse in the crowd, I'd see two big sacks of corn in a bicycle-taxi drawn by a young man with a shaven head. That lifeblood, all of it, my passion, my life in the balance for a bare few seconds. I'd go and sit down again, always at the mercy of any Pole who cared to denounce me; at the mercy of any Blue whom the Germans could suddenly terrorize into selling me; or at the mercy of more thorough checks.

But I was caught in my own machinery. Pavel, Pola, my father, of course my mother, and even Mokotow, all tried to confine my movements, restrict our crossings. Their words bounced off me: more than ever, crossing the wall, defying the butchers, making fools of them in my own eyes, had become my entire life. I was risking that life, but if I stopped hoisting those sacks of grain, the lifestream of the ghetto, I might as well be dead. To stop fighting in my own way, the way I'd worked out, would be to stop existing. So I crossed as often as ten times a day. The zlotys piled up. I handed them around, my father bought foreign currency. I changed them on the Aryan side, our profits soared. The ghetto's reception centers and Dr. Korczak's orphanage got their share.

In the evening, when I returned alone to the ghetto, they'd be waiting for me. Rubinstein the Clown would make faces for me, and the ragged children, their jackets held together by safety pins over naked flesh, would be there. The day after, in a week or a month, they'd be dead. I could read death in their eyes, and even if I saved those few children, there'd still be the crowd who gathered in front of the soup kitchens, who huddled by the curb: there'd still be tens of thousands starving in the ghetto. What more could I do? When I came home, as I went along Zamenhofa and then Mila Street, I'd groan with rage and despair. Yet they wanted me to stop! It would have been a crime to stop. And it would have been the end of me.

I hurled my sacks faster and faster, my movements became more and more restricted. In the streetcar, on guard, I worked out ways of perfecting my system, my organization. No one seemed to move fast enough, some of the porters were clumsy. Sometimes a sack would burst: grain everywhere. Passersby pounced on it, filling their pockets. I'd curse Pavel, Chaim the Monkey, Yankle the Blind, Trisk the Cart and Kive the Long. Not because of the lost goods, a few less zlotys didn't matter. I knew that not one grain would escape the children and the beggars, who would search the ground a hundred times, returning to the magic spot where a sack had broken. I cursed the porters because they could jeopardize everything. The Germans were never very far away.

One day, some visitors to the ghetto, soldiers on leave who came to watch us dying behind our wall began shouting. They had seen me holding my sacks: there were bullets. The porters vanished, some dropping their loads. I hesitated before jumping, a split second too long. The streetcar came to a halt. Two soldiers were already there, clutching revolvers, yelling, grabbing me. The streetcar moved off. I was caught. We soon reached the Dzika Street gate. Sentry boxes, police. The driver, a *graiek,* was taking it slowly as if giving me time to run away. How could I? There were four of them guarding me, insulting me. There were more shouts. I could see Mokotow the Tomb and Mietek the Giant fighting, then Dziobak the Pox waded in, with Rudy the Red, Pila the Saw and Wacek the Peasant; the Aryan passengers fell back on the platform. A woman was screaming. The driver braked again. The soldiers exchanged looks and shouted but the battle went on. A window was broken. They stopped watching me — a split second too long. I was already in the crowd and running down Niska Street. I waited a few hours, then joined Pavel, who'd managed to recover most of our sacks according to routine. I went out again. They were all at our meeting place in Dluga Street, laughing and drinking, and they greeted me with shouts. We downed some vodka: by now we had several weeks' work between us. We shared anecdotes, we shared a whole past. Today they'd saved me.

Mokotow took me aside: he had two new recruits for our gang. I trusted Mokotow the Tomb. A few days later I met Gutek and Brigitki the Card. Gutek, with his bullet head and short, fair hair, was a *Volksdeutscher:* on his left arm he wore a red swastika armband. But he'd been born in Warsaw, had grown up among the Jews in the Smocza area, all crooks of some sort. He spoke Yiddish, he was a gangster with a choirboy's face, a handsome Aryan youth who loathed the Germans. Gutek was Mokotow's first brainchild. Gutek took over the platform with his resplendent armband, his Nazi-style good looks, and acted as guide to soldiers on leave. He insulted the mass of Jews, mocked the old men and the rabbis with their beards and skullcaps; the soldiers would cluster around him, he'd name the streets, point to women and crack dirty jokes, and while the soldiers were leaning out one side of the streetcar laughing, I was holding out my bags from the rear platform. Sometimes Gutek even got himself invited for a drink, then when he came back to our haunt on Dluga Street, he'd spit with disgust and we'd console him.

Brigitki the Card was Mokotow's second brainchild. Brigitki was frail, diminutive, a creature with long hands and tapering fingers. Alongside Mietek the Giant or Pila the Saw, he disappeared, tiny, insignificant. Yet he'd escaped from Lvov Prison. After a few days I got to know the extent of his talents and contacts. Thanks to him and heavy spending, I had all the papers, all the armbands one could use. I had a United States passport, some Latin American passports, and I also had papers proving that I was a young Polish Aryan. But Brigitki the Card's triumph was presenting me with a *Volksdeutscher* armband and papers proving that I was Klaus Schmidt.

I became an impersonator and a conjurer: when Polish policemen were near, I dropped my guise of street tough. From a small, flat metal case in my left pocket, I took my swastika armband, which always had to be clean and neatly pressed. I slipped my armband onto my left arm: I was Schmidt, arrogant, bored and supercilious, talking Polish with a German accent. The Blues, the Polish police who maltreated Jews in public, hardly dared check on me. A few hundred yards further on, I had to become a hoodlum again. Hastily removing my *Volksdeutscher* armband, I adopted the casual swagger of a Warsaw teen-ager. Then, past the gate, if I jumped from the streetcar in the ghetto, I had to display my Jewish armband, which I kept in my right pocket. Thus, several times a day, I'd change my face, name, personality and language, but I always had to remain on guard, observing how I acted the *Volksdeutscher* or the hoodlum, and also keeping an eye on the enemy to decide what I'd have to do before he did. So I learned to have a dual, even triple, personality, as if I were in front of a mirror, acting and watching myself act. I was speaking and listening to myself. I was making gestures, and yet I was already somewhere else preparing others. Often, when I saw something, I had to pretend I hadn't noticed it. Only by such devices I survived.

Sometimes we all stayed in the ghetto at night, in spite of the curfew. I'd regale my gang with drinks, food and laughter. We'd shut ourselves in the Café Sztuka at 2 Leszno Street, and there in the smoke, singing away, we'd drink and fill our bellies. There were pretty girls to serve us. We'd rub shoulders with pushers, with the Leszno Street Thirteen, with Kohn and Heller's agents, with Gestapo informers, with collaborators, with smugglers like ourselves — as well as with the bakers, the princes in our prison. Eating and drinking: this was the great scandalous luxury of our privileged world. Sometimes I got drunk, but deep down my thoughts remained clear as a mountain stream. I got caught once in a raid one evening in the Café Sztuka: the Germans carted us off, made us strip, and mixed us in with some rabbis on their way to their *Mikva,* their Friday evening bath. The Germans herded us all together, men and women, and filmed us, their laughter echoing in my head. Now, even when drunk, I kept on guard.

Yet I had to drink with Dziobak the Pox, clink glasses with Ptaszek the Bird who was after my skin. And when we left the Café Sztuka, the Restaurant Gertner or the Café Negresco, our bellies full; whether Rudy the Red or Mietek the Giant was staggering over the snow covering Leszno Street; whether or not I was thinking of the oranges and bananas we had just eaten, in order to survive I had to see but not see the children in rags, the beggars who emerged from the shadows and put out their hands, uttering their tragic cry: "Have pity, Jewish heart."

To see such things and yet carry on as if you hadn't! Such was my life, always being two or three people. I could only keep going because I was defying the butchers. But to remain alive in that never-ending game in which the rules changed without warning, you not only had to stay on guard, own false papers, mobilize friends and accomplices, you also needed luck. The luck that gave you an easygoing German soldier, that left you an open door when you were trapped. But luck, in those days, was fickle, touchy: sometimes it allowed you only a fraction of a second. You had to make an on-the-spot decision or die. It never came a second time. Often you had to push your luck, even bet that it would come, and you had to wait for it as you were being beaten, silent, hoping. Sometimes it turned up just as everything seemed lost. Then you had to find the strength to dart forward and grasp it: you could not whisper, "I'm covered with blood, wait, I need a few minutes to get my breath back." Too late, the chance would have flown. You would die. I was young, observant, and I often pushed my luck and grabbed it. But sometimes it was a long time coming.

There was the morning the Polish police caught me on the Marszalkowska. I was alone. A mistake. Already, on several occasions, the arrival of Mietek the Giant, Pila the Saw and the rest had been enough to stall the Blues. That day they frisked me, found my armbands, and more important, my foreign currency, the dollars I was bringing across for my father. They bundled me into a corner of their van and divided the loot. The police, like the jackals, had it in for the Bedouins, too.

"What are we going to do with you, Jew?"

The big one gave me a kick in the ribs. They held a discussion: they'd robbed me, so I would be a problem. They weren't sure about handing me over to their superiors. Their only choice was between the Gestapo and the Jewish police.

Engine running, the driver looked inquiringly at the other three. They were remembering my *Volksdeutscher* armband, my Jewish armband and my foreign currency. They were baffled. They chose the easiest way out: the Jewish police, in the ghetto, on Gesia Street. They could have killed me. I'd won the first round. There were plenty to come. The police shoved me into a cell already crammed with about thirty wretches. I was beaten. In one corner an old man was praying. I was mad with rage: I was a prisoner of Jews and earmarked for the Gestapo because from time to time the Germans rounded up the prisoners or asked the Jewish Council to hand over several hundred workers; and Czerniakow, the president of the Jewish Council, collected workers from the prisons. From day to day everyone in that cell was sent to work camps, from which there was no return.

So I yelled, banged on the door, and when the guards came in with their clubs, I hurled myself at them, grabbed one by the neck, and while he was pounding me, I murmured "Zlotys, Pavel, and 23 Mila Street." They had to know outside where I was. The guards left me on the ground, covered with bruises. The Jewish police didn't pull their punches! I waited: I'd gambled, pushed my luck. Three days later I left the Gesia Street Prison: it had cost my father plenty. I left prison in the morning, as soon as curfew was over. Late that afternoon the Germans came for the prisoners. From the end of Gesia Street, the crowd watched them clamber into covered trucks. It was common knowledge they'd never be seen again.

"You were lucky," said Pavel.

He didn't want me to start again straightaway, but he'd more or less given up trying to make me see reason. The sight of that Jewish prison had disgusted me, had roused me still more. I held nothing against those policemen with their jackboots and their badges, aping the Aryan police. They were helping the butchers in the hope that they could soften their blows, escape themselves and, in the case of the best of them, even protect us. I'd seen them beaten by the Germans, forced to hop on one leg for hours, to play "frogs" in the street; forbidden to come within fifty yards of an Aryan policeman. Like us, they were condemned. Why resent them? Some of them no doubt had the souls of informers or butchers, but most of them were victims like the rest of us. The guilty ones were those who'd given orders to build the wall, who were killing us and starving us. They were the ones we had to fight. So I started again.

At first all went well. Several times a day I went to Aryan Warsaw, with its broad, clean, quiet streets; and back to the ghetto, with its filth, its crowds, its poverty, its rag-and-bone men shouting, "If you want to buy a rag, buy a new one."

Then fresh difficulties arose. A law banned the sale of goods to Jews, the penalty, a fine of a thousand zlotys: prices rose, dealers got scarcer. Patrols and checks were stepped up: the game got tougher. The stakes were rising.

While I was surrounded by my wall of thugs, my Mieteks and Mokotows, and while I was throwing my sacks to the porters, I hardly had time to think; but in the evening just before curfew, I made my last journey alone. I wanted to sleep in the ghetto: because of my mother, and because of Pola, whom I used to join in our hideout in the attic. Then too it was a kind of defiance or bravado to come back, with a box of cakes from Gogolewski's cake shop for my brothers, a way of showing my contempt for the butchers and of affirming my freedom. What's a life without bravado and defiance?

I was on the platform of the second car, enjoying the keen air. In the ghetto I felt suffocated: the gray walls and the stench of garbage and that bustling mass of people. The streetcar stopped at the gate, briefly. I barely gave it a thought: routine. The Polish policeman on duty on the streetcar was a *graiek,* a regular "cooperater" who earned far more from me than he'd ever dreamed. I glanced up at the soldier moving along the aisle, the soldier with the fresh, pink complexion, his cap hard down on his head; and recognized him by the long holster almost in the middle of his belly. It was "Frankenstein." He'd been seen one day in Dzielna Street, rushing along, clutching a revolver. He fired a shot, killing a man. Then he pulled out a notebook, scribbled in it; started running again, aimed, fired, killed another man. Then he walked calmly away, back to sentry duty at the ghetto entrance. Every day, it was said, he left five or six random victims dead. He was in front of me. He spoke in German.

"What are you doing there, Jew?"

I smiled, I felt a wound opening up inside me. I shook my head, I hadn't understood.

"What are you doing there, Jew?"

I looked him straight in the eyes and thought, "Keep calm, keep calm, Martin."

On the platform with me was a well-dressed man whom I'd noticed because he was wearing light-colored gloves similar to those my father had once manufactured, before the inferno.

"It's quite obvious he's not a Jew," the man said with a strong Polish accent.

Frankenstein kept staring at me. I shrugged, looking at the man.

"You know, he thinks you're a Jew," the man told me in Polish.

Frankenstein didn't flick an eye: his physical presence was crushing me. I shook my head, addressing both Frankenstein and the Pole casually, "That's a good one. I was taken for a Jew before. Two days ago."

Frankenstein took a step back.

"You're lucky you're not a Jew."

He jumped down from the streetcar, giving the leather bell pull a sharp tug. I was sweating all over, ice cold. The man started talking to me. The streetcar kept moving, Gesia, Zamenhofa. I didn't dare jump. Perhaps he was a Gestapo agent. Frankenstein's sudden appearance had made me nervous. I got off outside the ghetto and waited for a streetcar going the other way. I felt the squeeze was on. The Blue refused my zlotys, so I sat down, removing my white hat and overcoat. Frankenstein might board the streetcar again. My life would hang on a thread, the chance that he wouldn't see me. I was near the door, gripping the switch-blade knife Dziobak the Pox gave me, a white knife with tapered blade. The streetcar braked sharply, in the middle of Dzika, not far from Mila Street, where I should have been with Pola, loosening her fair hair, letting her stroke my face. *He* got on again and his boot almost brushed against my foot: all he had to do was look down. But he must have been looking straight ahead as he passed by. I saw his back, trench coat nipped in by his heavy belt. Once again I was outside the ghetto, alive, exhausted, wandering through Krasinski Gardens, hating myself for my carelessness, hearing Pavel's voice, Pola's and my father's lectures: knowing that my mother would cry all night, convinced that I'd been caught. That I was dead.

I hacked at the frozen earth: what an inhuman time, and yet man claimed to be man. We wolves, jackals, hounds! Frankenstein would be asleep now; he would surely have found his Jew. But when would *we* have guns, when could *we* yell battle cries? When could we avenge our dead?

I met Mokotow the Tomb at the Dluga Street café. He was rather quiet, there was a bottle of vodka in front of him, but his glass was full. I flopped down beside him, it was good to feel my arm against his.

"What's up, Martin?" he said coolly.

He pushed his glass over to me. I downed the vodka at a gulp, then we sat side by side, in silence.

"You're living at 23 Mila Street, right?" he asked.

I didn't speak but it was nice wanting to cry. He got up.

"I hope my ugly face won't frighten your mother," Mokotow remarked, and set off into the night.

I drank, then Yadia came. She had a small, warm room, with a stove into which she stuffed bits of wood. From time to time she got up and poked the fire, I watched her white skin, her broad hips turning pink. Then she'd lie down beside me again, tender and ardent, clasping me gently, rocking me and humming in an uncharacteristically solemn way.

I started again the next day, but things went badly. Ptaszek the Bird wasn't at the meeting place: Ptaszek had flown and for nearly a week Mietek the Giant and Mokotow scoured the Warsaw cafés for him without success.

"We'll have to be careful," said Mokotow.

But it was just one among many dangers and we had to keep going. So we kept on, throwing off sacks, paying the Blues. In the evenings I'd see Rubinstein the Clown, a little thinner, pulling a few more faces, and the children, rarely the same ones but all looking alike, struggling as best they could to survive a week or a month longer. It was the end of the winter and each of them was hoping to hang on till the sunshine: then there'd be one less enemy, the cold. But it was a bad time all right.

The streetcar stopped three stations before the ghetto and the Polish police leaped on the platform before we could make a move: without hesitating, they unloaded the sacks, shoving Pila the Saw, Wacek the Peasant, Mokotow and myself out onto the slippery road.

"The Bird," muttered Mokotow before he fell.

He was lying on the ground, bellowing as if he'd broken his leg. A roar from Pila the Saw as he ran away. Then Mokotow jumped up and dashed off. The Blues were yelling, charging in every direction and belting us. They took us off to the police station, where they searched us and insulted us.

"Are you the Jew?"

A German policeman had come in, I hadn't noticed him. It was obvious we'd been betrayed.

Wacek the Peasant got up without a word, as if he'd never seen me, but I trusted him, as well as Mokotow, Mietek and Pila. They were the ones I counted on. The German policeman looked as if he were a man, two eyes, a nose, an expression and gray hair. He didn't even question me, but started to slap my face: it was my first real beating; not yet actual torture. He slapped me on the mouth, nose, eyes. He slapped me hard with huge, thick hands, then brought me to my feet with a punch on the jaw, one in the kidneys, and doubled me up with a kick in the stomach. I fell to the ground: that was how my red-haired friend had died, for a few herrings. I did better than he and I knew by now that you could defeat the butchers; I was beating them every day. I'd done everything but watch them die. But I wasn't yet used to interrogations: I was far too concerned about well-aimed blows. I now knew that it took more than that to kill a man. "I haven't watched them die," I thought, and mustered my strength, shielding my head as best I could.

"To the Gestapo," said the German policeman.

I was dragged to an icy cell: bent double, trying to peer through swollen eyes, I waited. Mokotow and Mietek, Pila and Wacek wouldn't leave me here. I kept saying the words over to myself. The policemen carried me to the van. As they were about to sling me on the floor, I saw Marie, in her big fur coat: she approached slowly, not looking at me, but said, "Mokotow's here. He sent me."

Marie . . . I could see her long fair hair. Sometimes, when I went to visit Mokotow in Praga, she'd be sitting there, with a semi-ironic look on her face. She'd be praying and her brother would tease her.

"If you weren't a Jew," he'd say, "my sister would marry you."

She didn't protest but kept looking at me.

"But the Jews killed Christ. Did you know that, Martin?"

The van gathered speed, then braked hard. There was cursing, and Mietek the Giant dragged me out by my feet and flung me across his shoulder, jolting me as he ran. We regrouped in the Dluga Street café: they laid me on Yadia's bed. My eyes almost closed by my beating, I could barely see them in the little room.

"It was Ptaszek the Bird all right," said Dziobak the Pox.

Then Yadia came in and they left me: she didn't say a word as she went over to the stove to dip a handkerchief in some warm water to bathe my face. Then I slept. Mokotow came.

"You'd better get back to the ghetto. We'll go this evening. On the last streetcar, just you and me."

There were no snags: I made out I was a drunken Pole, between Mokotow and Mietek, who were laughing and shoving each other. At 23 Mila Street, they walked me up, because I couldn't have managed the stairs alone, but didn't knock.

"We'll leave you," said Mietek the Giant. "We'll drink to your health."

I leaned on the door, rapping gently; it hurt to raise my arm. Finally they came, and my mother clasped me to her.

"I've been very lucky, Mother," I muttered.

Luck. It deserted me, betrayed me, and then, stricken with remorse, returned again. But my parents didn't share the trust in it which I retained in my heart. My father, cautious, never slept at Mila Street, not wanting to risk an arrest aimed at me, a common smuggler, while he was taking on heavier and heavier political responsibilities, which he told me nothing about. But he had been tipped off by Pavel and he was there. I dozed, my mother kept tearful watch over me, reviling the men who picked on children. I could have spared her unnecessary suffering by showing a little kindness in the evenings. She'd realize soon enough that the butchers intended to send us all to our deaths. I recognized the way my father breathed when he was angry, in jerks. He stood at the foot of the bed, his arms folded.

"Martin," he said, "this time it's the finish. I've made up my mind, and I'm sticking to it."

He asked my mother to leave, closed the door and, still standing, his arms folded, talked about the Gestapo and their tortures. I was a child, I'd fought hard, helped the ghetto, my family, now I'd done enough. He had obligations towards me, and he asked

me never again to cross the wall without his permission. My eyes
and stomach hurt, I moved with difficulty, but I shook my head.
No, I couldn't.

"You're not to leave here again, Martin."

That night I managed to sleep. In the morning I felt much better: I could open my eyelids and see. Youth is the best cure of all.
But when I tried to open the door I found that it was padlocked.
I grew angrier by the hour. My mother passed me a letter from
my father under the door: he explained that he was waiting for
my promise. Until then I'd be fed through the window. At meal-
times I was lowered a basket of food from the apartment above.
My mother lectured me through the door. A day went by, then
two more; on the fourth, when I'd gotten back all my strength, I
went mad, fighting mad. Mokotow hailed me from the street.
Pavel explained that everything was going badly: the gang was
breaking up. Rudy the Red and Dziobak the Pox were fighting.
Pila the Saw and Brigitki the Card wanted to start their own firm.
All were drinking to excess. Mietek the Giant, Zamek the Wise
and Wacek the Peasant were planning to go back to chasing
"cats" and "Bedouins," who crossed the wall. "It's thirsty work,"
said Mietek. Mokotow was waiting loyally but warned Pavel that
he wanted to get cracking. I tried to come to terms with my parents, explaining I was becoming a laughingstock to the gang. Father didn't want to hear about it. I was in danger of death, he was
protecting me from myself. I insulted him for the first and last
time in my life, then sat down in a corner of the room. What was
the point of yelling? My father thought he was right, why hold it
against him? I had a wall, a new wall in front of me: as I wasn't
prepared to live without crossing it, I had to get around it, if I
could.

I started ripping up curtains, sheets and blankets; I braided
and knotted away. The rope looked strong. I pushed the bed near
the window. It was an old bed with convoluted legs, a heavy bed:
I attached my rope to it. It reached down one floor, we lived on
the third. I tied the rope to my thigh for safety: I wanted to succeed, not kill myself. I carefully inched my way down. When I
reached the second floor, I kicked in the window of an apartment.

I'd made it. I opened the door. Dr. Celmajster and his wife were finishing lunch.

"Good day, Mrs. Celmajster, good day, Doctor, do you recognize me?"

"They were rooted to their seats, petrified.

"Just passing through."

By then I was out the door. As I went downstairs, I had a good laugh as I repeated my greeting: "Good day, Mrs. Celmajster, good day, Doctor." I'd just made my final break with paternal authority. My father and I had to be equals now: I'd assumed equal responsibilities in defiance of him. A few days later, when I started crossing the wall again, we met at the Café Sztuka, like two friends who respected and liked each other. Mokotow the Tomb was waiting for me in the street: his presence gave me strength.

"Don't come here too often," my father said, "they're going to step up their raids. I had it from a reliable source."

We ordered vodka and clinked glasses.

"You could stay in the house," he said.

I sipped my drink.

"Of course, you'll be free, quite free to do what you want."

That same evening, I went back to Mila Street. As I kissed my mother I lifted her up; she was laughing; then I parted my two brothers who were squabbling over the chocolates I'd brought back from the other side.

Once again the days went by without any emergencies: only the constant threat of death and the sight of it in the streets. In Bonifraterska Street, on the outskirts of the ghetto, I saw a small boy, my brother's age, about ten, running along with a sack of potatoes on his back: a policeman caught him and shook him, gripping him as a farmer would an animal. He drew his sheath knife and stabbed him in the face: possibly he was trying to cut his throat, but the boy kept struggling. He ran off, clutching his bleeding forehead, then tottered and fell flat on the pavement. A woman came out, hurried over to the potatoes and began to pick them up. The policeman raised his gun and fired: a second body lay on the pavement.

I hurried on. What could you do? Clench your fists? Pinkert's men went by more and more frequently, pushing their cartloads of emaciated bodies. But Pinkert had also opened up a branch in Smocza Street, where he advertised expensive funerals: for twelve zlotys you could have undertakers in uniform. But we were dying too quickly for burials, we were being hounded like dangerous animals. When I was in Aryan Warsaw, I sometimes tried, in spite of the danger, to tear down the large posters showing a hideous Jew with a louse-ridden beard. "Jew-louse-typhoid," it said. We were germ carriers, vermin. So they disinfected us. It was our new torture, after the raids, cold, hunger and death. We were forced into freezing or scalding baths.

I worked with loathing. I locked myself up in my rage. How could you not hate those unconcerned Poles who strolled along the Marszalkowska? I could stomach only my gang of toughs, outlaws like myself. When my father asked me to take a message to Professor Hulewitz, near Nowy Swiat Street, I shrugged.

"He's helping us," he said.

I didn't answer. Who was helping us? The whole world was letting us die. Calmly, Father explained about the Polish resistance, its aims and its several branches. I went along to Professor Hulewitz's.

Luck again: the Professor was away, and that was how I met Zofia.

For months I'd been living with Dziobak the Pox and Pila the Saw, Brigitki the Card and Mietek the Giant. I'd been sleeping with Yadia. Men like them changed women more often than shirts. And Yadia was warmhearted, to anyone who didn't beat her too much. I had a sort of physical affection for Pola in our Mila Street hideout: we felt the need to reassure our bodies while the ghetto was silent. With the example of the men in my gang, and with my relationship with Yadia and Pola, I had no idea what love was when I met Zofia.

Then, looking at her, I began to laugh, easily, as if my muscles were relaxing, as if I were getting into a warm bath after feeling really tired, as if I were stretching out, rested, clean and new. She laughed back and we talked; not about the ghetto or the war, but about the old days, about the banks of the Vistula, about a circus which had come to Warsaw, in the square of the old town, probably in 1938.

"Theater Square," she recalled.

She showed me her books and a photograph of her father, a cavalry officer, now a Russian prisoner.

"We've only had one letter," she said.

Her mother had died during the siege of Warsaw, then she lived with her uncle, Professor Hulewitz. I was distraught at not being able to do anything for her, to get her father back; even embarrassed to admit that my own people were alive. We switched to more cheerful things. I talked about my mother, and as Zofia had never tasted a cholent, my mother would make her one. In the evening, when I left her, when I said, "See you tomorrow, Zofia, if I can make it," I couldn't have said when I first met her. It was as if she were part of my childhood, as if we'd always known each other, as if she'd been there in the old photos between my brothers, alongside my mother, smiling, in our house.

At that time you had to do things whenever you could: for about ten days we met regularly. Before returning to the ghetto, I'd go to her place and we'd talk and laugh. Then she came with me into the inferno. Maybe because there was the first sunshine of March, maybe because we'd stopped seeing horrible things, I felt that the ghetto wasn't as sinister as usual. We went to the theater, it was *The Miser*. Zofia laughed because they'd deliberately left out Molière on the poster, giving only the name of the Jewish translator: we weren't allowed to see plays by Aryan writers. Then we walked along the banks of the Vistula, lingered on Poniatowski Bridge: a few hours stolen from my rounds, which I made up by moving even faster.

"Yes," she said, "I feel I've always known you too."

She talked about her father, a strict Catholic.

"But not anti-Semitic. You'll see."

We went back to the ghetto, to the Eldorado Theater. I explained to her why everyone in the place laughed when a head popped out of the wings and asked nervously, "Everything all right?" It was the catchword of the ghetto streets, the question which passersby asked before they went anywhere, in case Frankenstein was tearing along, revolver in hand, or in case the Germans were rounding people up for the camps, the baths, or death.

"It's got to end," she said.

I was sure it would too, I was overjoyed listening to her, watching her toss back her fair hair which hung in ringlets down the back of her neck. She was the first woman whose hand I'd held, and we walked along swinging arms as if the war had never existed, as if I'd never been a Jew, as if the butchers weren't masters in Warsaw. We could dispose of the future as if it were our own.

The last time I saw her, Zofia said, "Perhaps when two people feel as if they've always known each other, it's true love."

We had never even kissed and we didn't kiss that evening.

It was a remorseless time: what you didn't take, you didn't get. There weren't any reprieves.

During the night of March 14 — there are dates you remember — my father knocked at my door: he now wanted to show that I was independent. He stood in the doorway.

"Be very careful tomorrow," he said. "They're on the warpath."

Why had he awakened me to say that? I was always careful.

"The Polish resistance has shot Igo Sym," he explained. "They're arresting the artists and intellectuals, making raids."

What did I care about Igo Sym, an actor who'd collaborated? We knew what the butchers did by way of reprisals, so perhaps if they were busy tormenting Aryan Warsaw, we'd get a breather.

"They've arrested Professor Hulewitz and his niece."

He shut the door. "It's got to end," Zofia had said. All I knew was the softness of her touch, and that we talked as if we'd always lived together. I lay there, motionless, in the dark. It was as if someone had slashed me open from head to foot and was doing it over and over again. There was nothing to be done that night: maybe the next day. Probably they'd shut them up in Pawiak Prison, in the ghetto. I could imagine the cell and Siwy saying, "You always wind up in Pawiak," Siwy who'd jumped from the cattle car before me. Then there'd been the parade in the yard, the SS, Himmler perhaps, and the black-bearded professor: "I'm not a traitor, I swear." Zofia was in Pawiak, and there I was,

BEFORE THE INFERNO

I can remember almost nothing of the fourteen years that came before, those years of childhood.

Martin (right) with his governess and one of his brothers

With his two brothers in Warsaw

SURVIVAL

September 1939: the Germans enter Warsaw. "They were everywhere. They were marching in serried ranks . . . slowly. They seemed invincible with their long black bayonets." PHOTOS BY U.S.I.S., KARCH. E.R.L.

"We wore armbands with the Star of David. They searched us in the streets, humiliated us . . ."

The building of the ghetto wall. At the foot of the wall, a small boy, one of the ghetto's young smugglers. PHOTOS BY U.S.I.S. AND E.D.J.C., ZIDOWSKI HISTORIC INSTITUTE

". . . the horrors of the streets and the suffering and the cold and children begging. Death was everywhere."
PHOTOS BY U.S.I.S. AND C.D.J.C.

being hacked, rent in two by that intolerable pain, worse than any beating. We were earmarked for death, that was the fate they had in store for us. Now I was sure of it. They were taking Zofia, my respite in our torment, from me: they were depriving me of her laughter, her gentleness, all that she'd revealed to me: a real life in which men would cease to be wolves. I lay there till morning, tense, unable even to recall the hours we'd spent together. I was pledged to revolt: Zofia, when will our battle cry ring out? Zofia, when shall we avenge ourselves?

We did everything possible to save them. The Polish police, my Warsaw gang and even the prison warders. No good: the hostages were hidden away in Pawiak and I lost hope. Every night I strolled around the quarter, if only to take one more risk for Zofia: I wandered down Pawia Street, Smocza, Dzielna, and Karmelicka. I'd squared the square. I was back where I'd started. All I could do was go home or drink. So I drank in one of the ghetto nightclubs.

Outside the Casanova, in Leszno Street, Rubinstein the Clown bowed to me and said, "We're all equal in the ghetto, all equal."

He gave a shrill laugh and added, "If they melt down the big fat ones, we'll have butter."

He made a face, then went off, repeating, "We're all equal . . ."

I could hear his cry fading away in the streets.

Mokotow the Tomb was the only one who knew. He barely left my side: we drank together but I never got drunk. I drank the way you take a cure, to try and get rid of the coldness within. It made me feel tense, knotted up. We waited day after day, then we heard that they'd all been shot. They'd only spent a few days in Pawiak. I'd circled the prison for nothing.

That day, it must have been in April, was beautiful. I went into the little ghetto, crossing the wooden bridge over Chlodna Street which had remained Aryan. I had to get away from Mila Street, as far away as possible. I made a careful check of the stairs, landings and cellars. It took a long time. Around Sienna and Twarda streets I examined the buildings, noted the positions of yards, then lay in ambush at the junction. Now and then, German soldiers, guarding the gate, walked up to it, rifles ready, invincible, lion tamers venturing into a cage. I waited. Finally the sound of boots on pavement: I saw the soldier's shadow. Clutching the knife Dziobak the Pox had given me, I sprang forward. But a woman I hadn't seen bumped into me. I slipped, dropping the knife. The soldier was yelling, *"Halt!"* I had to flee down Sliska Street. I could hear him running. He fired. I fell into a courtyard. He was on my track.

"Out you come, Jew!" he yelled.

I crept over to a stairwell leading to the cellars. I waited. Once again I saw his shadow. He was wearing a helmet. He was encased in leather and steel and seemed enormous. He inched forward and I sprang for his neck. I gripped him, squeezing with all my might, but he spun me around without even losing his balance. I felt his rifle butt in my left eye. My head seemed to explode but I kept squeezing and he finally fell to his knees, dropping his gun to try and free my hands. I kept squeezing but I could hardly see for blood, my blood. I took off across the yard, raced back along Sliska Street, heading for the bridge. My face swollen, I couldn't open my left eye. I reached Mila Street. The pain was good: it burned away the cold, and for the first time since I lost Zofia I felt life flowing back into me, surging, violent, full of hate. I'd held that neck, his helmet had cut my nose, but I'd squeezed and clawed away and the butcher had dropped to his knees. I was alive again. The cost was high. I'd lost my left eye.

Dr. Celmajster cleaned the wound. He examined the damage to the eyebrow ridge and pupil. Perhaps I'd still see shadows. But for all practical purposes I had only one eye from now on.

"It's your most precious possession, Martin," he said. "Look after it."

Dr. Celmajster came every day and, thanks to him, I healed quickly. On his final visit, he repeated his advice: he was talking about my remaining eye but I sensed that he wanted to say something else, talk about me.

On his way out, almost timidly, he said, "And look after yourself, Martin, right to the end. We only have life, and you, you young folk, are our life. Look after yourself."

When I was able to go out, get going again, I found we'd reached new depths in the inferno. We were no longer dying of cold, and yet more were dying: every day, people who'd starved to death were picked up in the streets; every day there were killings. Raid followed raid: people no longer dared go out but took to their cellars. I saw corpses, stripped of their clothes, lying in the streets, on the pavements. Karmelicka Street, near Pawiak Prison, had become, according to the ragged street children, "the forge of death." Hopes which my father had inspired in me of seeing the war come to a speedy end gradually vanished. The Germans were triumphant everywhere, in Yugoslavia, in Greece, and now they were driving across the plains of Russia: rumor had it that they'd killed all the Jews in Kiev. There was talk of *Einsatzgruppen,* of extermination squads with the task of liquidating the Jews. Yet, in Warsaw, our numbers increased: refugees amassed behind our walls, starving, destitute, desperate, describing the horrors they'd experienced. In the streets I passed a wretched, disheveled woman calling out a child's name: on the train to Warsaw her child had annoyed an officer, who proceeded to throw it on the track. The mother had tried to jump off but the guard had threatened to kill all the Jews in the car. By the time she'd reached Warsaw, she'd gone mad and was rushing about the streets. We were all gradually going mad! In the yard in Mila Street, I saw children tickling a corpse which had been taken there to await Pinkert's men.

I was still crossing the wall, but it was more and more difficult, more and more risky: the death penalty had been officially established for those who secretly crossed in and out of the stronghold of the ghetto. But I carried on: there were more children in the street, more wretched than ever. Some were barely three or four years old. I contributed to the *Centos* fund which tried to feed them, but who read the *Centos* posters which appealed for help? "Our children must live," they pleaded. But who could save so many children? Selfishness, corruption, indifference and impotence were our lot. Posters announced that eight Jews had been executed at the Jewish police prison in Gesia Street, the prison where I'd spent several days; it was run by Poles. Those people had died for not being able to pay a fine. A woman had been executed for a hundred zlotys, and yet the Café Meril, a few streets away, organized a dancing competition with a first prize of two thousand zlotys.

The butchers were trying to kill off pity among too many of us. They were trying to make us like the image they'd created of us. After that, they'd liquidate us.

When it first began to snow, they cut off the gas and electricity and reduced food supplies. In the streets, barefoot in the snow, the children could hardly put out their hands. At the corner of Leszno and Karmelicka streets, I heard their whimpers: deserted, orphaned, lost, they gathered to die.

How could I stop trying to cross the wall again and again? The street cars had stopped running. But I'd been expecting the decision for a long time, and was ready for it.

I summoned Mokotow the Tomb, Mietek the Giant, Zamek the Wise and the rest of them to the Dluga Street café. They'd got used to the streetcars, the easy pickings, the all-night drinking sessions, as well as the ghetto prostitutes.

"That's it, Mietek the Snip," said Dziobak the Pox. "Hide with your bank notes in Lvov or Warsaw. Pretend you're dead."

"You can hide, I promise you," said Wacek the Peasant. "I'll find you a farm near where I live, you can work, pay a bit, you'll pass for a peasant."

"They won't be here forever," said Zamek the Wise.

I listened to them: they really quite liked me.

"We'll start with Kozla Street," I said.

"Stubborn Bedouin!" said Dziobak.

Mokotow began to laugh happily.

"You're the one who pays, who takes the risks. You have to decide," Dziobak concluded.

Kozla Street, a ghetto block, looked onto Freta Street, on the Aryan side. The Germans had fixed narrow wire mesh across every exit, air vent and window. But we linked hundreds of funnels together, with necks the width of a nail which went through the mesh: I would shove all the funnels simultaneously against the mesh, they held, and we would empty the milk and sacks of grain which Trisk the Cart and Chaim the Monkey's porters then collected in Kozla Street.

Or at night, after curfew, we would drive a truck up to the ghetto wall. I chose the corner furthest from the gate in Parysowski Square; the Blues got a big rake-off. On the other side of the wall, in the ghetto, Pavel was waiting: we raised our ladders, and in the raw darkness of the Polish winter, in a few minutes, in total silence, we transferred our sacks. I sat astride the wall, on a plank which protected me from the fragments of glass embedded in the cement. As usual, I was keeping watch myself, they were my goods and it was my ghetto. Sometimes a patrol of German police would come on the scene, they'd fire, yell, I'd leap down, there would be yells, wounded men, the yellow flashes of rifle shots, and the goods which you had to try and remove. The goods were precious, they were worth men's lives, they were life itself. One night I had to go down a sewer near Parysowski Square, and hide there a whole day, but I saved two sacks of grain. So I turned up, filthy and stinking, at the Dluga Street café, dragging my sacks, to looks of astonishment from the men busy drinking.

"You can't kill Mietek the Cat," said Brigitki the Card.

It was true, I didn't want to get killed.

Pavel, Trisk the Cart, Chaim the Monkey and Yankle the Blind were controlling operations from the ghetto side. Oddly enough the telephone between the ghetto and Aryan Warsaw was still functioning. It was Pavel's weapon and mine. We didn't waste words.

"Which *meta* is cooperating?"

Meta meant the section of the wall where we were to operate, where the Blues would play along for an hour or two. Pavel had already paid them and he had also paid the gang of thugs who controlled the entire wall, underground customs men for smugglers; the rate was fixed by the sack and it was no good cheating. Pila the Saw and Mietek the Giant were flanking me, so that I couldn't be taken for a ride and hijacked.

Our truck would be standing ready in a shed, sometimes at the far end of Warsaw, near the East Station. The phone would ring, it was Pavel. I'd signal to someone to start the engine while I asked, "Which *meta* is cooperating?"

I'd race off and open the shed doors, cling to the frame, and clamber on top of the goods to join Mietek and Mokotow. We'd drive along prepared routes, without headlights, avoiding road-blocks. The lookouts, the "minders," would inform us, along the way, that the road was clear. The air made our faces smart and we had to cling with frozen fingers to the sacks as they rolled about. We'd drive on as if going in to attack, and our thrust would be made with all the precision of an assault: if we arrived too late, our *meta* would have stopped cooperating, other Blues would be there, ready to shoot us. I'd give my orders with hand signals and sometimes, in a few minutes, I'd have a few dozen sacks, more precious than gold bars, across the wall.

But then they strengthened the guards. Motorcycle patrols would stream forward, their engines revving. Our goods were "blacked," confiscated. I was wild with rage, I drank like a ma-niac. Then I switched to a new system. By special arrangement with Pinkert's men, I packed coffins with food, smuggled flour onto the carts loaded with corpses — which the Germans gave a wide berth because they were scared of typhoid. But when they realized that we were using our dead to save lives they bricked up the cemetery. So I switched plans again: I used the carts which oc-casionally passed through the gates to collect the rubbish.

It was a game of life and death. They were systematically tight-ening the noose around our necks and we needed more and more air. I provided a little of that air. But the stakes were still rising.

In the end I had to come out into the open.

In Pola's view it was suicide. She caught me by the hands. Pavel, dog-tired, was smoking in silence.

"Some people do it," I said.

"They're caught, nearly all of them, one by one."

But weren't we all going to die, "nearly all of *us?*" I got up, it was no time for discussion.

"Do you agree, Pavel, or don't you?"

"I'll be there," he said.

I ran out onto the stairs; at last I was going to start again, in a big way. I'd invested almost my entire fortune in the operation: I'd paid the Jewish police, paid the Blues, paid the Leszno Street Thirteen who, with my money, had paid the German police, so they claimed; I'd paid Kohn and Heller's men, the ghetto's official agents, who'd paid the German supervisors; I'd paid for a wagon drawn by two fine horses; and I'd paid for false papers and then for an import license from the *transfertelle,* the permit office.

Like all profitable ideas, my plan was simple: I wouldn't deal with a *meta,* a section of wall, but with a gate to the ghetto. So in we went. I was sitting on the goods, very high up: I showed my false papers and the Blue pretended to check them; he was "cooperating," the whole gate was "cooperating," I passed through several times: I had two hours, sometimes less, to make my way into the ghetto, guided by Pavel; I went into a yard, where scores of porters emerged from corners, cellars and stairs, and in seconds the wagon had been picked clean as a skeleton. Sometimes we even left one of the horses. One day, I went in with two wagons and four horses and came out with only two horses between the shafts. I was dealing with one gate going in and another going out. I went in through Dzika, at the end of Stawki Street, the porters would be waiting for me in the quarter with narrow streets like Wolyuska and Kupiecka streets, and then when I set off again for the Okopowa gate, I'd pass them, bent double, pedaling away, pulling their cabs filled with my goods.

I transported tons of grain and sugar. Once through the gate, I mingled with the crowds: from high above my load, as I looked down on Gesia Street with its hunched throngs of passersby, I felt like a monarch or benign spirit, bringing hope and salvation to his people.

But the stakes had never been so high. I was out in the open; each journey through a gate was a miracle. And luck is often fickle.

I'd stopped in front of the Dzika gate. Zamek the Wise was holding the horses' reins. I was sitting up on top of the sacks of grain, I could see Pavel, motionless in the thick of the crowd,

Pavel no doubt as worried as ever. The Dzika gate was playing along. The day was sunny at intervals, then they sky would cloud over. Sliding slowly down off the sacks, I could smell the grain: I had another load waiting, more grain, in a Praga shed. By now Mokotow the Tomb would have loaded up the other wagon, in anticipation of my return. I handed my papers to the Blue: I was a young Pole living in Powazkowska Street. He barely glanced at them. The German was in his sentry box. He was "cooperating" too. Everything was going well.

I heard the motorcycle police coming, they drove up alongside the wall. Gripping the sacks, I went on hauling myself up.

"You don't know anything," I told Zamek the Wise, to be on the safe side.

They braked in front of the gate, jumped off their motorcycles, and one of them aimed his automatic revolver in our direction; the other made for the sentry box. They all started yelling, the German and Polish *graieks* yelling louder than the rest so as to save their skins, the two policemen in their long leather coats shouting in our direction for us to climb down, show our papers and raise our hands. By now I was being struck in the ribs and on the head. I was holding out my papers, saying, "Why? I don't know anything."

Zamek didn't say a word.

One of the motorcyclists set off again, the other holding us at arm's length and striking us. I could see Pavel in the distance, at the end of the street. Despairing, he must have been furious with me for pushing my luck, daring it.

A car returned with the motorcyclist. It was me they were after. They practically ignored Zamek the Wise: obviously this was a betrayal, another one. We were flung onto the rear seats, beaten up, and we passed through the Dzika gate, down Zamenhofa into Dzielna Street. "You always wind up in Pawiak," Siwy had said, and I wound up in Pawiak. They searched me: I had too many zlotys on me to play the innocent. I got another beating, then a cell, alone. I'd lost Zamek the Wise for good. I sat in a corner, the darkest one: "Keep your strength, conserve your strength, don't panic." I kept repeating those few words to myself in an attempt to remain calm, but from time to time I was overcome by despair; I thought of my mother, of Zofia, and of Stasiek Borowski too.

A few hours went by. Then yells in the corridor; the door; the yard; a truck full of prisoners, silent with bowed heads. We drove off. I recognized the streets, the Nalewki Street gate, Aryan Warsaw and its free, untroubled passersby, then some trees, the pale green of spring. We were in Szucha Alley: Gestapo headquarters. I'd been there before, long ago, during my childhood when I'd hardly begun to discover the world *they* were building for us. I escaped. It had been luck. This time I was pinned against the wall of a cell in the basement, my hands above my head. Then some stairs, rifle butts, and a sunny, restful office, a man with well-combed hair, his hands on his desk, a long silence.

"Talk," he said.

The interpreter, near the window, translated.

I started: "I met someone in the street, I wanted to make some money, that's all I know." I told him my assumed name.

"Talk."

He wasn't even looking at me. I started again, I asked him to question me. I'd answer, but I was innocent. He didn't even wait for the interpreter to finish. He got up slowly, took a stick, a long, whiplike cane, and started hitting me. I could hear it whistling, feel it biting into my skin. How could I help yelling?

"Talk."

He went and sat down. I recovered my breath. I started again. Then he shouted, red in the face, got up, shoved me against the wall and I felt the muzzle of a revolver against my neck.

"Talk. I'll count up to ten."

Why die? My cheeks were on fire, my tongue felt enormous. It was choking me. Zofia was dead, and my mother had never given her the cholent which she made so well. Goodbye, my people. I hadn't uttered my battle cry, my cry of revenge. Goodbye, my people.

The door opened. Someone came in.

"I'm going to teach him a lesson," said the butcher, in German.

My hopes rose.

He counted and a shot rang out in my ears, fired close, by the visitor. I was still alive. Terror methods.

"You've got till tomorrow."

He took me to the middle of the room, doubled me up with a kick in the groin.

"I want the names of the gang and the soldiers who've helped you," he said. "Tomorrow."

What did he know? He didn't seem to know I was a Jew. I was back in a cell in Pawiak. Near me, on the slimy ground, a man in agony, his body black and blue, staring eyes, beaten, tortured almost to death, unable even to groan. Me, tomorrow.

But they seemed to forget me for four days. The second day, I took a chance and mentioned money to the Polish guard who was pouring our soup. He looked up, it was a fortune. He looked at me without revealing anything.

"Just tell a friend where I am. He'll pay you."

He was wavering; I repeated the figure.

"Who?"

I gave him the address of a shed in Praga, where I knew Mokotow would be waiting for me. The guard left: I'd gambled. All I could do now was hope. He returned on the fourth day. He smiled. Mokotow had ransomed me.

"The Tomb and the Giant are taking care of it," he said.

Mokotow and Mietek: now they knew. I had faith in them. I felt strong. But then the Gestapo came, the evening of that fourth day. I was fearful. A private car, not a truck. Another office, another butcher, tall, bald, well dressed, his face purplish in the garish lighting.

"You didn't say you were a Jew!"

Perhaps at the Pawiak prison infirmary where they had patched me up they had noticed I was circumcised.

"Jews always talk!" he said.

He didn't even have an interpreter, he was so sure that I understood German. I replied in Polish that I was innocent, that I spoke only Polish. His face went even more purple and he rushed at me, screaming. I could see the gold caps on his teeth.

"That'll do, Jew. You're finished!"

I knew that I wouldn't talk, ever; that he was going to kill me but that I would gain the victory of silence; that his bellows of rage were a confession of weakness. That he was cowardly, impotent, despicable; that he belonged to the world of mad beasts which get killed because they do harm; and that I and those like me were, whatever we did, whatever they did to us, in spite of the selfishness to which they had driven us, in spite of the qualms of many and the cringing of some, I and those like me were men with men's faces. The mad beasts couldn't conquer us even if they killed us. I had only one regret: not to be in on the kill when we finally cornered them.

Then they began: they formed a circle and flung me from one to another, as if they were trying to burst me, like a bladder. They stretched me out on a table and, two at a time, hit me with sticks and clubs. Then they thrashed me with leather thongs. They kicked me in the groin. Next morning, in Pawiak, I passed blood. This went on several days. They flung me in a truck and dragged me back to my cell by the hair. Then they started again the next day, or next night. On every journey, I kept hoping that Mokotow the Tomb and Mietek the Giant would attack the truck. But nothing happened: that *really* hurt; the loneliness. Then they placed my hands on a table and burned the base of my thumbs with their cigarettes, and "doctored" me by daubing my wounds with acid. They hung me up by the feet like an animal in a butcher's window. They *were* butchers.

I realized that if they continued, against my will I'd talk. I had to make up my mind. I contemplated suicide, but I was seventeen and eager to live. So I decided to provoke them with another gamble; to try my luck again.

When they dropped me on the ground and the red-faced butcher came sweating up to me, I said in German, "I'll talk."

He slapped his thigh, stroked my face with his whip and laughed.

"You see, Jew!"

He did as I expected, calling over the soldiers and the first butcher.

"Our little Jew's decided to chat."

He stuck out his chest and the others laughed. I got up. My ribs were aching, my hands stinging from the acid.

"He couldn't make a little Jew talk!" I shouted. "He thought he could!"

He closed in on me, his club raised. I gathered my strength and spat in his face.

"He couldn't make a Jew talk! So he's going to kill me, because he couldn't do it! He's going to kill me but I won't talk! He couldn't do it! He's going to kill me!" I yelled.

Then I shut my eyes. Nobody spoke and suddenly I heard him screaming: he was leaping around the room like a kangaroo.

"You'll talk, Jew, you'll talk!" he shrilled.

Then he yelled to the soldiers to leave. I heard them muttering. Suddenly there was silence: I was alone with him again.

"You'll talk, Jew!"

His face was hard up against mine.

"You'll kill me and you won't have gotten anything."

I spat again. He got up, pale, holding his revolver. He hesitated and my luck wavered, the luck I'd so often tested. Then he left. I was taken back to Pawiak and two days elapsed. My wounds were turning septic. I could feel death catching up with me, I could hardly move. Then, on the third day, the cell opened, and there was the butcher in front of me.

"You're brave, Jew. And you're smart. I'll make a deal with you."

I listened to him, it was simple: my life in return for my organization, my life for denouncing the Germans and Poles who'd agreed to "play along" with us. Why hadn't I the strength to leap at him? But my weakness helped me control my hatred, to formulate a plan.

"Get me some treatment first if you want to save my life. And get me Aryan papers."

I was haggling as if over a bargain because I had to convince him that the deal interested me.

"All right, Jew. We'll give you treatment. You'll have a nice life, like a real little Aryan."

He laughed at the thought of the bullet he'd fire. I quibbled again, refusing to give any immediate information.

"Treatment first."

I was taken to the hospital in Pawiak. A soldier stood guard at my door and Dr. Scherbel of the Gestapo called on me. He was a small, plump, mild, peaceful-looking man. Later I found out that he sometimes operated on prisoners without anesthetics, for "fun." One morning the Polish doctor who was looking after me and who hadn't spoken to me for a week, smiled at me.

"You're not doing too badly, but the Tomb and the Giant believe that typhoid would be the best thing for you, and I agree with them."

Happiness, sunshine, life came flooding back. I caught him by the hand. He squeezed mine back and winked. He gave me an injection. Two hours later, I was in fever, delirious; I was driven out of Pawiak. The Germans feared contagion. At St. Stanislas Hospital, in the suburbs of Warsaw, Mokotow the Tomb and Mietek the Giant gave the senior doctor the choice between death and a handsome sum of zlotys. One night, they lowered me from the window. I vaguely remember the rope dangling in front of the building. They substituted a corpse for me in my bed. Then they managed to smuggle me into the ghetto. I slept whole days and nights. Dr. Celmajster treated me with drugs he'd managed to acquire. Youth was on my side. So the days passed slowly and pleasantly. I let things slide. It was as if we were back in Senatorska Street, when being ill was pleasant, when I used to call to my mother in a hoarse, stuffed-up voice. At last both the nightmare and the dream had ended: I was left with some cracked ribs, a broken nose, and a few broken teeth. I couldn't straighten my arm. But I was alive. Out in the yard, the April sunshine was warm, the air thin.

I went out: the sight was unbearable. On the corner of Smocza and Gesia streets, a ragged specter standing by a corpse cried out at regular intervals, "A few pennies to bury my only son, Moniek."

I walked and walked through the inferno, and with each step my strength revived along with my hatred. That evening I'd decided to start again. But they didn't give me time.

They entered the ghetto at dusk on Friday, April 17. I could hear their footsteps, their angry voices. They weren't operating at random, but rounded up the "politicos," people who wrote, printed or read underground news sheets. They also took the bakers and the members of the "Leszno Street Thirteen." With the first shots, we climbed to our hideout. They shot the captives outside their doors. The following day, my father confirmed that extermination squads had begun to arrive in Warsaw.

The ghetto fell silent, expecting the worst. Then the alarm was over. I tried to link up again with my gang: but Zamek the Wise had disappeared after entering Pawiak, Dziobak the Pox had left Warsaw, Wacek the Peasant was selling produce which he brought from the country. During my long arrest and my sickness they'd lost heart. They were afraid, even Mokotow the Tomb and Mietek the Giant, to whom I owed my life. They'd made a lot of money with me, and they'd saved me. We were quits. I made a few more trips with Mokotow, but as the weeks went by, the difficulties became insurmountable. Large white numbers were painted on the ghetto wall every fifty yards. A Jewish policeman was on duty in front of each mark and guarded that section of the wall.

We had to find some other means of crossing. Then I remembered the sewers; but I was caught trying to prize up a manhole cover in Muranowska Street. Since April 17 patrols had been stepped up and the reign of Frankenstein as sole murderer was over. From time to time, Jews were hung against walls or in courtyards, as examples, on some pretext or other. The two helmeted soldiers who caught me made me raise my arms and pushed me into a courtyard at the corner of Pokorna Street. I shuffled forward. Had my luck deserted me again? A dozen men waiting against a wall with raised arms, four soldiers guarding them, others patrolling the street. The squad would soon form up and fire. I edged over to the wall, saw a glass fanlight, a cellar window at ground level. I inched towards it. "The first chance, Martin, always seize the first chance. There's never a second one."

I dived, fists clenched, into the pane of glass and landed on some crates in a dark cellar. Immediate shots, the familiar yells. I smashed in a door, climbed some stairs. No one. An unlocked door. "The first chance, Martin." In the room a little girl, dressed in white, thin, with taut yellow skin, motionless, cuddling a doll.

Dead. Starved. You've got to live, Martin. The yelling again. In another room was a large chest of drawers: I emptied one of the drawers, slipped the sheets and blankets under the weightless child, then curled up in the drawer, tugging on my belt to close it, levering with my nails to shut it completely. They hammered on the door with rifle butts. They fired, burst in, swearing, their hobnailed boots. No hesitation when they saw the child. They searched for hours, assembling the inhabitants on the stairs, yelling. I could visualize the women panicking, the beatings. But that was my law: to live, for that little girl who looked asleep. And for all the others.

Then silence. A command from the yard, where I should have been. A volley followed by a few scattered shots.

Hunger, cold, typhoid, beatings, occasional murders weren't sufficient. They needed mass slaughter.

Huddled in that drawer, fighting for breath, paralyzed by cramps, I knew that I hadn't done anything, or seen anything of the horror still ahead.

4

The Butchers Had Spoken

WEDNESDAY, July 22, 1942: the butchers had spoken. Groups of people were forming in front of the Jewish Council's posters, then scattering. Men running off, women screaming. One of them, sitting on the curb at the corner of Mila Street, was clutching her head, wailing and shrieking as if in a mad fit, her screams growing louder and then dying away. I could see my mother at her window. I tried to motion to her to stay calm. She was raising her arms to heaven. Rifle shots rang out in Zamenhofa Street, then the woman's screams again. Screams of the ghetto in its death throes.

The butchers had spoken: *they* wanted thousands of us each day for *Umsiedlung,* "transportation to the East." *They* wanted to "transfer" the population of the Warsaw ghetto, *they* wanted the Jewish Council to assemble the victims. *They* wanted . . .

I crossed the ghetto. Frenzy, terror everywhere. Shouts, pistol shots, men and women feverishly hunting for official documents that would enable them to avoid "transportation" for a few more days: *Lebenskarte,* the life-giving slip of paper, a medical certificate, or a sworn statement that they belonged to a Jewish policeman's family. Every document already had its price: rabbis were issuing fictitious marriage certificates: Jewish policemen were at a premium. Pola asked me to try and find her one, regardless of cost. Pavel bought a work permit. They imagined they were saved! At best they had a second chance. I walked to the end of Stawki Street. In front of the Jewish hospital, male nurses had just finished stacking up beds and tables: the patients were being brought down. Some were loaded into bicycle-cabs and carts. Others were carried on their families' backs. *They* wanted to use the hospital as an assembly center. *They* wanted it evacuated by that evening. And *they* wanted six thousand of us by six o'clock. How many tomorrow? *They* wanted . . .

The butchers had spoken, and yesterday's insecurity became a sweet, happy time of peace compared with what they had created with a few words. I went home to reassure my mother. How could I convince her when the whole ghetto was trembling, when some on our block, fatalistic and desperate, were already packing their permitted thirty pounds of luggage? As if the East which we had discussed could be anything but a step towards death! My father arrived, out of breath, overwrought, disheveled. He caught me by the arms, pulled me onto the landing, away from my brothers, who were playing by my mother, silent and helpless.

"The extermination squads are here," he said. "In Warsaw."

He clenched his fist.

"And we've no arms."

Then he calmed down a bit, gave me some labor permits. We were entitled to work in one of the ghetto's German firms.

"Factory workers may escape for a while."

For a while! That was how we'd hung on week by week, ever since September 1939. We'd hoped for Allied victories, thought the war was coming to an end. Rumors swept the ghetto, raising its temperature: Goering was dead; the English had razed Berlin; the Russians had destroyed the entire German army at the gates of Moscow; America, where so many of our people lived, would wipe them out. Yet *they* were still there. *They* were in control from the Atlantic to the Volga, from the Baltic to the Black Sea. Who cared about us dying.

It was up to us to escape. I ran, like thousands of others. Prisoners were already being marshaled in Zamenhofa Street. Refugees, old men, beggars, invalids and orphans rounded up, being pushed onto the road. Jewish policemen with raised clubs yelling orders: they needed six thousand heads that evening. Then the herd moved off and I followed it all the way along Zamenhofa, pathetic rabble in rags: poor people; thieves, children, cripples, old folk, the lonely flotsam from distant ghettos. Six thousand heads. As they moved forward, the pavements emptied. People stared at them in terror. They were us tomorrow.

Near me a woman whispered, "God's taking them. Thank God, their suffering's over."

I followed them to the hospital to find out. The cattle cars were there, lined up at the platforms, policemen yelling. I recognized the mighty Szmerling, whip held high dashing from the herd to report to the SS. Yet he was a Jew. Like them. Like me. They were shoved into the cars, separated, and if anyone shouted, protested or struggled, they got a blow from an iron bar, or a bullet. I watched, took it all in: tomorrow it could be me, my family. I wanted to find out because, in order to escape, to win, I had to know about the assembly point. The *Umschlagplatz*. A day ago, just a big intersection. A day ago the word didn't exist. But the butchers had spoken and the place had become the center of the inferno! A *Umschlagplatz!* A word of doom feared by all. Like a verdict.

I ran and found a carpenter. They were like gold dust but I had the money. I made him run too, tugging him by the arm. Everywhere, in every street, frenzied scenes, people making parcels, running off, coming back and finding themselves up against the bricks of the sealed-off streets, shrieking. The butchers had spoken and the ghetto trembled. Why didn't we have guns? Why were we letting ourselves be slaughtered? Back in our apartment, I took my mother and brothers aside. I wanted a safe hideout, much better than any work permit. The carpenter transformed the back of a cupboard into a door held by an invisible latch. Then we shoved the cupboard in front of the door of a room: a hideout for my mother and brothers, behind the bulging linen cupboard. I had another cupboard adapted for myself. I could crouch in it against one of the doors. I paid the carpenter. He had gray hair and thick hands covered with sawdust. He grabbed the notes, barely looking at me. We had to trust him. Our lives were in his hands and how could we be sure that he wouldn't trade them for his own?

I organized stores of food and a reserve supply of drinking water, then laid mattresses in the hideout. My mother watched me, submissive, resigned.

"It's going to be all right, Mother, I promise you. It's going to be all right."

I kissed her, hugged her, so that she could feel my strength, my courage, my certainty. I made them go in; my brothers were laughing. They wanted to stay in the cupboard. Finally I was able to insert the shelves, replace the linen, and close both doors. And sit down. Every night I would let them out and clear away the rubbish. From the street, shouts, sounds of running, Jewish policemen hounding passersby; probably short a few heads, which they were collecting at random. I saw one armed with a long club, chasing a woman, her arms in the air. She lost ground and fell. The policeman wrenched her up by the hair, dragged her along.

The butchers had spoken. Some of us had turned into savage beasts, others had gone mad, and more still were just passive bodies which the butchers grabbed. It was hard to remain a man. On Friday, the twenty-third, at 8:30 A.M., Czerniakow, the president of the Jewish Council, committed suicide, offering us his death as a cry of rage, revolt and despair. And as a sort of warning. But few of us heeded it. The police needed "heads," otherwise the butchers would shove the beaters themselves into the cattle cars that evening. It was every man for himself: one life for another's. It was hard to remain a *man*.

The streets emptied. The police squads arrived on the scene, climbing stairs, smashing in doors, dragging people from their beds or making for hideouts, betrayed by neighbors or relations. Then came the Ukrainians, Latvians and Lithuanians, hunters of Jews, vultures employed by the SS as falcons. The *Umschlagplatz* overflowed. The SS counted, and closed the doors of the cattle cars. So what, if a mother got separated from her children? Sometimes they were sorted on the square itself: those on the right into the cars; those on the left to work for the SS. Left meant hope.

I was caught in the street. Like thousands of others. Marched off in a column towards the *Umschlagplatz,* and herded into the hospital where we were corralled until the cars were loaded. It was then I learned that a man can become anything. The first two floors of the hospital were for the Ukrainians and Lithuanians: they camped there, killing and raping. On the upper floors us. Jews. Earmarked for the cattle cars; for the East, which some regarded as death and others claimed meant hope.

When the Ukrainians opened the doors of the hospital to drive us towards the cattle cars, the struggle began. We fought our way to the upper floors to gain a possible hour, or even a day. The Ukrainians fired at the windows from Stawki Street: bodies fell. Women shrieked, crazed men waved their arms about. The rooms were littered with filth and excrement. Men were sleeping on corpses. Some threw themselves out of the windows and the Ukrainians laughed as they waited to pick them off in the air, like birds.

I was caught. I escaped. Sometimes I escaped twice in one day. I'd bribe a Jewish policeman, take advantage of a momentary distraction, or get selected for the "left," the labor camp, and jump off the truck. Each time I was more determined, more certain I'd escape better prepared. I carried a rope wound around my waist, a knife and some money. As a smuggler, I knew nearly all the Jewish police, my *graieks*. They respected me, feared me, knew of my resources. They helped me.

But their prices soared as the butchers grew more demanding. I was captured in Niska Street by a croup of SS men. One of them, red-haired, his skin covered with freckles, was holding a long piece of barbed wire in his gloved hand. He closed on me, slashing my face several times. I was seared, bleeding. I said nothing. I walked on, remembering the *Umschlagplatz*. I thought only of the blood, the wounds which would single me out for the cattle cars. I had to keep silent, wait until the red-haired SS man left me for other victims. Once again I entered the *Umschlagplatz*. The scene was still one of frenzy: a small SS man, the smallest I'd ever seen, was standing in front of the cattle cars, smiling, separating mothers and children, wielding his lash. The Jewish police were alert for those who tried to escape to Dr. Remba's infirmary. In the center of chaos, the doctor and some nurses were trying to save a few men from the cattle cars. In that world of corruption and savagery, some human beings survived. The police shoved back into the cattle cars those who couldn't bribe them. I paid and waited several days for my face to heal, so that I could return to the ghetto.

Caught, paying, running away, caught again: day after day, that was my life. To survive, it became increasingly necessary not to see, not to hear. One day, in Karmelicka Street, they were throwing people into a van like sacks. An hour later, in Mila, a Jewish policeman was chasing a child: he finally caught it, grabbed it by the arm and shouted, "Got you!" Then the parents came out and they all went off together to the *Umschlagplatz:* children made good bait.

I wanted to kill. When I had the chance, I hesitated.

A Jewish policeman was in Mrs. Celmajster's daughter's room, tugging at the little girl, who clung to her mother and to a rocking horse while both of them shrieked. I went downstairs. I had to intervene. There are moments when, whatever the risks, you have to force yourself not to be a coward. I called to him, pleaded with him and insulted him. He had the glazed stare of a runaway horse. He raised his club so I charged at him, head down, hitting him right in his face. Flattening him. Mrs. Celmajster and her daughter huddled in a corner, both in the same position, their hands over their mouths. The policeman was lying there and I was afraid I'd killed him. I had dreamed of killing such men, who, to save their skins, handed over our lives to the butchers, their butchers. But now suddenly I felt close to him. He was a victim like myself, though in another way. When he got up I was standing in front of him holding his club. I shoved him into a cupboard and locked him in.

"I'll let you out this evening when their head count is over. Tomorrow go somewhere else."

His eyes were still bulging, terror-stricken.

"What about my quota?" he said.

"Tomorrow, somewhere else."

The butchers had spoken: every Jewish policeman had to produce his quota of four head a day, then five, then seven. They had spoken. That man had gone berserk.

Day after day the operation continued. My mother and my brothers no longer left their hideout. Pola took refuge in the attic. I shouldn't have gone out. I was defying fate. I roamed the streets, a scavenger. I went into deserted apartments even before the Ukrainians and Jewish police had left them. I followed in their tracks, in search of food. Sometimes I had to push aside a body of a woman who'd been raped and killed, a baby crying alone in a room. I tried not to take it all in: what could I do? I stuffed my shirt with whatever I could find, then went back to my family.

On the fourth floor of a building in Nowolipie Street, I came face to face with a Ukrainian, a straggler, a loner, a stocky looter with almost no neck. He caught me by the arm and shoved me out onto the landing. Not a word was spoken. Just his brutality and my apparent submissiveness. On the second floor, the open door of an apartment. He let go of me a second. I shoved him with all my might and slammed the door, holding it shut until he fired. I let go and dived into the opposite apartment, which was open too. He dashed up the stairs. I slipped into the apartment where he had been, leaving the door open, ready to fight, but he rushed down again. I waited a few seconds, then returned to scavenging, sniffing out food to take back to my family.

They still had us in a vise of hunger: smuggling had become practically impossible. Starvation was flushing people from their hideouts. And *they* knew it. In late July, they stuck posters up on the walls: those who turned up voluntarily at the *Umschlagplatz* would be entitled to six pounds of bread and two pounds of jam. Moreover, they said, the families would not be separated out there, in the East. That was when I saw the people who were really starving, those for whom bread and jam were a kingdom richer than life. They massed in front of the *Umschlagplatz*. The Jewish police didn't even have to hit them. I saw them, women in shawls, hollow-cheeked, laughing hysterically when they were handed the coarse gray bread, which they hurriedly raised to their mouths or ripped to pieces with their nails. That was when I saw parents who'd do anything rather than be separated from their children.

I was fascinated. I wanted to tell them to run away, shout to them that you could never trust the butchers, that it was better to starve to death. But they wouldn't have listened to me. And I was ashamed to speak, too: I didn't really know what hunger meant. I realized that most of them were leaving so as to stay with their families.

There were so many volunteers they had to turn some of them away. Those who hadn't managed to get into the *Umschlagplatz* pleaded, they wanted their bread and their jam. They wanted to leave the ghetto as a family. But they were sent away. A few days later, the ghetto was gripped by new rumors. The East was really the East all right, you could get food there, you could work there: some people had letters from relations stating that, although the work was hard, food was plentiful. I saw them again massing in front of the *Umschlagplatz*. How could they have fallen for it!

I hung about the streets as though hypnotized, following their docile, even cheerful columns. That was how, one morning, I saw the carts. The sun was blazing: after days of rain, the weather had taken a turn for the better and the ghetto was beginning to simmer in the heat. I saw them, Chaim the Monkey, Yankle the Blind, and Trisk. They were in a cart heading down Zamenhofa. They, too, were going to the *Umschlagplatz*. I walked along beside them, clinging to the cart.

"Trisk, Yankle, you're mad!"

They laughed.

"Anyway, we'll be safe, have food and work."

"What are you waiting for, Mietek?" said Yankle the Blind. "It's first come first served in the East."

"It's up to you, Mietek. Come on, we'll make room for you."

Chaim the Monkey was making his usual faces and waving his arms enthusiastically.

I pleaded with them to get off, to think, to wait. But they had answers for everything: letters from out East, the Germans turning people away at the *Umschlagplatz*. They were mad, duped, drunk. I jumped off the cart at the end of Zamenhofa. Goodbye, Yankle the Blind, goodbye, Chaim the Monkey, goodbye, Trisk. The butchers weren't just barbarians; they knew how to deceive, systematically divide us. Defeating them would be a long task. Only a few of us would survive to tell about it. I had to be one of them, at any cost.

Then the flow of volunteers dried up. There was no more bread and jam. There were raids again, streets sealed off, shootings. In Leszno Street, an Aryan Polish woman insulted some Germans who were rounding up children: a scream, a burst of fire. The roundup went on.

The inhabitants went to earth, buried themselves. The blistering sun seared empty streets. My mother and brothers were stifling in our hideout. It was a furnace; tar was melting in great lumps, the air was dead, water scarce. I tried to keep my brothers amused but they kept asking the same questions: Why? Why? They wanted to go out, they wanted to run around. I had to teach them silence; to lie down and not move when they heard sounds or voices. Sometimes a baby's cry had been enough to give away a dozen people. In the daytime I carried on with my roamings.

It must have been around mid-August, I was on my way home, when I heard singing. Soon I saw them, neat and clean, holding each other's hands: the children from the orphanage. Led by Dr. Korczak, the children were off to the *Umschlagplatz*. I'd applauded at their recitals, the entertaining scenes they'd enacted in charity shows at the Femina Theater. I'd been a regular contributor to the orphanage. Now they were off to the *Umschlagplatz*.

Dr. Korczak was striding forward with a fixed look, holding two small expressionless boys by the hands. I walked along beside him whispering, "Doctor, Doctor." I pleaded with him but he didn't answer, as if he hadn't recognized me. I walked to the barriers with them and watched them enter the *Umschlagplatz*. The cattle cars were lined up alongside the platforms and the little SS man was smiling.

"Come on." It was my father. He seized me by the arm and dragged me towards Mila Street.

"Korczak didn't want to frighten them. He's going with them."

I didn't answer. How could he have consented, not tried to hide the children? Why offer himself as a sacrifice?

"Don't judge him. Don't judge anyone. He's trying to save them, to protect them, in his own way."

We kept walking.

"They want to destroy us, slaughter our people, Martin."

Father talked on: our hopes, all we'd built over the centuries, the children, our future. They were systematically wrecking everything.

"They've got a plan: the East means death to us."

Outside 23 Mila Street, Father squeezed my arm.

"Survive, Martin. Remember. Today, forever."

He tried to procure arms, make contact with the Polish resistance: but arms were precious and the secret army's leaders often anti-Semitic. They hesitated, haggled. As if we could wait, when the ghetto was gradually emptying, when one by one the Jewish police were becoming more vicious as the SS threatened them each day with larger and larger quotas. I saw a Jewish policeman, ax in hand, smashing the doors of apartments, forcing out the inhabitants. I saw others dragging screaming women. The Ukrainians and Lithuanians went on raping and killing. They were hunting by night, too, now; gradually, spreading like a bloodstain. Silence pervaded the ghetto. Each day another section had to be flushed out: the apartment houses between Dzielna, Zamenhofa, Nowolipie and Karmelicka streets, then the little ghetto, then the buildings between Zamenhofa and Nalewki streets. The inhabitants sometimes had five minutes to come down into the streets, assemble under a hail of blows and move off to the *Umschlagplatz*. Afterwards, Ukrainian, Latvian and Lithuanian SS men and the Jewish police searched the buildings, looting, killing anyone they caught there. They smashed the furniture, wrecked the beds and broke through the walls: they looked for hideouts where families had taken refuge, for gold and jewels. They were hungry for gold, women and blood. Each day more safe-conduct passes became invalid: before long, work permits had to be stamped by the SS and the SD police. The frenzy reached new heights: everyone wanted to be in the last group allowed to stay. In one of the workshops run by the Germans I saw little girls, with the panic-stricken eyes of rabbits, faces covered with powder and painted lips, trying to pose as young women who deserved a work permit; and I saw old women with dyed hair. What had we become, into what macabre tragedy had we been plunged? For what fiend were we painting our faces?

Like the others, I kept an eye on my appearance: I had to look young and healthy. This had already saved me because I'd once again been marched off to the *Umschlagplatz* and bundled into the hospital. The screams of the women and children, the excrement heaped on the corpses, the intolerable stench; and the Ukrainians firing their automatic rifles over the crowd to drive it mad, grabbing a woman and dragging her away from her people and taking her off never to be seen again. I was back in the hideous world of the *Umschlagplatz* where men died in shame.

Twice I contrived to be selected for a labor camp, to climb on the truck and jump off. Now I knew which way they went, how fast and at what point to jump. You can learn skill at anything, even escaping death. On two other occasions I was shoved into the cattle cars. I heard grating sounds and the crash of the wooden door that suffocated us. I wasn't an apprentice anymore but a hardened criminal. We loosened the bars in the door of the cattle car, high up to the left, and several of us jumped out. The second time I carried a short saw. Because I knew. I didn't jump for fear of being shot. I hoisted myself onto the roof, making my way car by car to the rear of the train. I could hear soldiers singing and laughing, and a woman shrieking. On the next to last car I had to flatten myself: there was a soldier on guard between the two cars. I went back along the train in the opposite direction, crawling against the wind, and jumped off at the first bend.

Each time I managed to make my way back to the ghetto with one of the groups of Jewish workers whom the Germans still employed in Aryan Warsaw. Where else was I to go? My family was in the ghetto behind a cupboard full of linen, waiting for me at evening to bring them confidence, and to dispose of the accumulated garbage and slops. Without me, my mother and my brothers would have gone crazy. I had confidence: with each escape I gained strength, convinced that I'd survive, that, if willed hard enough, you could seduce fate to your side.

When my father got caught, I returned to the *Umschlagplatz.*
Escape from the Jewish police was my specialty. My father was sitting in one of the darkest rooms of the hospital, his face tense,
watching men lying in the blood and muck.

"Come on," I said.

He hesitated.

"Father, here. It's me."

I dragged him downstairs, and then to the *Umschlagplatz,* the
wails and screams. I'd got used to that sight. I knew the methods
of the SS, how they chose victims.

"Do what I do."

My father looked at me questioningly. I was confident, confident we were going to succeed. We were chosen for the "left." I
jumped on the truck, took one end seat, reserved the other so my
father could sit. As soon as the truck moved, I crouched down.

"Jump," said Father.

"Too soon. Wait! Follow me."

We jumped together, without even a shot, racing down an
empty street, hiding in a sunlit yard. The heat was overwhelming.
We washed and sat in the shadow of a wall.

"You're a master, Martin."

I laughed.

"You wanted to jump too soon, Father. The truck had barely
started."

We had a long talk, like brothers. I told him about my escapes,
the trains, my little saw, my knife, the rope around my waist. Father laughed, and I chatted away as if I'd been drinking. Then
we went back into the ghetto with the workers. The ghetto was
our battlefield. We couldn't desert it.

But the fight to survive grew harder and harder. Each time I
returned I found our prison mutilated, another quarter had died.
The deserted streets baked under the fiery heat of summer, streets
which I remembered full of people; Zamenhofa and Gesia every
stone of which I knew; streets where I'd seen Trisk the Cart and
Yankle the Blind striding towards me carrying sacks of grain;
streets where I'd felt like bursting with joy, proud at cheating the
butchers once again; Mila where I'd run clutching cakes from the
Gogolewski cake shop and whistling the songs of the ghetto;

streets where I'd been with Zofia, leaving the theater, drinking in Café Sztuka. Streets now deserted, the wind scuffing up an occasional black rag abandoned in the yellowish dust.

I suffered as I watched the gray-black, stooping, tragic crowd which filled the streets, I suffered seeing beggars, the ragged children. They still meant life, our life. All that remained now were things that mocked life; bare walls, people hidden and silent. In the middle of Gesia Street there was a piano, probably thrown from a window; farther along, furniture, some burst eiderdown quilts. I walked on not seeing the Ukrainian guards. Once again I was caught and herded into a column, shuffling along to the accompaniment of blows, towards the *Umschlagplatz*. Come on, Martin, come on, Mietek, you haven't come all this way to get caught. You're not going to let them master you.

I survived the ordeal of selection and clambered onto the truck; this time there was no jumping out. The road went deep into Poland, the countryside was obscured behind the white dust we churned up.

After a few dozen miles we stopped at a camp with huts and barbed wire. It was the Polish Army's former rifle range at Rembertow. My first camp. Days passed: my family was back in Warsaw. I tried to convince myself that they were still there, that my father would visit them every day. For the time being, there was no point in thinking about them: the only way to help them was to escape. All I ought to think about was escaping. Our work was moving sand, digging canals. In that camp the lowest scum of the ghetto had the best jobs. I had their friendship so avoided the hardest labor; only pushed wheelbarrows. We were continually beaten, but I was alive.

In the evenings I discussed escape with a young prisoner, Yankl Eisner. Every morning there were groups of Polish farmers at the entrance to the camp: they wanted our possessions in exchange for bread. Yankl was of two minds about escape: his father was with him. But my people were in Warsaw, I had to stay with them until the end. One morning I made contact with a farmer. The next day, as we went out, I sneaked into the bartering crowd, close to him. He passed me a cap, and I was a young Pole watching the disappearing column of prisoners. I saw Eisner turn back a couple of times. A simple escape. I still had to get back, skirting the main roads, crawling in ditches, at last joining the Jewish workers who were returning to the ghetto from Okiencie airport. Come on, Martin, come on, Mietek. Here's your long brick wall again, your streets, your tram tracks; here's 23 Mila Street. The cupboard was shut, linen piled high. I couldn't wait until night. I flung aside the sheets and blankets: my mother, my brothers were against the wall. My mother threw herself on me. My brothers clutched my legs. Alive.

So the days went by.

Father was alive too. Caught up in his underground activities, he made us rare visits. It was enough to know that he was with us in the ghetto: I was always with him and he with me, even if we didn't meet for days. Several times he talked about the East. They'd kill us out there. A man had managed to jump from the train and returned to talk: the rails faded into the wastes, to a deserted spot the peasants called Treblinka. Our people vanished out there, whole train loads; after a few hours the cars returned empty to Warsaw and the *Umschlagplatz*. They'd taken two hundred thousand of us in less than a month. Treblinka. That name grew in me like a weed and, hour by hour, I felt a wild anger seize me, well up in me, numb my brain, stifle me. I couldn't sleep, couldn't stay indoors, I had to go out and face them in the open.

And inevitably I was caught by the SS. There were a dozen of them standing, legs apart, in the middle of the road. They barely bothered to look at us, us Jews. With a jerk of a rifle they ordered us to line up. Quite a few of us had already been picked up in the streets and in the houses. Suddenly I saw a naked man come staggering drunkenly out, singing, and join us, laughing and dancing, then he left our ranks and started hopping about: the SS men laughed. One of them gave the man a push with his shoulder, the others stopped him: they wanted a little fun before they killed him. I leaped out of the column, to the steps of a house on the corner of Mila Street. I could already hear shouts and footsteps. I remembered the soldier I'd meant to kill. I'd lost that first chance. I got to the third floor and crouched behind the door. I knew those buildings, for weeks they'd been familiar territory. An SS man came nearer, walked past me, not even suspicious. I leaped from behind, grabbing his neck. I was strong now. The blows I'd received had hardened me, and the hands they'd burned, the fingers they'd crushed, knew how to grip. They were like my hatred.

He struggled but I didn't let go and he soon fell backwards in a sitting position, his heels drumming against the floor. I dragged him hurriedly down the courtyard stairs, blood running from his nose. My life hung on a few seconds. I took him to the cellar as shouts echoed outside. Some of the prisoners must have seized the chance of running away; there were bursts of fire, more footsteps. Shouts. They were looking for him. But it was getting late, already time for counting heads. Then the column moved off, the shouts vanished into the distance. So I buried the tall soldier in the beaten earth, my first victim. I covered over his body without hesitation or remorse. My father took the SS rifle, and asked no questions.

"Watch out tomorrow morning," was all he said.

They did in fact come back, sealing off streets, firing at windows, searching, killing, raiding, looting. All day I stayed in the hideout, relaxing. In the evening, after dusk, I went up onto the roof. It was cool up there. The sky spread out above me, blue and calm: after the blood, the noise, the heat and the horror, I lay down beside a chimney stack. The zinc roof was still warm and I dozed, the breeze in my face. The rooftops had become my new field of action. I crossed them in every direction, soon getting used to the narrow catwalk at the top between the two slopes, barely a foot wide. I walked along it confidently, and so was able to cross from Mila Street to Zamenhofa Street, from Gesia Street to Nalewki Street, I could follow Kupiecka Street and look down into the courtyards, and especially when the streets were raked by death, I felt free again.

I already knew every cobble in the streets, I could jump off a streetcar whatever speed it was going, I could tell a Blue who was a *graiek*, just from the look of him: it was the rooftops where I was now learning my way. A touch with my foot and I could gauge the resistance of zinc, wood or tile. I could jump nimbly, hide behind a chimney stack, lie on a sloping roof, hang on with my feet and observe the movements of the Ukrainians and the SS. The roofs grew familiar, friendly to me. They saved me, in spite of the Ukrainians and Latvians who also sometimes ventured onto them: they demolished them by blowing up sections of them so as to flush out families which had taken refuge in the attics. From my observation post, flat on my belly, I could see the smoke from explosions over by Dzielna Street, I could hear the grenades exploding on zinc. They'd probably come to my territory too, one day, but for the time being I was still king of the castle. It was there, on the rooftops, that I killed for the second time.

I was standing in the middle of the wooden catwalk when I saw his head poking through the skylight of one of the attics. A Ukrainian. His body emerged and, calmly, he raised his gun: he had time, all I could do was turn slowly around; why should he forgo the pleasure of taking a potshot at me? The Ukrainians are hunters. All this crossed my mind as I saw his head appear. Then, even before he'd raised his gun, I spoke: I asked the same question in Polish, German and Russian.

"Do you want some gold?"

I repeated the magic word, gold. The Ukrainians are thieves, and because I was a Jew, I had gold.

"Do you want some gold?"

Gold, gold. His gun remained poised. I edged towards him in order to reassure him. I told him about my hideout, my gold and jewels: my fortune in return for my life. He looked at me, I was unarmed, what did he risk?

"Where?"

I hadn't yet lost but I hadn't yet won. I pointed to the other skylight, at the end of the catwalk where I was standing, and where, if he wanted my gold, he had to venture.

"Get back," he said. "Don't turn around."

He was cautious. Gradually, his rifle still pointing in my direction, the whole of him appeared, huge, heavy, with long black boots nipping in his drill trousers below the knee. I took it all in, sized up the man I had to kill. He leaned against the chimney stack, I was two yards away, motionless, my arms half-raised. He hesitated. How innocent my face had become, how dull my eyes, how weak and cowardly I seemed.

"The gold."

I began again, pointing to the skylight. He took a step towards me, approached me cautiously, his finger on the trigger of his rifle.

"Don't move," he said.

Don't worry, Ukrainian murderer, Mietek the Cat's waiting for you. I leaped, feet out, landing on my hands, gripping the cat-walk boards, barely catching his chest with the toes of my shoes, but it was enough to knock him off balance. He fired a shot into the sky, slid all the way down the roof with a great yell, ripped off the gutter as he went over it, and gave another yell, though by now invisible. But who in the ghetto cared about a shot and a few yells? He fell into the inner courtyard and that gave me a few seconds' grace. I went down, dragged away his body and hid it under some crates, then at dusk, with the help of some Jewish police-men, I buried him. It was them or us: their war didn't allow for remorse.

The rooftops meant freedom: now I only left them at night to join my mother and my brothers who tried to sleep in the day-time. But my mother's health was bad: she suffered from being confined, she was dying from the unrelenting tension, she was ter-rified for her sons, terrified by the silence which pervaded the house. I'd no idea where Pavel and Pola were, I'd no idea where the Celmajsters and their daughter were. We were temporary sur-vivors. My father looked in when he could: he was trying to orga-nize resistance, he was telling everyone about Treblinka. But how could you fight back? Why struggle? Resignation, hunger, fear and illusion still hung over the survivors of the ghetto. And we had no arms. All that was left was a lonely struggle to survive, hunting for food in ravaged apartments, working up the will to keep going one more day, until the hours of darkness, sometimes earlier, sometimes later, whenever they stopped hounding us. Then, in the streets, shadows would flit past each other, looking for water and emptying rubbish; others would emerge from cellars, cupboards or hideouts for a breath of air before plunging back in when day came.

And day was pitiless; the heat was intense, and the stench of death hung over the entire ghetto. So I began the adventure of a new day, the wait for night, by going up on the rooftops again; I roamed them, warily, discovering new routes, venturing even closer to the front of the buildings. I'd dispensed with memory: each day was such an unknown quantity that I couldn't remember the previous one. My escapes merged into each other; the Ukrainian, the SS man, smuggling, Pawiak Prison were the stuff of the past; even if an event had taken place the previous day it was the past, and the past was meaningless. You had to live from day to day, with the determination to keep going until tomorrow. Anyone who looked back was a dead man: thinking about yesterday, when men were men, Zofia, the *droshkas* behind which I ran in Senatorska Street, was a fatal disease. My mother was prey to this sickness: exhausted, her hands resting in her lap, her eyes blank, she was remembering "before."

"Mother, Mother, please."

She shook her head, transported by her memories, immersing herself in happier days. I had to leave her because I had to keep watch, observe the movements of patrols, explore apartments. Because we had to eat, too. In the attic of a house in Gesia Street, I found Rivka. I didn't see her at first, cowering there in the darkest corner, where the roof sloped down almost to the floorboards. But when you've been on your guard for months, you get a sixth sense: I knew there was a living creature there, weaker than myself, because it was frightened. I searched the corner of the attic across from where she was, then I whipped around.

"Come on out or I'll kill you."

She gave a moan and I could hear her teeth chattering.

"Come on out."

She crawled towards me, into the daylight, looking up, her fair hair flowing down to her shoulders, then froze. But what had I become, to terrify a human being like that, what had they done to me? I knelt down, stroking her hair with an irrepressible desire to clasp her to me at once, to sit and weep with her. She seemed my age.

"You mustn't stay here, they'll come and get you sooner or later. You'll starve to death."

She knelt there, still trembling, staring at me like a bewildered animal, crazed with fear.

"How about your people?"

She shook her head, and then began to sob quietly, dry-eyed. She didn't need to answer. I stroked her hair, life flowed sweetly through me.

"Easy, easy now. You're alive."

She was still sobbing, still on her knees. I picked her up, held her to me, rocked her. I asked her name, Rivka, and she gradually calmed down.

"You're to come with me."

It wasn't very sensible because I was going to have to haul her across the rooftops to Mila Street, it wasn't wise because I'd have to feed her, take some of the air and space belonging to my mother and brothers. But why survive if I turned into a butcher too? I pulled her onto the roof: she started trembling again, rigid with fear, dizzy, unable even to walk along the narrow strip on which I was used to running. So I made her edge forward on her belly, yard by yard. "I can't," she kept saying, but she was making some headway. We worked our way along Nalewki Street, at an angle, towards the two inner courtyards, and hid behind the chimney stack to avoid two Ukrainians who were spraying the roofs, at random, with automatic revolvers.

By night, worn out, we'd reached 23 Mila Street. As I helped her to jump down into the attic, I noticed a strong smell of gas. I ran, with her following me: the smell was even stronger in our apartment, we opened all the windows, I flung aside all the sheets and blankets concealing the back of the cupboard, and raised the wooden latch: there they were, lying on top of each other. I dashed over to the window, slapped their faces and sprinkled them with water. Rivka helped me. Finally, slowly, they came back to life, vomiting, groaning. But there was still a strong smell of gas: I went down into the empty apartments below. I found the leak on the ground floor. There, lying on the floor of their room, all the windows closed, gas cylinders open, blankets along the sills to prevent the gas escaping, six people lay stretched out, dead, suicides. There were two curly-haired children who seemed to be asleep, one of them with his arms spread out above his head, fists clenched. I shuddered with rage and despair, what right had we to facilitate the task of the butchers like that? I stood there rooted to the spot. Rivka came. She freed my hands which were clenched in my hair.

We went back to my mother, Rivka was already one of us; my mother chatted away to her as if she'd always known her, my brothers played with her. Then they dozed off and Rivka climbed up with me onto the roof, alongside the worn chimney stack. We stayed there, holding hands. Suddenly the heavy throb of aircraft filled the sky. We stood up.

"The Russians, the Russians!" I yelled.

Rivka clung to me. In a few minutes, it was like broad daylight: the glowing flares fell slowly towards the earth, lighting up Warsaw, then bombs exploded over towards Praga. We cried out, calling for a hail of bombs, a holocaust that would bury the butchers, what did it matter if we perished too. But night returned, leaving us alone, exhausted, and we lay down beside each other.

It had been just another day, a good day because we were alive.

In the morning, the noose tightened around us again. At dawn, which promised a scorcher, I could see from my lookout spot on the roof Jewish police sticking up posters in Gesia Street. Then they moved off, and I could see figures leaving the buildings, coming down from the rooftops, meeting and running off again. I went down for the latest news: a new evacuation order had been signed by the Jewish Council; the inhabitants of Smocza, Gesia and Dzika streets had until ten that morning to quit their homes. They had to leave their apartments open. By ten, German and Ukrainian guards had sealed off the streets. I watched them as they moved about, as if doing exercises, as if the tearful women and frightened children didn't exist. Then they drove the column towards the *Umschlagplatz,* and in the deserted houses the hunt for those still in hiding began with a spate of looting. That evening we were still there, still alive.

In the middle of the night Pavel called out to me. I left Rivka, sliding down to the skylight, lying there flat on my belly, unable to see Pavel's face.

"They're raiding Toebbens and Schultz too," he said.

His voice came in jerks. He was talking in a way I'd never heard before, a mixture of rage and terror.

"They've taken Pola and my mother, and all our money."

I listened, beginning to distinguish his drawn features, the stubble on his cheeks.

"You'll have to stop going to the workshop, Pavel. They'll get you sooner or later, but they'll get you. Hide."

"No."

He'd yelled it.

"They're selling numbers," he went on. "They're going to let thirty-five thousand people stay on in the ghetto. I must have a number, Martin."

"Hide, Pavel."

"I must have a number, Martin."

We fell silent, I was lying on the roof, he was crouching in the attic. I waited.

"You have lots of money, Martin."

I didn't speak: he was whispering but his words were full of rancor.

"You've still got your mother, your brothers, your father. And you've got money, Martin. I need some tonight, a lot."

"Hide, Pavel."

"I know your hideout, I know it."

He was almost yelling. So they'd turned Pavel into an animal, too. I leaped down into the attic, gripping Pavel by the shoulders, shaking him like a rotten tree that needs to be uprooted.

"I'll go to the ends of the earth to find you, Pavel. And I'll kill you."

He didn't resist, he was sick with fear, Pavel, my friend, who intended to denounce us, whom they'd driven mad. I shook him by the throat.

"You'd better run, Pavel, a long way. Forget Mila Street."

Then I let him go and he fell down. He lay there a long time, then got up again without a word. I heard his footsteps on the stairs, the footsteps of my friend Pavel, who had kept watch for me in Zamenhofa Street, who had waited for me in Gesia Street; we'd shared laughter, joy and fear, we were brothers and I'd made his fortune by taking nearly all the risks. He thought that selling was ignoble, that by doing it you violated sacred principles. And now Pavel must mean nothing. I climbed back up onto the roof: they were sowing the seeds of cowardice in us. They wanted to destroy us and pollute us. Goodbye, Pavel, my Pavel, they've already killed you.

More days went by, more roofs were blown up. There was the cripple they flung with his chair from a window and fired at, laughing; the group which was lined up against the wall in Nalewki Street, starting to sing almost cheerfully, and then mowed down; the children's voices — which courtyard did they come from? — crying out in the night, how many of them were there? "Mummy, Mummy." I stopped my ears to them, hugged Rivka, and we made violent love, against our chimney stack, and fell asleep in each other's arms, protecting each other.

More days amidst the horror, then one morning, very early, David climbed onto the rooftops. I saw him waving hard at me, so I leaped from roof to roof, running towards the sensitive, smiling man who often crossed over to the Aryan side with my father to try and buy arms there. He was sitting there, his back to a wall.

"Still alive, Martin?"

He put his arms around my shoulders.

"They took your father the day before yesterday. There was nothing we could do."

He was already on his feet.

"Good luck, Martin. I'm off. They're still asleep."

He slid down through a skylight. I was alone. I could see Rivka unwisely standing there in the sunshine, waiting for me. My mother and my brothers were waiting for me too. I knew the rooftops: I'd skirted the fronts of the houses, clambered, gone past the chimney stacks. Rivka was there in front of me, worried.

"Never stand up," I said. "They'll see you."

She didn't question me: it was a time when everything seemed to go wrong. I led her into the hideout. My brothers greeted her with open arms, not saying a word. My mother rested her head against me.

"Martin, Martin, I can't, I can't go on much longer."

I rocked her like a child, gradually reassuring her, stroking her hair. How old I was. They were all so weak, so vulnerable, my mother, Rivka and my brothers, and I was old because of all the things they didn't know. Father taken away to the *Umschlagplatz* and Treblinka at the end of the road.

I left them, went back onto the rooftops and lay down in the shade. He'd escape, jump off the train, get back to Warsaw: anything I'd done, he could do, a hundred times over. All that day I let myself be more or less swamped by my memories: the last time we'd laughed together in that unknown Warsaw alley, after we'd escaped from the truck and washed ourselves in cold water; and before, when I'd met him at the Café Sztuka, with Mokotow the Tomb waiting for me, pacing up and down on the pavement, while my father was coming to terms with my independence. Without seeing each other often, we'd gone forward shoulder to shoulder all those years, always meeting again. He'd given me the strength. My will was his. We were part of each other, forever, and while one of us lived, the other would never die. Thank you for this life, Father.

Huddled there, gnawing my fingers, I suffered the intolerable pangs of memory. I wept.

There were a few days of calm. Chimneys smoked in the clear blue sky: summer wasn't yet ended and, probably, over there on the banks of the Vistula, children were running barefoot in the water. I began to hope: perhaps we'd be among the few thousand survivors? I started tearing about the rooftops, searching apartments again: I kept hunting in the chaos, chasing away rats, sometimes finding a set table, chairs knocked over, and food which I carried off.

But the respite wasn't for long, once again they sealed off streets for evacuation; there were still too many of us. Day by day, hour by hour, they closed in on Mila Street. I followed their movements, saw families driven down into the street, lined up and marched off to the *Umschlagplatz*. Now and again Ukrainians appeared on the rooftops, hurling grenades, firing volleys. We hung on. It was halfway through September 1942.

I was sitting wedged between two chimney stacks, concealed by them, listening to the shouts, watching the roofs over towards Nalewki Street. The Ukrainians hadn't yet explored that sector, I was expecting to see them appear there, so I'd chosen my lair in another part, near the corner of Mila and Zamenhofa streets, where they'd already been. I hadn't glanced down at the street for a few minutes. When I did, I saw them: Rivka standing very upright between my brothers, holding them by the hand and my mother behind her, clutching a few garments to her chest. They were in the middle of the column. When I opened my eyes again, I was lying in a pool of sweat, between the two chimney stacks. They were still there, not moving, trapped. Was it the carpenter, or Pavel, or chance? But why speculate, they'd got us. I had my rope, knives, short saw. I went down slowly, keeping calm. Go on, Martin.

The street was full of sunshine and dust. The Ukrainians were yelling, firing in the air in the direction of the rooftops, then letting rip with a few bullets, head high, and the column began to shudder, to waver. They let me cross the road as if they hadn't seen me. What was I to them? One of the 400,000 who were giving themselves up without a fight, not even trying to escape, who'd been cornered. I crossed the road, my head up: they didn't know who I was, why I was going over to them. I whose hands had been burned with fire and acid, I who'd managed to remain silent, to get sackfuls of grain across under their very noses, bribing the butchers the way you pay servants.

A Ukrainian pushed me into the column. I killed your twin, butcher, and I killed your SS master with these hands.

"Don't cry, Mother."

I went over to her, and one by one took away the clothes she was clutching to her chest as if they were her most treasured possessions. I made a bundle of them. I patted my brothers' heads.

"Here I am, Rivka."

She was as calm as if she'd finally reached her destination: I pushed her into the middle of the crowd: it was advisable to keep away from the edge, that was where you got hit. So we set off along Zamenhofa Street. Goodbye, Mila Street, goodbye, Zamenhofa Street. We were walking on torn clothes, scattered books; we were avoiding smashed furniture; we were treading on what had been the lives of tens of thousands of our people, the things for which they'd toiled, we were trampling on our own lives. The warm sun, still amazingly strong for September, beat down on our backs. I was walking behind my people, steering them so that they weren't driven to the edge. By this time we'd reached Dzika Street and I could see the *Umschlagplatz* and the hospital. I knew every cobble in the square and every one of the butchers.

"Rivka, you must run away."

She had a chance: I had money to buy her freedom. But my two brothers would never be able to leave the *Umschlagplatz*. So Mother and I had to go.

"You must run away, Rivka."

I whispered into her hair, her beautiful fair hair, hanging down over her shoulders.

"I can save you. We'll join you later."

I was talking as if lecturing her, but she didn't even look around.

"Run away, Rivka. It's now or never."

By now we could hear the yells of the SS, the slamming of doors, screams of terror and shots being fired.

I pleaded with her.

"Seize the first chance, grab it. After that, it's up to you."

By now I could see the cattle cars, the Jewish police ferreting about in the columns lined up in front of the doors, some people trying to slip away. The little SS man was still there, lash in hand.

"Rivka!"

She didn't answer, but without looking around, letting go of one of my brothers for a moment, she felt for my hand. She gave it a hard squeeze.

We weren't even taken to the hospital. They needed heads.

They were nearing the end of their task, they wanted to keep going, there wasn't a "left" or a "right" anymore, we all got into the cattle cars. I managed to help my people up into one which was only half full; so we all remained together, but by the time they'd shut the door we were in the middle, surrounded, and it was hopeless trying to get near a side. Mother, Rivka and I were an island, in the center of which were my two brothers.

We waiting, suffocating; the wails, screams, pleas for help.

Then the cattle car moved off and at once I started talking, trying to convince my neighbors of the possibility of escape, sometimes shouting, but I wasn't on my own this time, I was wedged there in the middle determined not to leave my brothers, mother and Rivka. I tried again, explaining patiently, gaining a few inches toward the skylight. But my brothers couldn't follow me and might have gotten trampled.

So I stopped talking, I gripped my mother and Rivka by the shoulders and put my arms around them. My brothers were close to us, gripping our legs. Mother was quietly weeping, her tears running down my hands. From time to time there were wild screams and the car lurched violently. I leaned over to protect my people.

The train was heading for Treblinka.

5

For This I Need Another Voice

THE train was heading for Treblinka. The journey took all night.

There was no grinding of axles, snorting of engines, rhythmic pounding of steel rails. The train made none of the reassuring familiar noises of a machine: that train wailed.

There were nearly a hundred and fifty of us, crammed together in one cattle car, unable to move, in the heat of that interminable Polish summer, sweating with fear. One man near me was praying, over my shoulder someone was bellowing insults at him and trying to hit him. Now and then, in a pause, you could hear a child crying. I was clasping Mother and Rivka by the shoulders, and my brothers were clinging to me. Through my arms I tried to pass on to them my tenderness and all my strength so that they could feel it, they, the ones I loved, to whom I couldn't even speak because the bellowing drowned my voice.

Then came thirst and men battling to get near the barred skylight; men ready to kill for a breath of fresh air.

Then the smell, the stench of physical fear. Some went mad. With dawn, I could see a woman tearing at her own face.

Suddenly the train stopped. Footsteps, voices, cars being uncoupled and shunted off. Waiting, the sun heating up the wood, the metal. Noises, more jolting, more cars. We moved slowly; then, again came to a halt. Grinding noise, blinding light, blows and roars as the car was emptied.

Treblinka.

The start of a new era.

For this I need another voice, other words. Every word to stand as a memorial to the thousands of lives which vanished, to the joy which vanished with those lives, to the sheer beauty of life. I need somehow to evoke my mother's look, my brothers' fingers clinging to me, Rivka's hair which I could already see a long way off in the column of women and children forming up under a hail of blows: there was my mother and there were my brothers and Rivka. Goodbye, my family.

This was the start of a new era. All I knew about Treblinka was the name but I knew that those I loved were going to die there.

SS men, Ukrainians holding lashes, cudgels poised to land on heads and backs. A loudspeaker, a cool voice repeating, *"Men to the right, women and children to the left."*

My head down to avoid the blows, I could see a small railway station, read the usual signs: Buffet, Waiting/Room, Toilets, Ticket Office. Everything was as spick and span as a stage set. Then further on I saw barbed wire covered with pine branches.

Goodbye, my family. They'd already disappeared into the huddled mob: gray hair, fair hair, curly hair: my mother, Rivka, my brothers. I knew, heart swelling up into my throat, that they would never come back. That I wouldn't be able to hold them an arm's length from death any longer. It would snatch them away. Perhaps Father had come here, too.

I edged forward, to gain a few seconds in which to understand, so as to choose my fate instead of submitting. Around us were prisoners, hunched, their heads disappearing between their shoulders, rushing in all directions, picking up the luggage, shoving us forward. One of them bumped into me. I caught him.

"What's going on here?"

He pulled away sharply, gave me a shove.

"Never mind, don't worry, just do as you're told."

I dodged blows, followed the line. Some old men were shown to an entrance with a red cross above it: *Lazarett.* The loudspeaker went on giving orders:

"Get undressed. Have a shower. Then you'll be moved to your new work sites."

I looked at the barbed wire, the cattle cars returning empty, the silent, anonymous prisoners. Here waited an unknown death.

"Take your valuables and your papers. Don't forget your soap."

I walked on into an open space where some men were already naked, and that was when I heard a loud, rhythmic sound, like a heavy engine with a dull throb, sometimes dragging, as if making an effort to turn over; an impersonal, monotonous beat: the pulse of the camp, which even the shouts of the SS couldn't drown.

Whips in hand, wearing black, SS men were walking among the naked, catching some by the arm and making them dress again. I still had my clothes on, so I eased over to them, pushing aside men who were having difficulty removing their shoes. I was being driven towards them by some force inside me shouting, "Go on, Martin. Go on, Mietek. That's where life is. Go on."

One of the SS men tapped me on the shoulder with his lash, singling me out.

I began to run along after the rest, carrying bundles of clothes to the sorting lot, helping to make up piles. Running head down, borne forward by those clothes, all that remained of men's lives. More cattle cars had arrived, the last section of our train, and the changing lot was deserted where, barely an hour before, there'd been a throng of naked men; the place where my mother, my brothers and Rivka had been, before disappearing into the hut. The loudspeaker again. I ran off again with heavy loads, as fast as I could.

With every step I came to know Treblinka: its yellowish sand, its all-pervading stench, its voices, its pulse: the engine pounding away in the northeast corner of the camp where, at the far end of an avenue of small dark pine trees, scarcely taller than a man, a brick building lay half-concealed behind a bank with barbed wire on top: a camp within a camp. On the sorting lot, I made separate piles of children's clothes, men's hats, spectacles, over-coats: every object had its pile and you had to rush from one pile to the next. The Ukrainians lashed out with their whips, and at times an SS man shot someone, or killed someone with his rifle butt. I scurried around stooping.

"Mind your face," a prisoner had whispered to me.

Then the breeze, bringing the sound of the engine closer. Over in that other camp they were raking sand. I could clearly hear metal prongs clawing at the ground. They were forever digging over there. We were assembled on a large open space, between the huts. The SS passed in front of us, the Ukrainians at our sides like dogs. And there *were* dogs too, huge ones, straining at their leashes. The SS pointed to men who then left the ranks and went off flanked by Ukrainians. Then we heard shots. We lined up for mess cans of water containing a few potatoes, and were shoved into one of the huts.

I was still alive. The stench in the hut was intolerable. Men were groaning, others prayed. I was sitting next to a man who was trembling, his eyes fixed, his fists and jaws clenched. He was wearing a red badge: a veteran of the camp.

"Where do they go?" I said.

He looked at me blankly.

"Where do they go, the rest of them from the train?"

"The gas chambers."

"Where?"

"To the lower camp, that other camp."

I huddled against the wooden wall. My people, thousands of them, Warsaw! And I was still alive.

Men were crying in the darkness. Then the sound of a box overturning and a death rattle. Someone began praying. A suicide. I made up my mind not to let life ebb away on its own, not to settle for a cowardly death. They were taking our lives; it meant that our lives were jewels. My people were dead; I held their lives in trust. They'd bequeathed me their past, what they could have become and what they had known of joy and sorrow. Through me alone, Senatorska Street might live on; through me alone, the ghetto hideout lived on; through me alone, Zofia's and Rivka's beauty lived on. Through me — and perhaps Father had come through too, maybe he was fighting on in the country or maybe he'd returned to Warsaw. And through me vengeance would live on. I'd decided to live. I *would* escape — for those I loved.

In the morning four bodies were dangling from the beams. We

were lined up on the parade ground and Lalka, the doll, the SS man, harangued us: we were nothing, less than dogs, we were worth less than the soil they'd bury us in, we were vermin. He was of the race of kings.

My first morning in Treblinka, and already the past was receding, already my time in the ghetto was merging with "before." Before the war, before my birth. By the second day I found out about life and death in Treblinka. I saw the *klepssudra:* men who'd been struck in the face, whose welts meant death. They were taken from the ranks and marked for the *Lazarett,* the "hospital." I saw prisoners killed with shovels. I saw dogs attack inmates. I knew why you had to walk with your head down, why you always had to run, do better, go faster: because the SS and the Ukrainians killed us to spur us on. There wasn't any shortage of us. The cattle cars arrived twenty at a time: three sections of twenty, a train. And the others, like Rivka, my mother, my brothers — the others who were my mother, my brothers, my relations, my family, my people — were shoved onto the platform, split up, men to the right, women and children to the left, stripped. And we helped them.

"What's going on here?" they asked.

"Nothing, it's all right, all right," we said.

I collected pairs of shoes; I gathered up clothes that reeked of sweat, I ran. I learned how to run my hands quickly through the pockets, find biscuits and sugar, put them in my mouth and swallow those crumbs of life without even chewing them. A twitch of the lips or the jaw and it was death in the *Lazarett,* or a bullet in the back of the neck. Or death from rifle butts or whips. I went down that avenue, the lovely avenue lined by black pine trees, which led to the *Himmelstrasse,* "road to Heaven," to pick up objects which some of them had dropped, to make the avenue attractive, welcoming, peaceful. I went and cleaned the filth from the walls and floors of the cattle cars. In the evening, on the parade ground, I saw more *klepssudra* leave the ranks for the *Lazarett;* I saw men even with unmarked faces picked at random with a glance and sent to their deaths. Death reaped our ranks constantly. Slowing down at work: death. Carrying too light a load:

death. Chewing a bit of food: death. They wanted to terrorize us. We had to feel their power bearing down on us as if from mysterious gods. They were our fate.

I found myself in the hut, alive, exhausted, winded, my mind empty, barely able to contemplate escape, because I'd had to remain so wary merely to preserve my life. I'd seen the high barbed wire; and beyond it a trench also filled with barbed wire; and another barbed-wire fence, and beyond it a circular path and a flat space a few yards wide also enclosed by barbed wire. Observation towers every two hundred yards overlooked this impregnable wall of steel. Escape that way was impossible.

There was still escape by death. That night, more men hanged themselves in the hut. When, for the third time, I heard a man dragging the box to help a friend die, I dashed over, grabbed him by the shoulders and shook him.

"But they *want* us to die!"

"If we all die, all of us, what'll we do?"

"What can we do anyway except die at their hands?"

He gave me a shove. I went and lay down, listening once more to the horrifying sound of a box overturning, the jerk as a body dangled, the death rattle. Then silence. Suicide was a kind of revolt, but it was the revolt of the defeated. You must live, Mietek. Live to cry out, tell the tale, have revenge. So that our people can live again through you.

The next morning, at assembly again, Lalka's speech: "You're less than dogs, less than dirt, vermin." We bowed our heads. They'd taken our people from us; they were forcing us to shove them onto the platform, to strip them. We met faces like our mothers' and looked away. Were we really vermin, as Lalka said?

So I kept on running, shoulders hunched. If we consented to die, Lalka was right. Martin, you've got to live. I kept running, lost track of time. How many days, how many trains? All those faces, men, women and children, their drowning gestures, those stolen biscuits which caught in the throat but filled the belly. The piles of clothes. Every evening, "You must escape." That struggle in the night to stop suicides. In the morning a man I'd saved going off between two Ukrainians to the *Lazarett*. And the *klepssudra* I'd tried to dab with sand and saliva in the night so the welts wouldn't show next morning, struck again and killed.

Time ceased to exist in life. They created another kind of time at Treblinka. It had no clocks, but was marked by the arrival of trains, the assemblies and the panting of the engine in the lower camp. I wasn't aware of how the sky might change during a day: my eyes saw only the yellowish sand and their boots. And yet, with death on the prowl, I observed the huts, the lay of the land; and the lower camp with its two entrances, one at the end of the *Himmelstrasse* through which our people disappeared, and the other an official gate used by Ukrainians and the SS. Then night would come. Waves of remorse mounted with hunger and exhaustion. Their faces loomed up: Mother, whose gray hair I saw in the column; my brothers — why hadn't I been able to do anything for them? Or for you, Rivka? Despair swept over us all and I had to struggle against those borne away by the current to voluntary death.

I was fighting that black wave. I had only one recourse: saying over to myself, I must live, live for those I loved, live to avenge myself and tell the world that Treblinka meant death. People still in Warsaw thought that they were leaving for the East and took the *Himmelstrasse,* as tens of thousands had done before them. Live, escape, proclaim, avenge. Those repeated words, piled on each other like stones, erected a wall against fear, despair and renunciation. Yet every day, weariness: Lalka's speeches, and the pressure of the butchers; every day, hunger, every day, the arrival of the trains and those barely glimpsed children whose clothes, like the skins of their lives, piled up; all those still-warm objects made a breach in the wall. And it had to be rebuilt, stone by stone, word by word: live, escape, avenge.

But no one lived long in Treblinka. I realized that. Even when I maintained my resolve in the face of the horror, there was chance; a blow in the face, an SS bullet, and that would be the end. You had to move fast. Every day I explored the camp. I became one of the *kommandos* who met our people when the cattle car doors slid open and they saw the little station, that stageset of a station painted on boards, which, for a few minutes — and that was enough — looked real, with its signs: Buffet, Waiting Room. A two-dimensional station. In Treblinka, life was just an illusion. I joined the *kommandos* who carried clothes to the sorting lot, who helped the men to undress.

I carried sacks full of women's hair from the huts, where the women first undressed and were then shorn with a few snips. Afterwards, they went off down the avenue of the dark pines, the *Himmelstrasse*. I made piles: all the objects were sorted, classified. Poor Jews from Warsaw, from the ends of Europe, crockery, fountain pens, photos of children. Mother, I piled up so many clothes like yours; brothers, I saw so many photos that resembled you! Each object was a sorrow; a life with its maze of joys and hopes, a dead life. And it would only be reborn through the living who could avenge it: living to tell what Treblinka was.

Come on, Martin, come on, Mietek. Live!

I joined the lumberjack *kommandos,* hoping to escape in the forest, but we were too well guarded. I joined the camouflage *kommandos,* who put pine branches on the barbed wire so the camp would disappear, so there wasn't really a clearing in the forest where hundreds of thousands of lives had vanished, there was just that engine scrabbling away at the yellow sand. I swept the *Himmelstrasse,* the huts, the platform, with the highway *kommandos.* And I escaped the *Lazarett.*

Then, one day — who knows how many days after my arrival, how many hours? Time didn't exist in Treblinka. One day I was put on a loading duty: the empty cattle cars were lined up along the platform and, always stooping, we carried the bundles of clothes inside. We filled the cattle cars to the roof. I dashed about, amid shouts, supervised by the Ukranians, the *kapos* and the SS. I jumped into the cattle car, shoving the bundles, and went off again to the huts to fetch more bundles, trying to make out where the SS and the Ukranians were, to see if I could slow down a bit, recover my breath, obsessed with my hunger and my tiredness. Suddenly, looking back at the platform, for the first time I saw the train for what it was: a train. A train about to leave Treblinka loaded with clothes. Then I ran faster: and my plan took shape: climb into one of the cattle cars, make a hiding place among the bundles, hide there, then leave with the train. I ran and jumped into one of the cattle cars, but the loading was over. I tried again, but bundles were against the walls on all sides. The SS came up and checked the loading, slamming the doors themselves when there wasn't any space left between the bundles and the wooden sides. So I had to leave the platform. I'd thought of it too late, I'd let myself get caught in their trap of fear, terror and exhaustion. I'd missed the chance, the first chance. The one you had to seize, Father. I had not been worthy of you. You'd have seized that chance. And that night, in my despair, I began to think that my father had escaped, that he was fighting on, that he'd hidden in the train from Treblinka.

From then on, loading bundles became my sole concern. I saw how to stack the bundles in a corner of the car, and make a rampart concealing the hiding place, as far as possible from the door; how to support the sides and let the bundles pile up. I was ready. But for the next few days there weren't any trains. Then I was transferred to the highway *kommando:* sweeping duties. I saw the train filling up and wasn't able to help load it. I was ready now but I'd missed that first chance.

In the evening, the black wave swept over me. I could see my people, I was back in Senatorska Street shifting sacks of grain, and Mokotow the Tomb was laughing. I was drinking the fiery vodka which Yadia poured out. I was holding Zofia's hand, laughing with her. The black wave swept over me, and I also remembered the Gestapo butcher who'd come to my cell at Pawiak and whom I'd beaten. Was it all for nothing?

In the morning I approached Kieve. He'd been a ghetto tough, a porter, a thief, once an ox, all muscle; thinner today, but still strong and tougher than most. When he opened his mouth there were only his gums, and a few black roots. He'd been hit with a rifle butt in the early days of the ghetto. We had never had the time nor strength to talk at Treblinka. I slipped into his corner before assembly. I shook him. He jumped as if I were death itself. Then he recognized me.

"You know the *kapo,* Kieve. We've got to get on the loading *kommando.*"

The *kapo* was a German Jew who knocked us about, possibly to spare us harsher blows, or simply to save his own skin; he had to hit us, or die himself. Kieve looked at me. We'd lost the habit of talking in Treblinka. One word could lead to the *Lazarett*.

"Kieve, if we're loading the train. Two of us . . ."

He gripped my shoulders.

I rapidly outlined my plan. He shook his head, rubbing his gums with mangled fingers.

"We'd have to be on the loading *kommando*."

"I'll talk to the *kapo*."

It was a long day. Two convoys arrived. Thousands of men, women and children. Their screams, their clothes, their hair. Hang on, Martin, hang on a bit longer. I charged about. In the evening, assembly. A long list, three *klepssudra,* then too many to count taken off to the *Lazarett*. The hut at last. Kieve.

"I spoke to him," he said.

I questioned him, uneasy, entrusting my life to Kieve, to the *kapo,* some apprehension nagging me.

"He didn't answer. He listened."

That didn't mean a thing, maybe just the caution of everyone in Treblinka. That night I slept badly. The noise of the engine at the lower camp never ceased, and I could see the beams of searchlights over to the northeast, behind the barbed wire from which no one returned.

In the morning, at assembly, more *klepssudra.*

Lalka made his speech: we were the scum of the earth. He called to some *kapos* and they ran up to him, their helmets clanking against their stiff thighs, and stood at attention. Then they passed among us. Kieve's *kapo* pulled me out of the ranks along with Kieve himself. Some Ukrainians surrounded us and a few other prisoners, but we didn't go to the *Lazarett:* we took the *Himmelstrasse,* the avenue lined with flowers and black firs which led to the brick building. With every step it became clearer: huge, austere, with a Star of David over its narrow door. It looked a bit like a synagogue. I hadn't seized the first chance. I'd put my life in others' hands. I'd lost. Fearful of having to pay for our escape himself, one day, the *kapo* had sent us to the *Himmelstrasse.*

As we moved forward, the sound of the engine became a roar and the grinding of metal on sand, a scream. The Ukrainians handed us over to other Ukrainians at the entrance to the lower camp. We crossed the barbed wire, and came face to face with the large brick building which had only one narrow door. On the right was the *Lazarett*. We walked around the brick building. And I saw the giant excavator plunging its steel arm into the yellow sand. The engine, dragging away, exploded in my ears. Guards shouted and prisoners rushed about carrying stretchers. The guards raised their whips and clubs, and I too began to rush to the stretchers which they were indicating. Rough canvas stretchers. Kieve took the other end and we ran towards the broad open doors on the sides of the brick building. Wooden doors, nine feet wide.

Then we saw.

For this I need still another voice, other words.

The bodies were naked, entwined tendrils; the bodies were yellow and blood had dribbled down their faces from their noses. They were my mother, my brothers, Rivka, all my people. We copied the others, grabbed the bodies and ran. We paused in front of the prisoners who, armed with pliers, were searching the corpses' mouths and extracting gold teeth, and ran over to the grave dug in the yellow sand. At the bottom, standing on the dead, prisoners were lining up the bodies, my mother's, my brothers', Rivka's body. Then we threw in our first body. Then more, still running, sometimes loading three children's bodies across a stretcher. The Ukrainians shoved anyone who wasn't running fast enough, who was carrying only a light body, into the grave. A hundred times over, I threw my mother, my brothers, Rivka, my people, into the bottom of the grave; and beyond, a few dozen yards away the excavator snorted, a monster digging in the sand.

I'd become one of the *Totenjuden,* death-Jews. I realized that the ghetto, the *Umschlagplatz,* the cattle car that brought us to Treblinka, the upper camp from which I came, were nothing. Here were the depths. The depths of life. The depths of man: because the butchers had men's faces. They were like those bodies I was throwing, they were like me. They'd invented this murder factory, these gas chambers, these new gas chambers so well planned with their nozzles, their white-tiled walls, their narrow entrance doors, and their sloping floors which ran down to the large door which opened; against which the bodies lay entwined. Our bodies. We were death Jews, dead too. Apart from our guards, we never saw a living person. Sometimes, in the distance, I could see, in the upper camp, the outline of a naked man running with a load of clothes. I was part of this kingdom of pariahs. When our food was delivered, the driver of the cart didn't come near us: he parked the cart at the entrance. One of us went to fetch it.

We were living with only the dead and the killers. Yet I had to survive. In the hut, surrounded with barbed wire, a prison camp within a prison camp, there was one suicide after another and every evening I tried to stop them. We had to stand witness. My voice would gain strength from those thousands of voices silenced by the gas and the yellow sand; my revenge would grow from those bodies with which we prisoners were lining the bottom of hell. Two or three layers of bodies and the excavator pushed sand over them. My life had to be another life for my people: those thousands of bodies we so roughly grabbed and flung on the stretchers.

Many of the prisoners seemed to live without knowing what they were doing, as if their actions had lost all meaning. They were shadows of men carrying out given tasks, amid blows and in fear. Others, like myself, lived and breathed resistance. In the evenings I wrestled with the suicides. We had to become a solid block of men who knew each other; a fist, which one day would kill before it was crushed. But the suicides went on. Death took its toll of our group.

One day. In the lower camp, on the edge of the grave, real time didn't exist, and even the rhythm of the upper camp ceased to have meaning. One day, when we'd removed the wedges from the gas-chamber doors, when the doors opened and we saw the sodden yellow bodies, when we began to drag them towards us, Kieve gave a howl of anguish and dropped the stretcher, grabbed a body and shook it as if to make sure that it had ceased to have any life, then ran towards a Ukrainian who fired. Kieve fell into the grave.

I didn't even look at the body's face. We, all of us, avoided the faces of the dead, refusing to look into them, refusing to see if we had known one of those faces.

Ivan, a huge Ukrainian with a tiny, squashed-looking head, was in charge of us. He killed indiscriminately. So I loaded on the heaviest bodies, two sometimes, to dodge the blow in the face which would make me a *klepssudra;* to forestall his command, "Down you go!" Into the grave. Ivan, before he fired, used to order the condemned man to lie in the grave on the still-warm bodies we'd just thrown in.

You had to run, keep on running. And we could scarcely breathe, and were famished. I selected "dentists" who worked quickly, who could inspect and deal with the mouth of a corpse in less than a minute — the corpse who less than half an hour ago had been a living creature with a head full of memories, a mind crammed with all the wealth of past lives. The finger slipped into the mouth and the pliers tugged. You had to choose a fast dentist because holding out a body at arm's length when you're on the verge of exhaustion was a cruel test. And a tired man would die.

So I ran, controlling my breath, gritting my teeth. Live, Martin, live. Kill them. The words filled my eyes, my mouth, my head. They were my drug and my food. At night when I heard that sinister word "Away," which meant that someone was going to remove the box from under the feet of his companion to help him die, I still tried to rush forward to stop it. Sometimes I gave up, conserving my strength in order to save my own life. I *had* to live. Sometimes a horror helped us. When they got the new gas chambers going, we had to wait a long time, because the stuff with which they were experimenting for the first time failed to work. So we got a little rest. Sometimes some crazy accomplice of a dentist would take a chance and let us through with only the merest pretence of stopping us. That dentist gambled with his own life. One of them, a thin young man with long, white hands was unusually skillful. He operated almost without looking, by touch. One day he passed me through with the bodies of three children barely five or six years old. An SS man, known as *"Idioten,"* because that was how he addressed us, came over.

"Why?" he asked.

"They were barely five years old, they couldn't have gold teeth."

I stood listening, terrified by the sight of a Ukrainian who'd followed his SS master.

"That's a good excuse," said Idioten.

He indicated the grave to the young man with long white hands. His body fell in at the same time as those of the three children.

For this I need . . .

Sometimes we found living children among the warm bodies. Little children, still alive, clinging to their mothers' bodies. We strangled them with our own hands before throwing them into the grave. And we risked our lives doing it because we were wasting time. The butchers wanted everything to happen fast. They rushed us so fast that suddenly there would be a silence when we'd completed our task and had to wait for the next wave. We heard it coming. We listened to the frenzied yells, the dogs barking. Sometimes we found men mutilated, their stomachs torn open by the dogs. Dogs trained by men.

I need another voice, other words to describe the shame that filled me, nausea, shame at still being alive; and the compulsion to live that possessed me; to live, to tell what we'd seen, what they'd done, what they'd forced us to do. The more savage they were the more convinced I became that they would be defeated, that it was inconceivable that their kingdom of death should become the kingdom of men. Their plague would cease one day. I'd be there, witness and judge for those strangled children. For those I loved. I ran, suffering when the bodies were heavy; from their weight we knew that those anonymous dead came from areas where famine hadn't been rife, areas where the Jews must have been caught in blissful ignorance.

In the evenings we returned, exhausted, reeking. Some grinned sheepishly, imbecilic, others taunted each other and fought, or hanged themselves. I couldn't sleep, waiting for that sinister "Away," listening for the SS. They came into the hut at night, accompanied by Ukrainians, to select victims whom they took from near the door and killed above the graves. In the evening some of the prisoners didn't even have the strength to drag themselves to the middle or end of the hut. They were volunteering for death.

At night I writhed with nightmares; waking, thinking I heard "Away" and the scraping of a box; seeing myself lying in the grave between my father and mother. In the morning I threw up reddish vomit, I felt cold, my legs trembling, my eyes misting over as if covered with yellow dust, the color of Treblinka sand. It took an effort to move my arms, to stand. Yet I turned up for assembly and ran with the others, my footsteps echoing in my head, their yells piercing my ears, red-hot needles. I picked up the stretcher. The sport began. New gas chambers were working at full capacity. Convoys kept coming, bodies piled up. I carried out my tasks as a death-Jew; teeth clenched, the muscles of my arms quivering, and every time I stopped in front of one of the dentists I was terrified I'd collapse at his feet. I kept my jaws locked, otherwise I'd have screamed; I kept running, throwing, even dragging my companion along, at top speed; the Ukrainians were watching me. If I relaxed, I was finished. To foil suspicions, cruel eyes, I loaded on the heaviest bodies. "They're sacks, Martin, go on, Martin, keep going, survive." A jerk of the hips and I lifted the stretcher, running towards the dentist. Running meant life.

I held out almost to the end. We'd had a long day. The gas chambers had been full, the bodies heavy. It was now my last trip, the gas chambers were empty.

"Quick!"

I gave the dentist an imploring look as I whispered the word. He flicked open the lips with a finger. I passed on.

"*Halt!*"

Idioten was close beside me, lash in hand. He called the dentist. A gold tooth gleamed. He went down into the grave without being told. The excavator was working near us and I didn't even hear the shot. Idioten raised his lash and struck me. I hung on, trembling from head to foot, then tipped in the corpse. I knew that I couldn't hold out longer. Fever had me in its burning grip; maybe I was already doomed anyway, my face marked by Idioten.

THE INFERNO

In the streets of the ghetto. PHOTO BY C.D.J.C.

WEDNESDAY, JULY 22, 1942.
THE BUTCHERS HAD SPOKEN

"They wanted thousands of us each day for *Umsiedlung:* transportation to the East. I saw women in scarves, hollow-cheeked, laughing hysterically." They agreed to leave for six pounds of bread. The butchers herded the inhabitants into columns: women, children, the disabled. The Jewish police (in caps, armbands on sleeves) had no choice but to obey. PHOTOS BY C.D.J.C.

UMSCHLAGPLATZ

"The butchers had spoken and this place had become the center of the inferno." They loaded the cattle cars. After the long journey on the train came the halt on a single track: Treblinka. PHOTOS BY C.D.J.C.

"YOU'LL FIGHT, MIETEK"

Sunday, April 19, 1943, the ghetto rose up. The butchers withdrew, then set fire to the ghetto. "Now you could hardly tell day from night." It was a fight to the death. PHOTOS BY C.D.J.C.

GOODBYE, MY PEOPLE

"My father lay among the stones of the ghetto, a stone of the ghetto."

Es gibt keinen jüdischen Wohnbezirk — in Warschau mehr !

"The Jewish quarter in Warsaw no longer exists." This was how General Stroop headed his report to Himmler. PHOTOS BY C.D.J.C. AND U.S.I.S.

Maybe I would be a *klepssudra,* ordered out of the ranks at assembly. But they ignored me and I managed to drag myself across the floor of the hut, to the far end, crawling on my hands and knees, half-dead. A man came over to me and pulled me away from the middle of the floor. I looked up and showed him my face.

"*Klepssudra?*"

It was dark. He leaned over and ran his fingers down my cheeks.

"Nothing there," he said.

Sometimes people lied to discourage suicides in the night.

"I won't kill myself," I said.

"There's nothing there, I promise you."

I lay there, trembling convulsively from fever and nausea.

"Are you ill?"

I tried to retch.

"You must keep going," he said. "Where are you from?"

The black wave of memories was surging up. He sounded like one of my ghetto toughs. I began to talk, half delirious. About smuggling, crossing the wall a hundred times, the wholesome-smelling sacks of grain, Frankenstein, the Café Sztuka.

"Abram's also here," he said.

Abram! Abramele, we called him. We used to pour into Abramele's restaurant like a torrent — Dziobak the Pox, Mokotow the Tomb, Pila the Saw, Zamek the Wise, Pavel — the Pavel of before that August night — and I. Abramele would set the table for us, smiling at the thought of what we were going to spend with him, teasing Pavel.

"He works in the kitchen," he added.

"Who are you?"

"I'm Moishe. You knew Trisk the Cart?"

Yankle the Blind, Chaim the Monkey, Trisk: I'd seen them riding in a cart down Zamenhofa Street to the *Umschlagplatz,* deaf to my warnings. I'd joined them, a little later, here in Treblinka.

"I'm from Trisk's family. I'll help you."

So, in that kingdom of death, a man branded a thief said those words, "help you," those words which meant extra risk, in a place where to survive at all was a miracle.

Moishe was in with the *kapos* and he ate better, thanks to Abramele and the killer Idioten, who, for some reason, was protecting him. To hold out at Treblinka you needed the *kapos*, who weren't constant victims of blows, work, chance and hunger.

In the morning, at assembly, the fever was still with me, but I recovered hope. Still, when the Ukrainians and SS came, I lowered my face. Maybe Moishe had lied, maybe I was *klepssudra?* But they looked at me and didn't pick me out.

That day I was spared the gas chambers and the graves. I joined the highway *kommandos;* I gardened, I turned the handle of the well and the prisoner who was working alongside me helped me, pressing on the handle himself when all I could do was lean on the steel bar above the deep shaft that smelled so fresh and moist. I'd become one of the privileged caste in the lower camp. But like all prisoners, we could be singled out for death at evening assembly. The next day I again escaped the gas chambers. A *kapo* took me to the kitchens, and to Abramele, always cheerful, good for a laugh.

He didn't even look surprised to see me again.

"Mietek! All of us are coming here," he said. "The last table for Mietek!"

He took me to a safe corner.

"Eat quickly," he said, suddenly serious.

I swallowed some potatoes, still hot, with hunger greater than my fever. I managed to rest a little, I gained a few days saved by others who remained men. Leaning on the handle, kept going by my silent comrade, I was convinced that men would eventually triumph over the creatures of darkness who were slaughtering us.

But Abramele, Moishe and I remained death-Jews, subject to the whims of our masters and the demands of the "factory." We were on temporary reprieve. Each time a convoy arrived, we were shoved towards the graves, towards the wooden doors of the gas chambers, and we took up the canvas stretchers again, to the pounding of the excavator as it clawed more graves out of the yellow sand. I kept going. I followed Moishe. The fever still in me, I lifted and carried light bodies, guided, protected and borne along by Moishe. Idioten turned a blind eye. And thanks to Abramele, I got a few extra potatoes.

One evening Moishe failed to return to the hut. Ivan had shot him, near the kitchen, because he wasn't running fast enough. I realized again that my turn would come if I didn't escape. There was no survival in the lower camp. Next day, at the graves, Idioten warned me. My stretcher wasn't loaded heavily enough. But instead of shooting me, Idioten made me stand to attention in front of him.

"If you scream, Jew, I'll kill you."

He beat my body, avoiding my face, possibly in memory of Moishe. I didn't cry out. My life was spared. But I was ordered down into the grave, to stand on corpses and line them up as though they were wood; to trample on those who, half an hour earlier, had been human beings full of hope and fear.

Some prisoners who worked in the graves went mad. Others asked to die. I hadn't much time left. I was close to the end of my life. The butchers had already noticed me; I had been around too long for a prisoner. I was bound to make the mistake for which I'd die.

I sat in the hut: I'd been fighting just to survive but that wasn't enough. The rules of the game meant that I was losing. I'd missed that first chance by not jumping into the clothes train. Now I was near the end. I possibly had a few days more, maybe only hours. All that I'd done, all my energy, anger, vengeance, would come to nothing if I consented to die. The butchers would have won: no point in those victories against them, at Pawiak and in the ghetto. Nothing, hundreds of thousands of men would have died for nothing. I had to escape from Treblinka. That was the only victory that mattered. It would make me the witness, the avenger, the man through whom my people, all my people, would live.

I kept repeating these words, these conclusions, to myself to spur myself on, to give myself strength. I had to do it alone: Moishe was dead, Abramele doubtful, the others might fear reprisals. I had to rely on myself alone. At night, I worked out plans. Getting through the barbed wire was impossible and the *Himmelstrasse* out of the question; no one could get through the gate of the road to heaven. That left the west exit, used by the SS and Ukrainians. But it was far from our barracks and was sure to be guarded. Yet it was the only route of escape from the lower camp to the upper camp. Then chance the train again. There was no other way. This plan was crazy, but I was living in a crazy world. I had to succeed or die.

Would they leave me time? Fate would decide. For a while, thanks to Abramele, I managed to stay in the kitchen. I thought of killing an SS man or a Ukrainian, putting on his uniform and passing through the door. It was an impossible dream. I waited; every hour alive was a card in my hand, and having a definite goal gave me strength. I was sent back to the grave; I worked like a machine, running, shifting my feet impatiently in front of the dentists. I mustn't die. I must hang on.

I kept going. How many hours or days? Human time didn't exist in Treblinka. I kept going until I saw a truckload of SS men make for our huts, singing. They went in to where the gold was accumulating, the gold the dentists extracted from corpses' mouths and which the Ukrainians often stole. I spoke to Abramele who knew what went on.

"The SS just come and help themselves to gold. Jews are rich, you know, Mietek."

He started laughing.

I observed the truck. No one guarded it. I saw it move off, SS men jumping on board, slapping each other on the back. And it drove through the west gate without even slowing down. It disappeared behind the huts in the upper camp. Hope lay there.

That night, I worked out my plan. That night, like every night, men hanged themselves. Several times I heard the word "Away"; and the box scraped against the floor. When silence returned, broken only by men having nightmares, I slipped over to the hanged men, went to the box and took them in my arms, my dead comrades who were to help me. At Treblinka you hanged yourself with your belt: and I needed belts. I released my comrades, and removed their belts. I joined several belts together into two long loops, winding them around me as once, in the ghetto during the evacuation, I'd wound a rope around me to escape from the hospital and the *Umschlagplatz*. In the morning, no one was surprised to find bodies lying on the floor. What were three dead to those who dealt in hundreds?

That day I went back to the graves, trembling. Martin, you mustn't die today. I kept going, I ran. I placed two, three bodies on my stretcher, gasping. I ran to live. The following days — how many of them? — I stayed near the kitchen holding a spade, fearing the assemblies, a glance from drunken Ukrainians, some fatal piece of luck.

One afternoon when the sun had disappeared behind the trees, the horizon in Treblinka, a truckload of SS men returned, spewing yellow dust. They pulled up in front of the hut and jumped down. I was just a blob. Their minds were on gold.

I propped my spade against the hut, and glanced around. I was going to make it.

The whole of my life, all those dead lives of my people were there to protect me. I couldn't help making it, because I had to. I dived under the truck. I looked for rods, jagged surfaces, and slipped the belts over them, passing them under me, tightened them clutching the steel with my fingertips, pressing my face against the metal, clinging there with all my will, all my life. That truck was my flesh, my shield, my mother, and I hung there between the wheels, in a womb from which only death could tear me. But I feared my body. My muscles were quivering, the belts were biting into my neck and legs. How heavy my famished body! An agonizing wait. I could hear laughter, the crack of their boots on steel and wood. The engine suddenly burst into life close by me, the truck began to vibrate and finally moved off. Only yards and I nearly screamed. My foot was touching the exhaust pipe. I shifted and became part of that vibrating machine-mother now jolting and smothering me.

I held on. Thank you, hanged comrades, thank you, Moishe. And you, the stranger who pressed on the well handle. Thank you, Abramele, for those potatoes, now the strength in my wrists and fingers today. Thank you, my people. Thank you, bodies in the grave, children strangled by my own hands to spare you slowly suffocating to death under humid bodies; thank you for giving me faith, and for that truck that drove on and on. I'm shivering beneath you, machine-mother, but I'm hanging onto you and nothing will make me let go. Go, Martin, go, Mietek.

We drove across bumpy sand, engine roaring, my mouth full of dust. At last we stopped. Shouts, the yelping sound of assembly. I could hear the SS boots on the ground. They must have jumped down. I had to wait, cramps racking my muscles. I could hardly unclench my fingers. The two loops held me at the neck and ankles or I would have fallen to the ground. I hung on. Men were talking, walking past the truck, then night and silence cloaked Treblinka. I waited. I could see the beams of the searchlights sweeping the barbed wire; now and then the door of a hut banged. I untied one of the loops and slid to the ground. Oh, the joy of touching the ground! Resting my back in that sand in which were buried all my people. I loved the earth with my body, my bruised neck and stiffened arms. But I had to be careful. I clung to the truck, only letting myself rest on the ground when I felt that I'd scream from the pain in my muscles. I heard a sound by the side of the truck, too late to grab hold again; I clutched the little capsule of cyanide which Moishe had given me. I didn't even look, expecting a flashlight, a shot. Then I felt a body against me. A German shepherd dog, sniffing peacefully. I started stroking it and it licked my hands. It went away, then returned, innocent in the night. In the narrow passage of the factory, where five doors opened onto the gas chamber, other dogs were poised to kill. Which was the beast, dog or man? You could do just as you liked with dogs as well as with men. There were no men, no dogs, no cursed race, just men who'd become butchers, others who'd trained them, and maybe societies which had produced more butchers than others.

The dog disappeared again. I was afraid it might bring its master. Then, still clinging under the truck, I calmed down. I had to wait. If the truck drove away, I'd stay with it. If not I'd seize the moment, the first chance.

Dawn brought cooler weather. Mist drifted across the ground, an omen of good luck. There was a burst of machine-gun fire from an observation post near the lower camp. Probably only Abramele would notice my absence, for a moment. For the butchers, we had no names, no numbers, no faces; we were working dead men, objects that sometimes cried out and stained red when a bullet struck. We were nothing. I could hear the engine of the excavator as the shovel bit into the first layer of sand. They were digging a new grave. My comrades were about to line up, the *klepssudra* stepping out of the ranks without being told, the others running with loaded stretchers.

I'd gotten away from the lower camp, that bit of the *Himmel-strasse* from which no one returned. But I'd gotten away; now I had to break from the upper camp too. It was my vow. And listening to the excavator digging new graves, being away from and yet among my friends standing on the dead, I felt renewed strength. I'd make it.

The mist had thickened. Lalka's voice, announcing our end, our nonexistence, reached me: it was time for assembly. I waited, wrapping the belts around my body. I was about to risk losing everything. Voices, speaking Yiddish, near the truck. I crawled over to the wheels. I saw a group of prisoners, about twenty yards off. I stood up, stood by the truck, keeping an eye on the Ukrainian guard. I walked over to them in the mist, legs stiff, arms like lead. I bumped into a wheelbarrow and clutched it. No one could have wrested it from me. A prisoner turned.

"Where are you from?"

I nodded. "Later, later."

He hesitated, shrugged. I stayed with that group, a highway *kommando*, for a while, then, at assembly slipped away. I had to lose myself among the prisoners. My chance lay with the butchers' cruelty, their regular executions of the men they picked out of the ranks every evening and took to the *Lazarett*, men who had to be replaced. In the upper camp, as in the lower, there were no names, no numbers, no faces. I collected my soup, like the rest. I won. I was no longer at the bottom of the abyss.

In the upper camp, I started to live again. To live in spite of the horror, because I'd known the graves and the "factory," because I'd come out of that last place where the living never go, because I still had hope. I kept telling myself, as I ran, that even here, as in Pawiak, as in the Gestapo headquarters in Szucha Alley, I had beaten the devils, the lords and monarchs of death. With no weapons except my heart and will. Go on, Lalka, tell me

I'm scum, vermin, carry on in your smug little puppet's voice. I'm the man and I'm going to win.

I now had only one aim: to join the *kommando* loading the cattle cars. I had to proceed with caution, alone, trying to learn the workings of the camp, observe the *kapos* and the *goldjuden,* "golden Jews," who formed the camp aristocracy. I had to move fast, hide my face, become invisible. I had to conserve my strength: I rapidly searched the clothes we carried to the sorting lot, swallowing biscuits and sugar without moving my jaws. I removed labels from clothes, so that they became anonymous. I hid a sharp knife found in a leather jacket. I worked with almost all the *kommandos.* I carried sackfuls of hair, sorted into colors. Then I drew duty in the *Lazarett;* and again met living death. The hut was on the east side of the camp, near the sorting yards — marked with a huge red cross. The waiting room was clean, with comfortable armchairs and led into the "consulting" room. A prisoner in white coveralls brought in the latest arrivals. The room had a large exit, hidden by a curtain behind which was an armed Ukrainian and a pit. I collected the bodies of old men, still trembling, as they died; and the bodies of children and disabled. The grave all over again, but finally I managed to escape and lose myself in other *kommandos.* Once again I watched the trains arrive, the frenzied looks of mothers and children. They'd catch me by the arm.

"What's going on? Where are we?"

"It's all right, all right."

What could I say? What could I do? I saw faces that I seemed to know. When I saw healthy-looking men with a chance of being selected for a *kommando* I whispered, "Don't get undressed."

We weren't meant to breathe a word to the new arrivals, we weren't even to notice them. A prisoner in the blue *kommando* near me was hailed by a woman's voice, a heartrending mixture of joy and terror.

"Schloime, Schloime, it's me!"

I knew he hadn't moved, that he was keeping busy in order not to hear, I heard his footsteps dying away and the voice calling, "Schloime, Schloime, it's me!"

Booted feet followed Schloime, whose face I hadn't even seen.

There was a shot. How could you trust a prisoner who'd seen his mother or sister arrive?

"Schloime, Schloime!"

I cleaned out the cattle cars, removing the bodies of those who'd died of thirst: children, old men. Chalked on each car was the number of persons it contained: 120, 160, 145. Back at the *Umschlagplatz,* an SS man, possibly the little one with the lash, had been going about his task. Each convoy left me horror-stricken. It was as if my mother, my brothers and Rivka were getting out again, as if once again I was going to lose them, let them die. Now I knew, I'd returned from down below, where the excavator was at work, where the dogs were yelping in the halls, where sometimes the children weren't yet dead when the big wooden doors opened. I knew. With every convoy, it was my mother, my father, Rivka, my brothers, my people, who were shoved out on the platform. I was powerless.

Sometimes men and women cried out, "We're not Jews!"

Like bewildered animals, they rushed towards the Ukrainians or the SS men, screaming in terror, "Polish! Not Jewish! Not Jewish! Catholic! I hate the Jews!"

They died even sooner, from a bullet; or suffered the common fate. Here, in Treblinka, it wasn't the Jews they were killing, it wasn't a particular race they were exterminating. The butchers wanted to destroy mankind, and they'd decided to begin with those men known as Jews. All men were condemned. Only the butchers and their dogs remained alive. In Treblinka, it was mankind they were wiping out. But to conceal this vast undertaking more effectively, the butchers had tried to cloak mankind under the name Jew.

So the Poles who jumped down onto the platform shouting, "Not Jewish, not Jewish! Catholic!" died. I listened to the frenzied cries of men who had probably been seized in the vicinity of the wall, or who looked like Jews. They were going to die without realizing that their faith or their race wouldn't have protected them for long: some day or other they would have had to choose between the fate of a beast or the life of a man. I discovered in Treblinka that, Jew or non-Jew, there was only humankind.

That was also something I had to tell about outside. Time

passed. I tried to stay with the *kommandos* working by the platform: this meant the horror of the convoys but some hope of the loading train and escape. One day, the Ukrainians shoved me over to the changing lot: part of the red *kommando* was working there. You had to help the children and elderly undress. They moved awkwardly, shattered by the journey. They questioned me. And I knew! I was probably the only prisoner in the red *kommando* and possibly the only one in the upper camp who had seen. I knew their fate. But I had to harry my brothers and my mother. I had to keep saying, "It's all right, all right."

I could picture their yellowish bodies lying in the grave. There was nothing I could do.

Among the *kapos* was a Jew from Warsaw, one of the gang which controlled a *meta* of the wall and made us smugglers pay "duty" in order to get our sacks through. I'd already spoken to him.

"You're Mietek," he'd whispered.

Then there'd been a long pause.

"Your grain wasn't much use to them."

It was his voice, both friendly and desperate. You had to take a chance. One night we were sitting shoulder to shoulder in the dark at the far end of the hut.

"I've been down there."

He asked no questions: a good sign.

"Do you hear?"

The excavator was clawing at the earth. There had been two convoys that day. Jews were turning up in ever increasing numbers from every corner of Poland; even farther away.

"It's digging graves."

I started talking. I mentioned Abramele and Moishe, whom he must have known in the streets of the ghetto.

"Mietek, never talk."

He gave my knee a squeeze.

"Never talk. They have spies."

I'd found a man.

"I must get into loading the cattle cars, the first load."

We remained side by side until assembly.

"Never talk," he repeated.

I didn't see him again. I'd changed *kommandos*. Then one day, as we were dispersing, he hit me on the back once, twice, yelling, "Come on, move!"

He shoved me toward the loading *kommando,* led by another *kapo.*

We set off for the platform, the *kapo* hurling insults at us. The train was there, cattle cars open, empty; bundles ready for loading.

Thank you, fellow prisoner, Thank you, man.

The plan was the one I'd worked out long, long before. I loaded the corner of a car, stacking bundles, just enough to be a busy, anonymous ant in the trail. Then I moved away from the corner with its niche and filled up the rest of the car, the prisoners behind me piling up the bundles for me to stack. I was leaping, climbing, shoving. A *kapo* was yelling, Ukrainians and SS men marched up and down the platform. Prisoners were stooping, swarming, running, jumping, loading. I was alone in the car for only a moment: but it was enough. I dived into my niche, shutting myself in with a bundle, my arms supporting the pile, pushing against other bundles with my back and head. I was aware of the dull thud and pressure of more bundles building up, squeezing me against the side of the car. Then silence, my right hand clutching my poison capsule, my left gripping my knife. Voices. A shot. An SS man or a Ukrainian shooting a prisoner as an example. In my hiding place I no longer heard the excavator; it was as if I'd already left hell.

The creaking and slamming grew closer; SS men were shutting the doors. A moment's silence, shouts, probably a car not fully loaded. More creaking and slamming. My car. A wait. The train moved, then stopped again. Another wait.

A wait as long as if all those lives, lying in their sandy graves, were joined together; a wait as long as an assembly when I was sure I would be a *klepssudra:* as long as that race from the gas chambers to the graves when the fever was with me; as long as my torture at Gestapo headquarters; as long as the moment when they yelled "Men to the right, women and children to the left" and my mother, my brothers and Rivka were separated from me. As long as my death in Treblinka.

I felt a cold draft through the wooden sides. The train was moving.

There was a grinding of axles and a snorting of engines, then the rhythmic pounding of steel rails. That train made all the familiar sounds of a machine.

That train was a cry — our cry to life.

6

I'd Tell Them about the Umschlagplatz,
the Cattle Cars and the Graves

THE train kept moving. I was pressed hard against the rough
wood, groping at the side of the car, the wood against which
so many of my people had pressed their foreheads, their lips, on
which so many of my people had broken their nails between Warsaw and Treblinka. I made an effort to control myself, not to be
carried away by the excitement, mingled with fear and anguish,
which tempted me to dig a hole in the wood, smashing it with my
head, sticking my knife in anywhere, ripping away with my teeth
and hands the boards that divided me from free air. I gradually
controlled myself, recovering my breath, collecting my thoughts,
working out a plan. I began by enlarging a chink between two
boards, to look through; and suddenly there was the western horizon, a dark red strip with no observation posts or barbed wire to
mar it, only the black mass of forests half-obscured by dusk; cultivated fields shrouded here and there by drifts of grayish mist; the
vast countryside, unblemished, no helmeted men, no corpses, no
columns of stooping prisoners. I couldn't stop staring at those silent, drowsy, peaceful expanses of innocent land dotted with stag-
nant marshes, on which men had built Treblinka.

The train slowed to a crawl. I was seized with panic. We were
passing through a station. On the lighted platform, soldiers were
eating, their weapons, packs and helmets stacked against the
walls. Some, holding mess cans and sprawled near the tracks, were

AREAS OF POLAND

which Martin Gray covered after his escape from Treblinka (Zambrow and Bialystok areas), then after the uprising of the Warsaw ghetto (Lublin area).

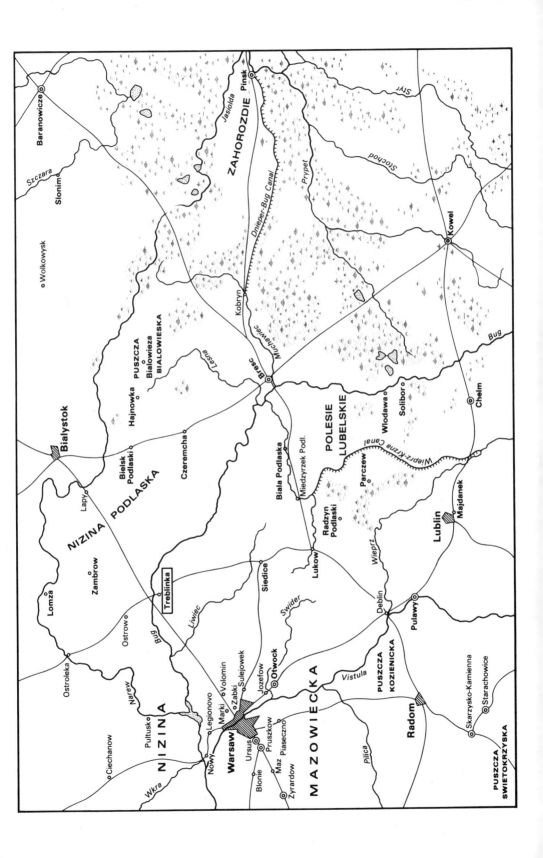

looking at the train. I was sure they'd see my eyes and rush forward, yelling. I gripped my knife: I'd never go back to Treblinka. Then the train gathered speed again, plunging into the countryside and the night. I began to dig, whittling away at the boards, splinters in my fingers, sweating. Once again we passed through a station, deserted, barely indicated by two flashing yellow lights. Back in the night, I strained against the bundles of clothes. With a loud crack the boards gave, damp air blasting me, my hiding place filled with the noise of the train and the smells of the countryside. I had to hurry before another station, full of soldiers, came along. Clinging to the boards, I slid out of the car, clutching the side, staring into the night. I didn't worry: for years my life was mostly leaps in the dark. I'd just come from a place where only objects were friendly, men cruel: how could I be afraid of leaping into the night? The speed, the earth, the darkness, even the stones would be kinder than the beasts with human faces I'd known back there.

I jumped, head cradled in my arms. I rolled off the track and landed in a grassy ditch full of icy water. I listened to the night, the breeze in the undergrowth, the lapping of water. I pulled myself to the edge of the ditch and remained there, my face in the rich, damp soil, gulping in the scent of the grass and water, trying to forget the stench that clung to me, the stench of death, the stench of the graves, the stench which permeated my clothes; of Treblinka. I rolled in the grass, rubbing my face with leaves, drinking from the ditch, shivering at the sounds of things far away from the panting excavator, which had filled my life for weeks.

I walked across fields all night, wading marshes with mud clinging to my legs, thrusting aside the lower branches of clustered small black firs, which dotted the plain. A stack of beets made me shudder, as if it were one of those piles we made on the sorting lot at Treblinka. In the morning, swathed in mist, I watched the sunrise. I entered a forest and lay down under the trees at its edge, gnawing a beet, exhausted. Beneath me, the earth. I pressed my belly, my legs, the palms of my hands into it, so it could give me strength, restore my sanity, teach me life again. I pulled up strips of moss and watched the brown worms. I watched some patient ants. I rediscovered.

A day. Another night. Finding with my eye and senses that Treblinka had left nature untouched and allowed some men to work behind their horses. One day, another night. Not to forget: Treblinka, my mother, my brothers, Rivka, and the yawning graves, so that my world could be restored alongside them and so that I could relearn how to move in it. By the second morning, I'd lost the haunted frenzy of a man at bay. I'd tell my people of Treblinka, avenge myself; live. I washed in icy marsh water, then skirted the wood. I had to get used to looking at faces again. In order not to betray the dead of Treblinka, I had to learn again how to live like a human being: to forget Treblinka in order not to forget it.

It must have been about noon of the second day. The sunlight had turned yellow. I left the shelter of the forest, cutting across fields towards a road, towards a stationary cart with wooden wheels, loaded with beets. A peasant was sitting on its side, a red-faced old man with his cap tilted back. He'd seen me but went on eating, gray bread and bacon.

"I'm looking for work," I said. "I need it. My parents are dead."

He chewed slowly. He shook his head.

"Nothing," he said. "Not a hope."

"I can turn my hand to anything, I need it."

He went on eating and shaking his head.

"Maybe the other side of the Bug."

Back there, little more than a few miles, back there at Treblinka, my comrades were running to the graves, throwing in children, back there Ivan and Idioten were killing. Maybe Abramele was already dead. I wanted to shake the peasant by the shoulders and tell him where I'd come from, tell him about the "factory," the convoys, the wrenched teeth, the children, my mother, Rivka. But all I said was, "Can one cross the Bug?"

He stood up. He had a stoop and moved slowly. Pointing, he explained in a mumble how to find the ford.

"You don't want to go over the bridge, eh?"

His eyes twinkled, ironic and conspiratorial, not expecting an answer. I thanked him. And as I left he called me back. He went to the rear of the cart and returned with half a round loaf and a chunk of bacon.

"I've enough for myself."

I took the bread and bacon, my hands full. I skirted the field, headed back to the forest. There I sat propped against a tree, laying the bread and bacon in front of me. Thank you, peasant, thank you, man, for helping me return to your world. I ate slowly, relearning the taste of food into which I could sink my teeth and chew, not just swallow quickly to avoid the blow that killed, was still killing in Treblinka. Thank you, peasant, thank you, man.

That evening I forded the Bug.

I walked on. The forests, the fields, their hard mounds on which I stumbled, the dusty roads, and the ditches in which I sometimes flung myself to avoid a German truck; I got to know Poland by traversing its soil, by sleeping under its trees, by hiding in its icy waters. I got to know the blank faces of peasants, the hand that gave bread and the one which threatened to strike you, I got to know villages with low, thatched houses, churches where the men stood apart from the women in their black shawls. I asked for bread, for work. I stole potatoes that had been buried in straw to protect them from the frost. I stole matches and, on the edge of the forest, made a fire, laid the potatoes in the ashes, and burned myself on their skins, I warded off the cold with branches, trying to sleep and failing: my people were before my eyes, all my people, a community of the dead. I spent nights haunted by nightmares, endlessly throwing my mother, my brothers and Rivka into the grave. Then I lay down beside them until invaded by the chill that later woke me. I went a little further into the forest, to avoid bogs. I made another fire to warm myself, but they were still there, and once again I had to start throwing them into the grave. Sometimes, after hours of sleeplessness, I reproached myself for still being alive, for having eluded their fate. So I clung to my father's memory: in Senatorska Street I used to hang around his neck. He'd start whirling around, and soon I'd feel as if I was going to be hurled a long way, a long, long way, against the walls. I clung to him, clutching his neck, screaming with terror and delight. In the forests, on the far side of the Bug, I clung to my father. "You must live, Martin," he'd say. And he wanted to live too. He must be alive. Day after day, I convinced myself that, like me, he'd escaped from Treblinka to fight on and avenge us.

I walked north, to get further away from Treblinka. I passed near villages: Srebrna was one, strung out along the side of the road, the barns of sod cottages almost abutting the forest. Behind the last house stood a peasant, leaning on a fork, watching me. It was evening. I'd been walking since morning, my face was streaked with white dust. He beckoned me over.

"Do you want work? Threshing grain. I'll give you bed and board."

I agreed and he showed me to his barn in the dark night.

"You can sleep there, fix it up how you like. I'll give you a shout tomorrow. My name's Chmielnitzki."

I wasn't used to trusting men. I scouted the barn, carefully unnailing boards which faced the forest and replaced them: if I wanted to run, all I'd have to do was give them a push. Chmielnitzki looked a decent sort but men's faces could be deceptive. At dawn, in the mist which I could smell, I studied Chmielnitzki, busy on the threshing floor. Then he shouted to me and work began. Hard work: my mind was free. Only my hands were occupied, washing down the horses and cow; threshing grain, lifting the flail. I could see Ivan with his club raised, I was crushing ears of corn, he was crushing heads; when I currycombed the horse's soft, shiny hide, I was thinking of our lacerated skin, or bruised flesh; when I threw the dog his can of potatoes, chunks of bacon and crusts of bread, I knew that, in Treblinka, men would kill for a handful of such food and that, in the ghetto, hundreds of children had never eaten as much. In the evenings, at table, watching Chmielnitzki and his mother munching away silently, I sometimes felt I was going to vomit. I couldn't swallow. I wanted to yell out, "Do you know what they did to my mother?" But I held my tongue, declined their bread, and prayed like them before and after meals.

Chmielnitzki didn't talk much during the week. But he drank on Saturday. Then while his mother was saying her rosary he'd go into a monologue, or sing, and as he liked an audience, I'd sit there in front of him longer than usual, in the yellowish glow of the oil lamp. Normally he didn't ask me any questions, happy just to talk. However, one Saturday, the third I spent at his place, he'd drunk more than usual. In the afternoon, a photographer from Zambrow came by and all the peasants collected in front of each farm, on the threshing floor, girls in white shawls next to the young men. Chmielnitzki nudged me.

"What about you, Mietek?"

I tried to refuse but Chmielnitzki wouldn't have it.

"For once we've got a worker from Warsaw! Come on, Mietek!"

I was photographed with the rest. In the evening he was practically drunk.

"You were scared, eh, Mietek, you were scared of the photographer."

He was cupping his chin, his eyes half-closed.

"You wouldn't be a Jew?"

His mother crossed herself.

"We don't like Jews here, Mietek. They killed Christ."

His mother crossed herself again.

"But there aren't any Jews left, boss, they're dead, *kaput*."

He banged his fist and spat on the beaten earth floor.

"Go to Zambrow and you'll see them, as fat as ever. Here, on this side of the Bug, we're in the German Reich. They're big, fat Jews. They pay off the Germans with gold and we're the ones who get requisitioned."

He poured himself out a glass of vodka.

"If you're a Jew, Mietek, I'll kill you."

I began to laugh.

"All the Jews are dead, boss."

Chmielnitzki's mother went on saying her rosary.

"I'll kill you, Mietek," he muttered.

Then he slumped over the table and began to snore and groan.

It was a clear night outside, the north wind had blown away the mist, it was cold. In the barn, below the loft where I was staying, the horses were pawing the ground. I made sure that the boards I'd loosened were easily detachable. I'd have to leave one night because Chmielnitzki was just the sort of respectable man who'd kill you or denounce you. But I was ready for him, I'd sensed the threat. Others, maybe thousands in Zambrow, were no doubt believing blindly in the mirage of the East; they were "adapting," waiting for the end of the savage whirlwind which had been unleashed. They didn't know anything about Treblinka and one day they'd be shoved into the cattle cars. And here I was, doing nothing, only thinking about my own life.

On Sunday morning, I attended Mass with the rest. Chmielnitzki was silent once more, standing next to me in the chancel, kneeling down at the elevation of the Host, bowing his thick peasant's neck, an honest, simple man, who could kill. We lingered on the square; I went from group to group, taking aside one peasant or another and encouraging him to talk about the local Jews. All of them said that the Jews were living undisturbed in Zambrow and in other small towns.

"The Germans are protecting them," one of the peasants would sometimes say. "They need their gold."

I had to leave as soon as possible, warn the people of Zambrow, tell them about Treblinka. Chmielnitzki harnessed his horse, as he did every Sunday morning: he was going to the next village to visit his brother. His mother was wearing her pleated black skirt. I held the horse, handed the reins to Chmielnitzki and watched them until they'd disappeared behind the forest. Then I dashed into the house, breaking down a door to find the large chest in which Chmielnitzki kept his clothes. I took some black boots, a jacket, and some bacon, bread, potatoes and matches from the storeroom, made for the forest behind the barn, and ran north, towards Zambrow.

I walked all day, all night, all the next day. Hunger and tiredness didn't bother me: I had to get to Zambrow before the Germans began their work of extermination. I'd already wasted too much time. To get my bearings, I left the fields and the forest and followed the road. Sometimes I was in such a hurry that I ran: I'd know how to talk to them. I'd tell them about Warsaw, the *Umschlagplatz,* and then about the *Lazarett,* the graves and the excavator; on I ran: so then we'd arm ourselves and maybe we could take Treblinka by surprise and free the prisoners.

On the road, in the middle of the forest, I saw a group of men working, some whistling, others talking. I seemed to recognize Jewish songs and Yiddish words. Crawling flat on my belly across the moist earth, concealed by scrub, I crept up on them. They were Jews all right, some were wearing black skullcaps, others had Stars of David sewn on their clothes. They were the first Jews I'd encountered since Treblinka. Possibly a *kommando* from a nearby camp. I looked for the Ukrainians or Germans guarding them. But there were no soldiers on that straight run through the forest, only those men, filling potholes and digging ditches along the main road. I retreated, made a detour, leaped onto the road, and walked confidently towards them, digging my heels into the ground. They gradually stopped working and watched me approach, two or three took off their caps and looked down. I stopped among them.

"Where are your guards?"

I spoke roughly, addressing an oldish man. He hesitated, glancing to left and right for support.

"But we're a free *kommando,* young man."

I looked at them blankly: Jews, free, a few miles from Treblinka?

"Free? But you're Jews?"

Some of them resumed work. The old man smiled at me.

"We go back to Zambrow every evening. The Germans trust us."

I'd tried everything in Treblinka, I'd joined the lumberjack *kommandos,* the camouflage *kommandos,* hoping to escape surveillance by the guards, yet here were these Jews in the middle of the forest; they'd only have to go a few yards and they'd be lost in the trees.

"You go back to Zambrow every evening?"

I repeated those incredible words. Then I went up to the old man: with his horn-rimmed glasses he looked like a doctor or a professor. My face was close to his and I could tell from his scared eyes that my anger was visible.

"I've come from Warsaw. All the Jews are being killed back there, I've come from Treblinka, there's a factory there where we're being gassed to death, everyone, women and children."

The others had drawn away and I looked at their stooping backs. They didn't want to hear. The old man's face was tense, he was trembling.

"If you don't run away at once, they'll send you to the factory, you and your children. So go!"

I went from one to the next, I grabbed one or two of the stooping men by the shoulders, making them stand up, shaking them.

"Go! Go!"

I shouted, ran back and forth among them. They drew away from me and immediately went back to work as if I didn't exist, ignoring my shouts and insults. I'd dropped my bag of food, I was waving my arms about, then I stopped: I saw their furtive looks as they started to lift a tree trunk which had rolled half across the road. I recovered my breath.

"Listen to me, I'm a Jew, a Jew, like you! You've got to believe me: they're killing us, all of us! Do you know about Treblinka?"

They didn't even look up.

"You've got to believe me!"

They carried on with their work as if I weren't there, as if Treblinka were just some lunatic's nightmare. I sat down on the side of the road, not even seeing them anymore. The butchers had got hold of our minds too. Yet my hands had held hundreds of bodies, why didn't they look at them, why didn't they understand?

"Here's your bag, young man."

The old man was standing in front of me. "You don't believe me?"

He smiled.

"It's all different here. Zambrow's part of the Reich, the Germans need us, you understand. Warsaw and Treblinka aren't occupied territory, they're in Poland. It's different here. Take your bag, young man."

He was talking to me as if I were a stupid child. I threw my bag across my shoulder.

"Which way to Zambrow?"

"Straight on, straight on. Five miles."

I looked away from them, rage and bitterness welling up in my throat: didn't men understand disaster until it hit them? Didn't anyone ever listen to witnesses? Had my people died for nothing? I walked on into the sunset, crying in frustration. They had to listen to me. I'd speak out again, tell them about the *Umschlagplatz*, the cattle cars and the graves. I'd tell them about my mother, my brothers and Rivka. But would they understand? Just as in the days of the Warsaw ghetto, the butchers had cunningly set snares of hope. They knew that Treblinka was inconceivable: they'd given each of us the illusion of privilege. Those Jews in the forest imagined, as many had believed in Warsaw, that they were useful to the Germans, that they enjoyed some special status.

By now I could see the houses of Zambrow framed on the horizon. I passed carts and an occasional truck. I was going to speak out. I had to speak out, but I'd no illusions about being heeded: the Jews in Zambrow wouldn't arm themselves and march on Treblinka. How could I have asked it of them when the whole world had allowed us to be murdered? But I had to try. Back there the excavator was still digging away. I walked on, crossed a wooden bridge over a muddy river, entered the town which had many sod or wooden houses like the ones in the villages, then made for the narrow streets where the ghetto was sure to be found. At the end of one street was a sign, some stanchions holding up a few strands of barbed wire and a passageway with a single Jewish policeman guarding it. This was the beginning of the peaceful ghetto of Zambrow. I walked through the gate, the shops were open, quiet groups were standing in front of the synagogue, old Jews were chatting. Already I could see death, sneering death, perched on their shoulders, dogging their footsteps, laying hands on their ears and eyes. I was going to speak out but I wouldn't let myself get caught. If they refused to listen to me, I'd survive, I'd survive, alone if necessary, and there'd be at least one man to avenge us.

I went up to one group. A fat little man with round face and shiny red skin was addressing a respectful audience: his hand was beating time, conducting his words.

"That's war," he said. "They can't give us everything we need but they need us."

He was talking, the others were meekly assenting, solemnly nodding their heads. Several times I heard the word patience, and I was reminded of the Jews in the forest who'd also said, "They need us."

"Treblinka. Do you know about Treblinka?"

I was in the thick of them, facing the speaker, my vagrant's bag over my shoulder.

"A few miles from here, there's a factory, graves . . . and they're extracting gold teeth from our people."

I spoke to complete silence, I could hear them breathing, then the speaker suddenly closed on me, his face livid.

"What you're saying can't be true. It's impossible. The Germans aren't mad. Why should they kill us, while we're paying them, working for them? It's in their interest to keep us alive here in Zambrow. You're the one who's mad, mad, you're out of your mind!"

He shouted the last few words then went on.

"It's impossible, the Germans aren't mad! Even if they wanted to do what you're saying, the world wouldn't allow it!"

I tried to continue.

"Don't listen to him, he's obviously a lunatic!"

He dragged them away and I was left there watching them, the speaker was making a speech, his hand raised, and I saw some of them laughing and glancing back at me. They didn't want to believe me because the abyss was terrifying, so they preferred not to see, not to know; they couldn't believe me because it was impossible to imagine Treblinka. A healthy man can't understand that he's doomed. Those good people had no idea of the butchers' murderous lunacy. They talked about self-interest, reason, practicality; but the butchers wanted extermination.

I went from group to group, told them about my mother, my brothers, Rivka, the scraping of boxes at night in the huts. I mentioned the yellow sand in the graves, the strangled children, the dogs, I described the excavator, the *Lazarett,* the clothes in the sorting lot, Idioten, the SS man, Ivan the Ukrainian. Sometimes I felt that my words were reaching the Jews who had sought refuge here from Warsaw, that I'd convince them; but the horror was too great. I couldn't show them the corpses, my hands were only hands, who'd have guessed that they'd lifted hundreds of bodies? My words were just words. Sometimes someone, eyes fixed, bathed in terror, said, "But what should we do?"

I thought I'd won. I told them about the forests around Zambrow, attacks on German trucks, how we'd seize arms, how we'd join the Armia Krajowa, the secret national army which the peasants had mentioned. Then the women walked off, the men shook their heads.

"They're all anti-Semites," someone said. "We'd be in their hands. The peasants would denounce us, the partisans would kill us. Here in the ghetto, we're together."

Another of them remarked, "The Germans aren't that mad."

Still another added, "And then the war won't last forever."

An old man winked and said, "It's so cold in Russia."

They laughed, rubbed their hands and wandered off. Once again I'd failed. What a nightmare to know, to be sure that you're right and not to be able to convince people, to sense that before your eyes the men for whose sake you're talking are closing their ears, that your words are bouncing off them! What a nightmare it was to feel so helpless!

I slept in lofts, at the backs of yards, and begged food which was handed me with a pitying smile. I was a sort of tragic clown, the mournful clown Rubinstein of the Zambrow ghetto. In the morning, at dawn, I was outside the synagogue, preaching tirelessly, buttonholing passersby and trying to convince them, but as the days went by my words lost even their original impact. I was already part of the scenery; I was too young to be heeded; and as long as life went on peacefully and the free *kommandos* returned safely every evening from the forest, I was regarded each day as that much more of a raving lunatic, one you shouldn't believe if you wanted to go on living. One evening, a tall, thin girl, her black hair hanging down in pigtails, stopped me in the street, then began to walk with me.

"I believe you." She had a firm, keen voice.

"I'm from Warsaw. I knew Dr. Korczak. I saw the children leaving for the *Umschlagplatz*." She lived in a tiny room, more or less a cellar. We spent whole nights side by side, talking about

Warsaw. She wanted to know all about Treblinka because her family had left in a cattle car at the end of July. I didn't give her much hope: in any case she didn't want it. She didn't want to run away or fight: just to know what her fate would be and that of the children she was looking after here in Zambrow. We held hands in that dark, freezing room, I trying to restore her zest for life, she trying to strengthen my will to fight back.

"Mietek, you must survive, for us," she kept saying. "You go and fight. You avenge us."

Her name was Sonia, she was thin, desperate, heroic in her desire to know and endure.

"You must go, Mietek, you can't do anything here. They don't want to know. If you stay, an informer will denounce you to the Germans one day. You mustn't die, Mietek, you know too much. You're our memory."

One night, she asked me, simply, to make love to her, because she was going to die and she wanted to know about that side of life. I took her frail, trembling body in my arms, it was burning with all the years that she wouldn't live. Then we laughed and cried, and had a little feast, potatoes cooked in the ashes in the stove, and a sip or two of vodka. Sonia, with her rumpled hair, white skin and bright eyes, was beautiful.

Next morning, I was on the square again, in front of the synagogue, moving as usual from group to group, when I noticed a Jewish policeman who seemd to be looking for someone. Intuition? I went over to him: I'd learned from the ghetto, from Treblinka, that one way to disarm danger is to head straight for it.

The policeman almost bumped into me. He was holding a photo.

"Do you know him?" he said. "We're looking for him."

He showed me the photo. There I was, in front of one of the houses back in the village, on the threshing floor, in the middle of a group of peasants, my face with a circle around it, me, Chmielnitzki's thief. I took the photo.

"Yes, yes, he's still up there, on the first floor, in one of the offices."

I pointed to the house next door to the Judenrat. The policeman snatched the photo from me and made for the building.

A few minutes later, I was out of the ghetto, another few minutes and I'd left Zambrow. I went back to the dusty road, the forests.

Goodbye, Jews of Zambrow, farewell, heroic Sonia. I live for them, for you too. I'd done preposterous things for them, taken crazy risks in that ghetto, every morning in front of the synagogue. I told you everything: all I had left to offer you was my freedom. What would have been the good of that? I decided to fight, for my people, for you, and for you, Sonia.

After two days' walking, I got a job with a peasant in the village of Zaremby. His name was Zaremba. Zaremba was a gentle giant with milk-white skin and fair hair: I never saw him take a drink. In the evening, after the meal, he read books which the priest gave him, to his mother and sister, historical novels or lives of the saints. Marie, his sister, would sometimes cry and the mother would gaze delightedly at her children. Sometimes I'd forget that I was a Jew on the run. I told Zaremba I came from Warsaw: I didn't have a Yiddish accent. He took me to the priest, a young, thin, lively man. A few days later, I went to the church to fetch books for Zaremba and to bring some eggs. The priest made me talk about Warsaw. It was easy inventing a life similar to that of Mokotow the Tomb or Wacek the Peasant. Then I told him about the ghetto, and a Jew whom I'd known well who had gone in for smuggling, until the Germans had caught him and had taken him and his family to Treblinka, a camp where, it seemed, Jews were being exterminated.

"The Germans have unleashed evil," said the priest.

One day he handed me a printed sheet, an Armia Krajowa leaflet.

"It's the Polish national army," he said. "Do you want to help us?"

I took the leaflet. At last I was going to fight.

"But don't go on too much about your Jewish friend." The priest smiled. "The A.K. crowd aren't exactly in love with them."

Had he guessed? I didn't say anything, and I began, at nights, to dash from farm to farm, distributing leaflets that smelled of fresh ink. On Sundays, the group of *Akowcy* (members of the A.K.) met openly in front of the church. Almost the whole of the village supported the A.K.; the Germans didn't often come this far into the countryside. People discussed the communiqués from the exiled Polish government in London, the triumphs of the Allied armies. There was never any word of the persecution of the Jews. They didn't exist. So for the time being, I held my tongue: the main thing was for me to fight the Germans too.

"What about arms?"

"It's not time yet, Mietek. They'll come."

In the evenings Zaremba tried to calm me down. Marie would smile at me but I was thinking of Rivka whom I'd left on the platform at Treblinka, of Sonia whom I'd left at Zambrow. Zaremba would read on.

Towards the end of one of the first days of heavy gray clouds, when we thought it was going to snow, Zaremba said to me, "Tomorrow morning at four, harness the horse to the big cart. I'm going to Zambrow."

He didn't add anything but he seemed anxious. In the morning I was there, the chill mist like light drizzle on my face and hands, holding an oil lamp.

"I'll go with you, if you like, boss."

"Don't you move from here."

He leaped onto the cart, I went with him as far as the road. The place was in commotion. Carts from the entire village were milling about, peasants yelling to each other: the mayor had ordered them all to go to Zambrow with their carts.

"It's probably the Jews, they're going to be transferred," they explained.

Some were cursing the mayor, others the Germans, but most of them were cursing the Jews.

I buried myself in my work all day, sweeping out the stable, tidying the hay, working so as not to think of Sonia and the people of Zambrow.

Zaremba returned long after nightfall. He handed me the horse's reins without a word, not even glancing at me. When I got back to the kitchen, his mother and Marie were staring at him, motionless, silent, petrified. Zaremba was drinking straight from the vodka bottle. I flung myself at him and snatched the bottle from his hands. He didn't even resist.

"You're right, Mietek. Why drink?"

"Was it the Jews from the ghetto?"

He nodded, then he began to speak slowly, in his normal manner. From time to time he brushed away his tears with the back of his hand, saying, "What could I do, Mietek? There was nothing to be done, except obey."

He'd seen the SS and the guards surround the ghetto, forbidding the inhabitants to leave; he'd heard the shots; he'd seen women jump out of windows; old men lying on the ground, arms stretched out, killed one by one with a bullet in the neck; children cut down by bursts of automatic rifle fire, girls dragged into yards by the Germans. Goodbye, Jews of Zambrow, farewell, heroic Sonia. Then the Germans, with rifle butts, had forced the Jews up onto the peasants' carts and the convoy had moved off towards some old barracks on the outskirts of Zambrow. Zaremba had heard screams and shots before leaving for the village. I stared at his face in the hope that he'd tell me that some had gotten away, that there'd been a miracle at the last moment, that Sonia was alive.

But no, Zaremba said, "What could I have done, Mietek? I couldn't do anything, I let them kill the children. Do you hear, Mother, the children, the old people?"

We remained silent. His mother was praying, Marie was kneeling in front of the crucifix. I got up and laid my hand on Zaremba's shoulder, Zaremba who was twice my age, but who'd only met savagery for the first time that day.

"That's the way it goes, boss. You couldn't have done anything. You must get some sleep."

I went out to the barn where I slept. I had been helpless, like Zaremba: I had let it happen. All night I tortured myself, accused myself of failing to convince people, of failing to fight, of failing even to rescue Sonia; all night I bit my knuckles to stop myself from howling with despair, reliving my time in the ghetto, Pawiak, Zofia, Rivka, the *Umschlagplatz*. The butchers hadn't killed me but they'd sowed the seeds of death in me. I had to defend myself against that too.

In the morning, the mayor came. A tubby man, with plump hands and a freckled face; a merchant and moneylender, he cheated on the weight of grain; an informer, he had his hand in the requisitions demanded by the Germans. He came into the barn where Zaremba and I were working. He looked at me and I knew what he was thinking. That man was my enemy.

"Zaremba, you and your man must go to Zambrow. The Germans will give you a *Kennkarte*. They're calling in old papers. They're doing a check. There are Jews hiding everywhere."

I hadn't had any identification since Treblinka. I felt the vise closing on me. Zaremba went to Zambrow the next day, telling me to visist the *Kommandantur* the day after; I fabricated excuses, put it off from day to day. I found it hard to work out a plan. Maybe I should throw caution to the winds, go to Zambrow, ask for a *Kennkarte;* or maybe I should wait. Drained by my nightmares, I couldn't make up my mind. By then the mayor had come several times:

"How about your *Kennkarte?*"

I realized that I couldn't delay any longer: I had either to run away or try and obtain the document. When Zaremba went to Zambrow to hand the Germans the grain which he owed them, I went with him. We unloaded the sacks in front of the store on the main square, some distance from what had been the ghetto. We dragged them inside; the job done, I'd go to the *Kommandantur*. Zaremba went back into the store, I waited for him near the cart, and suddenly I saw the mayor pointing me out to two German policemen. Too late. I'd hesitated, I'd forgotten my father's lesson and the lesson of Treblinka, I'd let others decide for me. I had excuses, but I knew that in the tribunal of mankind excuses were meaningless. I couldn't run away, the square was deserted, the police armed with rifles. The mayor stayed back, his arms folded, watching them close in on me, and I stared at his shifty little eyes. I observed his smile, his smug look, and I became myself again: you'd like me to die, informer! So I'd live. I wouldn't miss any chance.

"Let's see your papers."

One of the policemen stepped forward, he spoke excellent Polish. Calmly I began to explain that I was from Warsaw, my sick father had kept my papers.

"To the *Kommandantur.*"

Once again I was in their hands, but the doubts which had been assailing me for days had vanished. Now I knew what I had to do: fight to live, run away.

In the *Kommandantur* I was bundled into an office, and I recognized their faces: the faces of men with the arrogance of strength and power, their flat voices, their eyes, just like the eyes of the officer who'd killed my red-haired friend for a couple of herring.

"Your cap, Jew."

I didn't move: few Poles understood German. The officer, a thin man with slicked-back dark hair, knocked my cap off with a blow from a ruler. I picked it up and put it on his desk. He knocked it angrily to the ground, shouting. They all had the same voices. I began to speak in Polish, making excuses. He flung down the ruler on his desk, cursed the Jews, Poland, and called an interpreter. An oldish officer entered.

"Where are you from, Jew?"

"I'm not a Jew."

I told my story, talking quickly, mixing up the details. I hadn't any papers, my father and mother were in Warsaw, I was here to work and to eat. The interpreter sounded human and I watched him as he translated: he even attempted to back up my words with his gestures, trying to convince him too. Now and then he gave me an encouraging glance. The officer was sitting at his desk, playing with the ruler, of two minds, half-convinced.

"So you want a *Kennkarte?*"

I felt I'd won.

"I want what I need to be able to work."

There was a knock at the door, a civilian looked in.

"What now?"

"It's about last night's robbery."

The man came in, a Pole, with a slave's stoop. He was working at the *Kommandantur:* he and the officer discussed the vanished sacks of grain. I was in a corner, aware that the situation was changing. The Pole turned to me and the officer suddenly noticed me again.

"What do you think, a Jew or a Pole?"

The man hesitated.

"A Jew. He winked at me."

I denied it, I hadn't done anything, but the officer was already on me, hitting me. I was paying for the grain thieves.

"Make sure," said the officer.

The man closed in on me. I stared at him: he could save me or doom me, he had power over my life and over the memories of all my people that I was keeping inside me. He had power over what remained of thousands of lives because of me. But he too had the face of a man with the bulging eyes of a beast. All I could do was leave it to him.

"Circumcised. A Jew. I told you, I'm never wrong."

The Pole laughed.

"Teach him a lesson," he said as he left.

I again tried to protest, to explain that I'd been ill, had an operation as a child, but they didn't listen to me, I was talking in desperation. The interpreter was translating, I could sense the anxiety in his voice. The officer stopped him.

"We'll jog his memory for him."

Some soldiers came in and I became the center of a ring of fists and boots, the target for a storm of blows. The officer was asking me questions for the pleasure of hitting me. He made me lie down on a bench, and each time I groaned, he struck me harder with his whip. Then he grabbed me by the hair and pulled me up.

"Jew, you're to give us the names of the partisans known to you. You're to tell us where the Jews are hidden."

I shook my head. He grabbed my hair.

"You're stubborn, Jew."

They started hitting me again. When I came to, I was lying on the floor of a cell, my face and back bleeding, my body black and blue. I tried to get up but couldn't, so I lay there thinking of my people, going back over the whole of my life. Had I escaped from Treblinka only to wind up dying here in Zambrow?

I heard footsteps and voices, after what were probably hours of broken sleep and nightmares.

"Get up."

The officer stood framed in the door. I made an effort, fell back, I reminded myself of the graves at Treblinka. I bit my tongue. I stood up, leaning against the wall. Behind the officer I could see two soldiers and the officer-interpreter. They were conferring. I could hear the interpreter arguing.

"If you kill him here, you'll have to bury him. The simplest thing would be to take him back there."

He came into my cell, forced my arms behind my back, handcuffed me and removed my boots.

"He won't escape, I promise you."

The officer hesitated, then went away. The interpreter, that man in German uniform, had saved my life. He pushed me outside and two soldiers flanked me: it was night, snow had fallen, I was stumbling forward, we were heading for the country. The interpreter was behind me, I turned.

"Can a Christian, a man, let me die?"

"There's nothing more I can do."

He was speaking quickly, his eyes lowered, his voice tense, emotional, obviously worrying about the suspicions of the two soldiers who wouldn't understand an officer entering into conversation with a Jew.

"They wanted to kill you. You're going to the camp."

My bare feet stung in the snow, and with every step I had to concentrate all my energy, all my will on a single end: to lift one foot, then the other from the snow; not to fall down. I had to walk to the camp because the soldiers wouldn't drag me there. I wanted to talk too. I gulped down air until my heart was ready to burst and my stomach ached.

"Officer, you seem to be a man. Listen to me. You saved my life. Listen to me."

Boots tramping the snow. Was he listening to me?

"You've got to know about Treblinka, to understand."

I was talking wildly, my words coming out jerkily when I ran short of breath. The sound of his boots. Lights. Barbed wire around a large building that looked like a barracks: Zambrow camp. A sentry took a step forward.

"Another one," said one of the soldiers who'd accompanied me.

"You could have kept him."

The interpreter came over to me, removed my handcuffs, quickly clasped my hands in his.

"Run away, run away," he whispered.

The sentry began to yell, "Run, Jew, it's cold! Do you want me to warm you up?"

I ran, the soldiers laughed at my awkwardness, but I didn't fall: everywhere *men* still existed, some disguised in butchers' uniforms.

Shouting and laughing, the sentry prodded me to a hut in the yard. A butt end against the door.

"Herr Doktor Menkes, a client for you. One of your little brothers."

The doctor was one of those privileged prisoners whom the Germans tolerated for a while because of their services. Fat and neat, Dr. Menkes was medical supervisor of the Zambrow camp.

"You were lucky."

I undressed with difficulty. He rubbed lotion on my back: I was shivering with cold, pain and weariness.

"Where are you from?"

He had a gentle touch. I talked: Warsaw, Treblinka.

"Get up. Get dressed."

His voice had changed.

"If you breathe a word of that propaganda in the camp, do you hear, I'll get them to shut you up."

He shoved me outside, again telling me to keep quiet, throwing me out as if I had some contagious disease. Then, in the dark, he called me back. He handed me an old pair of slippers.

"It's all I have."

His voice was normal again. It was almost gentle.

"You'll see," he added, "it's not like what you think here. So keep quiet and don't make a nuisance of yourself. We'll all suffer if they get annoyed. But I assure you, I am not going to let you cause any trouble."

The snow had become hard. It was difficult getting my swollen feet into the slippers. I was exhausted, my body one great aching wound. How could I, why should I go on talking? Menkes led me to a hut.

"Don't forget," he said.

I'll never forget the blindness of some people, or the shrewdness of the butchers who manipulated their desire to live, their cowardice, their kindness, their selfishness. I'll never forget that long dark room at Treblinka in which men tried — like me — to sleep away from the entrance where I also tried to identify those elbowing each other in order to shift a yard further away from that door. No one needed to explain here in Zambrow camp as at Treblinka, that the SS men would come every night. Commandant Bloch himself made the rounds, with his huge dog whose hackles rose as soon as he saw a prisoner. Bloch would enter, and in the silence of the hut point his foot at one of the prisoners.

"Are you cold, Jew?" Or, "Are you warm?"

What did the reply matter? The prisoner knew. He'd go out to "warm himself" or "cool himself" awhile. He never came back. In the morning, on the parade ground, shivering, snow whipping up into our faces, Commandant Bloch, dog at his side, would say:

"Jews of Zambrow, fear nothing. I will take care of you. I have to keep you Jews alive and in good health, to exchange for German prisoners of war. But watch out, Jews. I must have obedience, total obedience."

Men and women who watched Bloch come at night, who heard the shots, who watched a prisoner huddled in a ball on the ground, his hands over his face, trying to avoid Bloch's dog, still believed in speeches! I realized that there were men, perhaps most men, for whom there was no greater horror than the truth.

That first evening I had no strength to fight. I slumped near the door. Let death come. That night Bloch did not come to our hut. The next night he came and pointed to two prisoners. I was already with the ones at the far end, determined to survive.

It was a transit camp for Jews of Zambrow, Lomza, Sniadow and Czyzew: waiting until their grave back there in Treblinka was ready. I saw a few inhabitants of the Zambrow ghetto: the orator who kept raising his hand as he talked in front of the synagogue; now still beating time confidently, hardly any thinner. One night I slipped over to his bed. He was dozing; with his plump cheeks he looked like a pink child. I shook him. He instinctively raised his arm like a boy caught doing wrong. I wanted to talk about Treblinka again, and hadn't I been right about the Zambrow ghetto?

"What is it? What is it?"

"Nothing. You're taking too much room."

He protested but moved over, and I spent the night beside him. He wasn't able to accept the truth. It was about to destroy him. Let him find out for himself. I later looked around the camp for other men with whom I could talk. There weren't many of them. When I finished describing Treblinka, most of them shook their heads.

"It's too late. Our children are with us. Do you want us to abandon them?"

I would set off again, cautiously, preaching escape and revolt. I checked the sentries' rounds, counted the rows of barbed wire. Flight was possible. Simple. It was cold at night, so cold that the soldiers in the observation posts kept to their sentry boxes. I saw them, greatcoat collars turned up, climb the wooden ladder and disappear into the shack that protected them from the wind. I also noticed that Jews arrived at the entrance to the camp and were allowed in, without being checked. Every day some arrived who wanted to join their families or who could no longer stand being hunted or who believed the propaganda and hoped for humanity from the hunters. I worked out a lunatic plan, which had a kind of logic. I'd run away, get bread from some peasants, return to the camp, sell some of the bread, and run away again, buy clothes and papers, and so avoid all checks, maybe even manage to get back to Warsaw or join the partisans.

For days I scoured the camp for wire cutters, naturally without luck. I stole a pair of scissors from Dr. Menkes's hut. The same evening I hid at the foot of an observation post. The beams of the searchlights didn't meet there, leaving a patch of shadow supposedly guarded by sentries. They were keeping warm. I waited. Motionless. My bare feet in my slippers. I heard Bloch's dog barking in a hut; he was making his rounds. Then silence. I clawed at the frozen earth, lived an eternity finding weak sections to break in the barbed wire; tore my clothes and my skin; crawled, listening to the silence and sweating even in the cold; then made for the trees. I was free. I walked to a village. Dawn, low clouds threatening snow; the wind had dropped. I knocked to ask for bread.

The peasants looked at me in silence. "Bread, bread."

They saw my red hands, torn jacket, worn-out slippers, and handed me some hard, gray crusts. A peasant woman, huddled in shawls, gave me a bowl of hot milk and a bag. We didn't talk: my body had turned red and blue from the blows and the cold, and my clothes, everything proclaimed *Jew!* But they gave me bread. Thank you, Polish peasants. I slept in a stable near the animals, taking a little warm milk from the cow in the morning. My bag filled with bread, I left for the camp. The next day, I told myself, I'd be out again with my German Reichsmarks. I didn't even feel the cold. As in my ghetto days, when I crossed the wall again to return home, I was defying the butchers. The sentries peeped out of their huts.

"I'm a Jew. My parents are here. I want to come in."

A wave: an animal making its own way to the slaughterhouse. I sold my bread. As in every camp, trade was organized. I handed the lion's share of my bag over to buyers who would then resell it in small quantities. That evening I had a little money. I slept, but once again, I'd missed my chance. In the morning, at assembly, Bloch halted in front of us. He was wearing a long black leather coat with a fur collar, fine boots, slapping his gloved hands and we were motionless, dying of cold.

"Jews. I'm hurt. Jews. Some of you have betrayed my trust. There have been escapes. German property has been stolen. You'll pay, Jews!"

He chose a dozen men, among them the orator of Zambrow, stooped, defeated. Bloch lined up the hostages.

"Jews. These men are going to die because of you. They could have ended up in America but they're going to die."

The soldiers were there, fifteen men, helmeted, buried in greatcoats; huge beasts. A light snow was falling. Bloch took his time, relishing his own words. Our lives were in his hands. He could play with them.

"Go on, Jews. Go join your God."

He made the hostages turn around. I was watching the orator from Zambrow, his astonished scarlet face, his raised hand; I thought he was going to speak but the soldiers were already lining them up. A dozen bodies in the snow. Bloch's dog barking. But we hadn't seen the last of the commandant. He had fathers brought out, those with children in the camp.

"Jews, you love your children. Animals love their young, too. Your children's lives are in your hands. You'll be on guard every night. One Jew every twenty yards. You and your children will pay for escapees. Jews, I have spoken."

That same evening, the new system was in operation: unbreachable. I tried to talk to the Jewish guards. I explained that we were all going to die; that we had to attempt something together; that our fate was as linked as the fingers of this hand. Look at it, brothers: with it I've strangled dying Jewish children to spare them death beneath the yellow Treblinka sand. Hear me! We must all try and escape together, now. You won't save your children by accepting the laws of the butchers! But nobody listened. How could I blame them.

I wanted to get through in spite of them but realized they'd prevent me because, in their eyes, I was a young idiot, a coward who would betray them and deliver them to Bloch's vengeance. Yet I wanted to escape for them too, for all those in the graves of Treblinka.

I toyed with alternatives like hurling myself at the sentry who often stood alone in front of the entrance. For a whole day I watched the soldier, but when I was ready to spring another came and they stayed side by side. The next day there were two sentries, permanently: once again my plan collapsed. Back in Treblinka, the excavator must already have dug our grave, my grave. I *had* to escape! I bribed a peasant who delivered potatoes to the kitchen. I took his place on the wagon, but realized from the way the soldiers looked at me as I was leaving that I'd failed: with my ragged clothes, my slippers, I could only be a Jew.

"What the hell are you doing here?"

I hurriedly made up an explanation: the peasant had asked me to drive his wagon to the gate. I got down, receiving a few kicks.

"Clear off, Jew! Move! Clear off!"

Another day wasted; another day bringing Treblinka nearer. In the morning I was ready to try anything: I'd leap on the two soldiers at the entrance, stab them, run; maybe they'd miss when they fired at me. The assembly went on interminably, Bloch passing through our ranks, unleashing his dog on a prisoner who wasn't standing at attention; then an officer asked for workers; painters and carpenters. I raised my hand: maybe this was my chance.

We went through the gate and the barbed wire. In front of us was the open road. But two soldiers flanked us, the fields were bare, running would have been suicidal. Rounding a bend I saw more buildings, behind barbed wire and a wooden fence: the officers' and soldiers' barracks. We had to repair one of the buildings. The guards divided us into small groups: I said I was a painter, and I found myself with three others in a long, empty hallway; without supervision. Through a window I could see a forest behind the fence. I went into the yard: deserted. By the gate at the end of the fence, a sentry box. We were alone. I came back. The others were already at work.

"There isn't anyone."

All three stopped, surprised by the excitement in my voice.

"No one! They've gone! We could cross the fence."

I opened the window. One of them rushed over, pulled me back, shut the window and stood in front of it.

"It's forbidden to open it," he said. "If you've come here to try something, forget it."

He didn't even dare use the words "run away."

"Why?"

One of them, an older man, began speaking slowly.

"You're young, on your own, but we have families in the camp and we'd have to pay for you."

I talked about Treblinka; hurriedly, because my mind was made up. These men would never leave. These men would die. They'd agreed to the butchers' law without knowing it, refusing to know it. I knew. I'd survive. They'd pay for me, yes. But we were all condemned to death, so whatever they thought it was either flight with me, or death in Zambrow camp, or Treblinka. Goodbye, my brothers.

I worked with them acting nonchalant to make them forget what I'd said. I sang and whistled. Then I went out to inspect the barracks, convinced that the chance had to be seized; now. Barbed wire, the fence, some other buildings, one of them a wooden hut with tarred roof: the latrine. I returned to the hallway, back to work, wandered out again. The only place I could hide at the very last moment was in the latrine. To climb the fence in broad daylight was too risky. I must wait for approaching dusk.

I had to choose now: to plunge once again into the unknown, to break with the precarious but organized life of a camp and its routines; to leave men whose faces were growing familiar; to accept their curse and their sufferings; to break away from the community that we'd formed in spite of ourselves; to accept their belief that I'd betrayed them. I had to choose to live to keep faith with them. Choose to be alone in order to remain with them, all of them, the dead of Treblinka, and of the ghetto, and those who would soon be lying in the graves but didn't yet realize it.

So I hid in the latrine. Supposing the soldiers came? The hut was bare, with just one hole in the boards over the pit. I prized up the boards, there was a gap between them and the frozen surface which I broke with my heel: below lay the ghastly mire of countless men. I laid the boards to one side, ready to plunge in. How slow, night! I could hear shouts, *their* dogs barking, *their* voices. I slid in up to my waist then to my neck, my stomach retching in numbed disgust. Don't think, Mietek. Survive, Mietek. I replaced the boards above me, resting my arms on the frozen horror around me as it gradually melted. Outside, the dogs were near the hut: a soldier came in, boots crashing on the boards lit by his lamp. He spoke to his waiting comrade.

"Jewish swine! Not a word to Bloch."

I heard his boots scraping the ground. His shit fell on my back. Then the other followed him in. More shit. I didn't move, couldn't breathe, didn't exist: Mietek, *they're* going to lose. You'll survive it all and no one will pay for your escape after all because they're afraid to admit it to Commandant Bloch. You've won, Mietek. What does their shit on your back, their shit around you, in which you're plunged, matter? Keep going, Mietek, survive.

Dogs barked. Soldiers came to the latrine: silence gradually fell over the camp. I waited, motionless, for hours in the slime. Then I pushed up the boards, hoisted myself up and managed to climb out, stiff all over, the *beast himself* clinging to me, to my clothes and skin. Outside, the cold assailed me and I began to shiver. I was so heavy and awkward with all that weight on me. I staggered to the wooden fence: eight or nine feet high. I tried to climb it once, twice, a dozen times. I reached the top of it, then slipped; *their* weight preventing me from jumping. I cleaned myself to become lighter, dried myself and rested, but there would soon be daylight. I realized I'd never climb the fence. I began to follow the fence in the direction of the sentry post. My only hope was to attack the soldier.

I edged forward. With fifty yards still to go my hand fell on a strip of wood: a door in the fence had been sealed with boards in the form of a Z. You can make it, Mietek. I climbed slowly, levering myself up on the boards, taking time to recover my breath before jumping down on the other side. Free. I crawled, walked, then ran, plunging into the snow, crossing fields, towards a light, a peasant's house where someone was already working. I knocked; a man's heavy tread. My life in his hands. His huge frame. He drew back, raising his arm to his face: my stench.

"I've plenty of money," I said at once, stepping forward, "more money than you'll ever see. I want to wash and some clothes."

I produced my sodden notes: he hesitated, glancing at the money then at me.

"Come on."

He showed me into the stable: the women came down as another man entered, stocky, heavy-jawed.

"Water," ordered the man who let me in.

I held out the notes and began to wash. I was drying myself when the two men came back with clothes.

"You'll need a lot of money for these," said the stocky man, "plenty!"

The other glanced down, as if afraid to look at me.

"You're a Jew. You've got more money. Let's have it."

I had to hand over my remaining notes. They took away my future, the money for which I'd risked so much. When they were sure they had it all they gave me the clothes.

"Off you go now," said the stocky man. "Get moving."

They were stronger. The man shut the door behind me and I was alone in the dawn, robbed but free. I had to start again.

I crossed fields and forests, plunged into the snow, slept in barns. Like a fox I stole eggs and chickens; I followed the railway tracks, sold what I'd stolen to the signalmen at the crossings, since they didn't care particularly for the peasants. I stole bacon and bread and peasants chased me as far as the forest, ready to slaughter me like a pig. I lived on plunder and hope. Sometimes I'd work a few hours or a few days for peasants. Or I'd knock on doors, all innocence, muttering the ritual formula, *"Niech bedzie Pochwalony, Jesus-Christus,* Bless you Lord."

And they'd reply, *"Na wieki, wiekow, Amen."*

Then I'd sell them sacks of jute, precious in those days of scarcity, which I'd just stolen from the steps of their barn.

I met beasts with men's faces, and others who gave me bread and hospitality for the night, who risked their lives to shelter me from the snow and rain. Thanks to them I kept hoping. They talked to me about the partisans of the A.K., whom I already knew about, as well as of Jews who were somewhere in the great forest of ancient trees, so tall you couldn't even see their tops, in the vast forest which the Germans never entered and which stretched forever, south of Bialystok. I walked in the direction of that forest: the Puszcza Bialowieska. If Jews were fighting there, and if my father was alive, he'd be among them. I passed through the town of Lapy, and reached Bialystok: Jews were still living in the ghetto, blind, deaf, convinced, like those in Warsaw and Zambrow, that they were of use to the Germans, that they had a different status. I preached as at Zambrow. Sometimes young men listened to me when I said that we had to fight, to join the maquis. Several knew the area where the Jewish partisans were hiding, but they didn't want to leave Bialystok. They weren't prepared for a sudden break in their lives; they weren't prepared to recognize that their choices had narrowed: to guerrilla warfare, or death in Treblinka with all the others.

Then I left Bialystok and headed for the Puszcza Bialowieska, finally reaching the tall trees that screened the sky. I walked on, stumbling into snow-covered potholes, whistling and singing Jewish songs, living on potatoes. Then one day I saw them advancing through the trees. I sang at the top of my voice in order to be recognized. There were a dozen of them, two or three with revolvers, living in huts made of branches, begging food from the peasants, hiding more often than they fought. We talked all night: *they* believed me. They stared at me, riveted, across the flames of the fire, and I could see the horror in their faces. I had to describe Treblinka over and over again. Then, as I finished, one of them, Isaac, a thin young man with a heavy black beard said, "Did you know that they fought in Warsaw, Mietek?"

Fought, in my city? I went over to Isaac, grabbed him by the shoulders and plied him with questions.

"They fought in the ghetto?"

Some peasants, returning from Warsaw, had told them about an uprising, a battle with the SS. That was all they knew. My father was *there,* I felt he was, I was sure of it, now. There, in our city. I couldn't sleep; I was nagged by the cold and above all by the urge to leave for Warsaw. Isaac wanted me to stay but how can you stop a river flowing to the sea? We embraced several times. In those few hours we'd become brothers and I was afraid for them. I knew they wouldn't be able to survive long like that, with no organization, no food, no arms. But they'd fight with their bare hands, I knew that, too. Goodbye, brothers. Our lives were full of goodbyes.

I left the great forest. One Sunday, with everyone at Mass, I entered a village, searched the houses, stole some food, and found, in one of those wooden boxes where peasants hid their money beneath their clothes, a Polish passport in the name of Lewandowsky, and a few banknotes. I ran with those possessions, without remorse. I was at war. I needed that money and passport to get to Warsaw. I took the night train at Hajnowka, climbing to the roof of a car, clinging, despite the ice, to the searingly cold metal. Once again I was in Bialystok, it must have been the end of January. They in the ghetto were afraid now. There was talk of the Warsaw uprising. Fear of reprisals here. A sense of the German grip tightening. I begged a little money, slept in cellars, altered the photograph and date of birth in the passport, and preached again, but I had only one overriding aim: not to get caught in the trap of the Bialystok ghetto, to reach Warsaw and to fight there. If my father was alive, he must know that I would return to Mila Street to avenge our people.

I left Bialystok just as the Germans were beginning the first "transfer" to the East. Bialystok's turn had come.

I took the train to Warsaw. The Germans got into my car at Lapy, checking suitcases and papers. Near me was a big leather bag. They opened it: full of bacon. I disowned it. But the other passengers disowned it too, and the Germans chose to take me to the *Kommandantur*. The soldier walked along beside me, unconcerned, untroubled; what was a little black marketeer? In a deserted street I gave him a kick in the belly, then another, leaving him bent double, hit him again, then tore away. At the end of the street I ran into a Polish couple, who must have witnessed my assault.

What makes you trust people?

"This way," called the man.

I followed them back to their place; we talked over tiny glasses of vodka. I talked first. I'd been right to trust them: the young woman wept hearing me describe Treblinka. The man shook his head, resting his fists on the table.

"To go to Warsaw," he said simply, "there's the frontier of the Bug. On one side occupied territory, on the other the general government of Poland. And nearby, Treblinka. Checkposts everywhere. Better head south, towards Bielsk Podlaski, then towards Siedlce. You can slip through that way."

The young woman wiped her eyes.

"We know all about the trains," she said with a smile, "we're couriers for the Armia Krajowa."

We drank on.

"You can help us a lot," said the man.

I wanted to get to Warsaw, soon, at any cost, but they advised caution. Their area was being closely watched. I stayed three days in their apartment, then we left for Brzesc. There I saw real fighters, I learned what it was to be an officer responsible for the lives of a group of men, who has to make decisions on his own. I learned that war was tough. The young woman shyly confided to me.

"Don't let on you're a Jew. It's our secret, between us. The A.K. men hate Jews as much as Germans. But we need them to fight the Germans."

They fought well against the butchers. I met Captain Paczkowski, known as Wania; and Mieczyslaw, known as Bocian. They gave me my first weapon, a heavy Colt. At last, at last I was to fight. I still wanted to leave for Warsaw, but I also wanted to learn how to make war, to fight better alongside my people.

Captain Wania and I walked along frozen rivers, crawled through forests, put explosives on railway tracks and sawed through telegraph poles. Then we were captured. Once again I escaped, jumping off the truck taking us to the prison in Pinsk. I had to hole up in Brzesc, switch hiding places, hang around and postpone my return to Warsaw so as to take part in the liberation of Captain Wania organized by Jan Ponury.

Jan had come from Warsaw. He was a born leader, one of those men who wear their nobility and their courage in their faces. I told Jan I was a Jew. I described Treblinka. He listened to me with clenched fists, too. He'd parachuted in with Wania, sent from London by the Polish government-in-exile: he had not realized the scope of the exterminations. He, too, advised me to conceal my origins. I realized that I couldn't stay in the Armia Krajowa: I wanted to move out into the open, for my people, with my people. Wania's liberation was my last operation with the A.K. We planned the attack on the prison in Pinsk with Jan. For the first time I ceased to be a fugitive and became a hunter, an observer, a fighter, noting the movements of guards; knowing that on a given signal we were going to shoot the sentries I was watching.

We drove up in front of the prison. One of us, dressed in SS uniform, gave the order to open the gates. We leaped out, slit the throats of the soldiers on guard, and opened the other door. Jan Ponury gave us our commands by whistle. We spoke no Polish, giving the impression that we were Soviet partisans, to avoid reprisals. We smashed the doors of cells and the prisoners rushed along the galleries towards our trucks. We were giving them back their lives. What a joy to triumph, to let our battle cry ring out, to begin the age of revenge at last!

We freed Wania, tortured, wounded, but alive. From the Armia Krajowa I learned how to handle arms and something of war. Now, I'd paid my debt. I could leave.

I drank with Jan Ponury, to our friendship, to our struggle. He was a soldier building his army with whatever men he could find; so what if there were anti-Semites among them! After the war he'd have to build another Poland. We drank. I was from the Warsaw ghetto. I'd left Rivka, my mother and my brothers in Treblinka, Sonia in Zambrow, so many others in the yellow sand. If my father lived, he'd be in Warsaw where our people had already fought. My place was there. With my people.

"Go on, Mietek, go on. You're right. You must never hide your colors, what you are."

We embraced.

Two days later I was in Warsaw.

7

Our Lives Had the Resistance of Stone

MY city, my streets, my past: there were the East Station, Praga, the market where I had sold gloves, streets I had run down. And the Vistula, Poniatowski bridge, the quays, Laidak the cat. And Zofia, squeezing her hand: it was all centuries ago, another life. A streetcar went by. I wandered slowly; everything was going along normally. Was it possible, during the centuries that had passed, everyday men and women had quietly begun another day: work, meals, children, love?

Everything became gray and blurred. I was in a sad, embittered mood. I felt the injustice, selfishness, indifference and ignorance around me. The streets of Warsaw, the passersby, the waters of the Vistula and the stones in the bridge; the whole city proclaimed my loneliness. What were *we* to those strollers, those playing children? Nothing! We didn't exist, my mother, my brothers, Rivka, Sonia, Zofia; and you, too, orator from Zambrow, dead in the snow. And you, dentist with skillful hands at the bottom of your grave; and you, my brothers covered in yellow sand. This indifference, this self-absorption were killing you for a second time, burying you deeper than at Treblinka. In New York or even farther away, who could know? Who? Or care.

I crossed the Vistula and roamed the city, almost like old times. Before approaching the ghetto I wanted to get the feel of life in Warsaw. I wandered all the way down Dluga Street to the white-fronted Gogolewski cake shop, then to the café where the gang used to meet. I went in: there was another Yadia, similar to the one I'd known, full breasts and a ready laugh, broad hips; men who looked like Pila the Saw, Brigitki the Card and Zamek the Wise were catching her by the waist. I drank a glass of vodka, listening to the laughter, the bursts of conversation: around the tables they were talking about "cats" and "Bedouins" who had gone to ground on the Aryan side and whom they were going to hold for ransom. Laughter. Other *Schmaltzowniki,* those who were growing fat on our blood, had taken over from Dziobak the Pox, Mietek the Giant, Rudy the Red, Ptaszek the Bird. Selfishness, indifference and cowardice: the butchers still had allies, the dark side of man which can transform him into a beast.

I left, crossed Krasinski Gardens, and went down Swientojerska Street, then Nalewki, slipping back into my hoodlum's swagger to mislead the gangs on the lookout for Bedouins and to deceive the Blues, Ukrainians and Germans still at the foot of the wall.

But their very presence excited me: it proved that the ghetto was still alive, that my father could be there too. We *had* to come back, to proclaim our survival and ignite a beacon in the heart of Warsaw so that *they* would know we were living; so that the world would learn that we were being slaughtered. Fight and fight again: I was more than ever convinced that this was our only way to survive, to save our people, those covered in yellow sand, in oblivion, forever. Our only way to bring them back to life again.

I went back to Praga and knocked on Mokotow the Tomb's door. I trusted him. Nobody. I waited, hiding in a cellar, knocked again. It was his sister, Marie. She looked at me. Not recognizing me, I felt she was racking her brains, hoping my name was about to float up from the depths.

"Mietek, I'm Mietek the Snip."

She gasped, then put out her hand and gently stroked my face.

"Mietek, Mietek, you're so thin."

She stared at me, reading from my features, my skin, the centuries through which I'd traveled.

"You're alive."

She made me sit down, gave me food, then, as she walked around me, stroked my hair, my face and my shoulders.

THE UPRISING OF THE WARSAW GHETTO
(APRIL 19 TO MAY 8, 1943)

●   Bunkers

←   Attacks by the insurgents

⇐   Advance routes of the German troops

18 Mila Street: Mordekai Anielewitz's command bunker

23 Mila Street: Martin Gray's home

"Tell me all about it, Mietek."

I shook my head. I hadn't the strength to face my dead, here, with her.

"More than you can ever know or imagine. All murdered. All my people. Tell me about you."

Mokotow was working as a truck driver and had joined the Armia Ludowa, the partisans' popular army. Maria began searching through piles of linen in a cupboard. She brought out a small, badly printed newspaper: *Glos Warszawy,* organ of the P.P.R., the Polish workers' party.

"I handle distribution, Mietek."

I didn't hear Mokotow return. I felt his heavy hands on my shoulders.

"I knew you'd be here one day, Mietek."

We embraced. We hadn't seen each other for months but Mokotow, once the scourge of the Bedouins, was now a militant worker. He sat down in front of me and we took a good look at each other.

"Have you come far, Mietek?"

"Far."

He poured me a glass of vodka.

"But not for nothing. Your people are fighting now. They've become lions."

My father was there, I was sure, sure. Yes, we were alive, yes, men would triumph over the beasts, just as Mokotow the Tomb's darker half had been cast aside.

"It started in January. They attacked the Germans with boiling water, boiling oil, stones and bottles, and weapons, too. There are so few."

I was drinking but the warmth I felt wasn't alcohol. At last, at last our battle cry was ringing out.

"It happened near your place in Mila Street, in your area, Mietek. The Germans ran, stopped the deportations. There's been shooting every day."

I got up.

"I'm sure my father's there."

Saying it out loud for the first time made me doubly convinced.

"I'm going there, Mokotow, now."

He advised caution. The streets were full of blackmailers, denouncers. They hounded anyone who looked suspicious, robbed and killed. When a Jewish family managed to find rooms on the Aryan side, for twenty or thirty thousand zlotys, gang after gang held them for ransom.

"Jackals! Vampires! They give addresses to each other and share profits. Then, when they've squeezed the orange, they denounce them and collect a reward. That's it, Mietek."

He dismissed them with a wave of his hand.

"And the others, Pila the Saw, Dziobak . . ."

"A band of jackals."

Marie came up to me and caught me by the shoulder.

"Stay here, Mietek. You can fight with Mokotow, join the Armia Ludowa, if you like."

But Mokotow already had his cap on.

"When you've come from where you have, Mietek, it must be hard to wait."

I kissed Marie, drank a final glass of vodka. Mokotow and I took the street to the ghetto.

"Every evening some of the *Placowkarze* come back down Leszno Street. You can try them."

Several times, in the old days, I'd slipped in among the Jews returning home from working outside the ghetto in the daytime: the guards didn't check very closely. Who'd be crazy enough to return to a prison if he didn't have to?

Mokotow and I went along Leszno Street, formerly one of the main streets of the ghetto, now one of its frontiers. The buildings in Grzybowska Street, Krochmalna and Ogrodowa were empty; their inhabitants had filled the cattle cars at the *Umschlagplatz,* then the graves at Treblinka.

A column of Jewish laborers, escorted by German soldiers, was moving down Zelazna Street. I noted the hollow cheeks, bowed backs and ragged clothes of the *Placowkarze.* I embraced Mokotow.

"Good luck, Mietek."

The column halted in front of the entrance to the ghetto. A

few Poles were there, idlers, thugs, Bedouin hunters. I rushed forward and my people closed around me, stooped, looking at the ground; a meek slave. The column set off again through the gate. I was home, back in the ghetto.

It was empty, deserted, anemic, languishing but still alive.

The column of laborers was joined by workers from Toebbens and Schultz, then at Nowolipki Street everyone dispersed. The streets emptied, everyone vanished into the dusk, without a sound, into the silence of a deserted town. I ran. I recognized the cobbles, the doors. I was journeying through my past as if it were a stage from which the actors had disappeared. At the corner of Dzielna Street, lay a group of young men in wait. They accosted the workers, handing them leaflets which some refused but others stuffed into their pockets. They gave me one. Even before I could speak to them they scattered. I went into a courtyard and read the text. It was wholesome bread; clear water; a transfusion of blood:

> *Zydowska Organizacja Bojowa*
> Jewish Fighting Organization
> *Jews! The German bandits will not leave you in peace long. Gather around the standards of resistance. Take shelter, hide your women and children, and join, with whatever means you have, the fight against the Nazi butchers. The Jewish Fighting Organization counts on your wholehearted support, moral as well as material.* WARSAW GHETTO, 3 MARCH 1943. MAJOR, J.F.O.

I kissed the crumpled paper and ran through the streets: I went to meet them, I went to meet *him*. The only place he could be was among the fighters. Like me, my father who had set me his example, who, from the very start, when we used to walk through Krasinski Gardens, had known what the Germans had in store for us. That text was his voice, mine too, which had been pleading in Zambrow and in Bialystok for weeks to no avail.

The streets seemed empty; but the farther I went the more my eyes grew accustomed to the darkness, and the better I could see heavily laden figures, stooping under sacks and boards, running from one street to the next. I went back down Zamenhofa. I soon reached the corner of Gesia: every foot was familiar, the front of every house was still the same, here the columns had formed up for the *Umschlagplatz*. Mother, brothers, Rivka, Pola and you too, Pavel, Pavel of the night before you abdicated, here was the heart of my life, here I'd killed, these were my rooftops, here I held you against me, Rivka, here was the heart of my already distant life, here Dr. Celmajster's daughter screamed out, and here on these rooftops David put his arms around my shoulders and said, "They took your father yesterday. There was nothing we could do." Here was the heart of my cruel life. I stopped at the corner of Mila and Zamenhofa, I looked at the window as if my mother might have been there, stretching her arms towards me, her frail arms, hope and fear, her hand giving a small, shy wave. I could see her eyes dim with sorrow and anguish. I'd never forgive them for my mother. Never. I walked down Mila, entering it as if it were a dark cave. I climbed the stairs of No. 23.

I stopped, sat down, shadows flitted past, grazed me. In the courtyard, a sound of hammering; I could hear tools clinking on the ground, sawing noises. I went down again into the yard; over by Kupiecka Street a group of men was digging and paving. They'd formed a chain and were passing sacks, buckets and planks.

"Don't just watch, give us a hand."

The man was holding a heavy piece of timber and pointing to the other end. I took it and worked with the group till dawn: the idea was to build two bunkers facing Kupiecka Street, communicating, by means of a number of tunnels, with the courtyards in Mila Street. I worked and worked, unaware of time, forgetting where I'd come from; as did all the others, working like me, frenziedly, as if the Germans were arriving that morning, as if the fates of all our people depended on that bunker. It was true, the fates of our people did depend on the bunker and all the others being built in every street of the ghetto, islets of resistance and survival, a ghetto beneath the ghetto.

Dawn came, soft, pale blue. Two figures crossed the yard in our direction. They were moving slowly. The men stopped working and gathered around them. I put down my saw and joined the group. One of the two men spoke.

"These bunkers, comrades, are like our heart, our life. It's not just for us, but for the world, they must know. With these bunkers, it's up to us to hold on, hold on for a week, so our voice can be heard, down the centuries."

I knew the urgent, metallic quality of that voice. I went up closer. Behind the speaker I saw a gray-haired man, his head drooping as if with tiredness, a tall man with his hands behind his back. I went even closer, jostling a girl out of the way: she swore at me, he turned around. He was alive.

We were like one person, arms entwined, chest to chest: his beard against my cheeks, like old times in Senatorska Street. I drank his salty tears and mine flowed onto his hands as they clasped my face. Where were we? Why the war, the ghetto, Treblinka, why man's folly, the savagery of the beasts with men's faces, why, Father, Father, Father, why those graves, those dead children, when there is such joy in feeling your hands, in finding your body alive. Father, why this world, why such turmoil?

We wept in each other's arms, in silent communion, and my cousin, Julek Feld, who'd come with my father, Julek Feld, the P.P.R. delegate, stopped talking.

The circle around us had grown and everyone was crying, for us, for their own lost families; everyone was crying for joy and sorrow. Then they left us. We stayed in the middle of the yard, holding each other by the shoulder. Before leaving, our comrades shook my father and me by the hand, as if to convince themselves that everything was possible; that maybe one day in a ghetto courtyard, or maybe after the war, they, too, would find one of their people.

They left us. Still holding each other by the shoulder, we went upstairs to the place where we'd hidden our defenseless loved ones. The apartment had been ransacked, the fake cupboard stood there gaping, smashed in the room that had been their hideout: my brothers' books and a knitted shawl which my mother used to throw over her shoulders were still in one corner. We were holding each other by the shoulder and hadn't exchanged a single word. The others spoke for us, Julek Feld had explained. I wanted to talk and talk, but the words wouldn't come, I had so many things deep inside me, torments, questions, so many unshared fears and horrors I'd never dared to go too far into because I was afraid they'd drag me down with them. I wanted to talk about them, say that it was unfair that her shawl, that cupboard, those books were still there, whereas my mother and my brothers weren't; that life was meaningless, that the world didn't deserve meaning because dead things survived and those you loved all died. We were holding each other by the shoulder, not daring to speak of all those days in Treblinka that I wanted to talk about, all those questions I wanted to ask.

"Father, Father."

"Go on, Martin, go on. You mustn't be afraid to cry."

I sobbed against him and he against me. I wept until the sentences came freely. Then I told him everything. By then we'd stopped crying, we were sitting on the floor, facing each other, legs crossed.

"That's right, Martin," he'd say from time to time.

When I paused, he respected my silence for a while and then said, "We must keep going, Martin."

"What about you, Father?"

He'd managed to get selected at the *Umschlagplatz* for a labor camp.

"Thanks to your advice, Martin."

He'd escaped from it and returned to Warsaw.

"You weren't here anymore. No one was. But, Martin, I knew you wouldn't give up. I knew. I had faith."

All day we stayed there talking, exchanging words and looks, sharing experiences. Then night fell and once again came the sound of hammers, spades and saws.

"Now, Martin, the time has come to fight. You must take your place."

Father got up and stuck out his hand, giving me a sharp tug as he used to in Senatorska Street when I pretended I wouldn't get up or sit down to table. He kept hold of my hand.

"Martin, you must fight, because it's our duty. We must fight to the last. Most of us will perish. You must try to live. Live, Martin, live for all of us."

We embraced. Someone was sawing in the yard. We'd had a

whole day to ourselves, almost an eternity in those troubled times. We couldn't ask for more.

That night, I described Treblinka to the members of the Jewish Fighting Organization. The ghetto knew by then that it was an extermination camp, because others like myself had escaped from it; but I was the first to return from the lower camp. I told them about the excavator and the graves in the yellow sand, about Ivan and Idioten. Then I asked to join the Organization.

Now came days of feverish activity. We needed money, arms and men; we had to silence the cowards, win over the faint-hearted, punish the traitors. Even then, in spite of the evacuations, in spite of what was known about Treblinka, in spite of the *Umschlagplatz,* in spite of the January fighting, some people, those who had obtained a "number" from the Germans, the right to live, went on hoping that they could hold out until the end of the war by obeying the butchers.

I saw workers from Toebbens and Schultz volunteer for "transfer." One March night I stuck up some posters: the Organization explained that we had to sabotage such "transfers" in order to cheat death. The next day the Germans pasted them over. Toebbens and the corpulent Schultz organized meetings for their workers. "We need your work," said Toebbens and Schultz from high up on their balcony. "But since you can't stay in Warsaw itself, we've selected other areas for our workshops, Trawniki and Poniatow. You'll get work and bread there." Schultz and Toebbens gave their word of honor.

We had to challenge such speeches; but sometimes, going into shops, I heard the last few respectable shopkeepers whom the Germans had tolerated talk about us as "hotheads" and "young puppies" who "invited trouble and persecution."

But it was no time for respecting opinions: I'd come from Treblinka, Zambrow and Bialystok, I knew what moderation was worth. So I formed a group to raise contributions for the Organization. Sometimes, all we had to do was ask, sometimes we had to produce a weapon, sometimes leave with a hostage. We took Wielikowski, son of one of the three members of the Judenrat, and got a million zlotys. We commandeered food from the shopkeepers. We killed German looters, soldiers who'd infiltrated the ghetto. We sentenced to death and executed traitors, such as Jacob Hirszfeld, who was manager of Hallmann's workshop.

We were fighting for a world of men, and we knew that our victory would be merely to *fight,* not defeat the enemy: because we were an island, a tomb, a ghetto surrounded by indifference and hatred, encircled by the enemy; and we had no arms. It was there, in the J.F.O., that I met the men I'd hoped existed: Mordekai Anielewicz, Michel Rosenfeld, Julek Feld, Ber Brando and Aron Bryskin, and so many others who thought like me that keeping faith with the dead of Treblinka meant struggle and revenge. But we had no arms.

So once again I took the road to Aryan Warsaw, but today our grain was revolvers and grenades, rifles and bullets. I waded through the filthy water of the sewers. At first I had an Aryan Polish guide, then after a few trips I got to know this new geography. I'd known the lay of the streets, the streetcar routes and the wall, then the rooftops. Now I was exploring the twilight world of underground canals, unmarked intersections, identical criss-crossing passages which perhaps led to some endless maze, even to madness. The sewers became my streets, my new freedom.

I joined Mokotow the Tomb: he was waiting for me at an agreed exit, keeping an eye on the approaches, warning me if a policeman or Bedouin hunter was in the vicinity. As soon as he raised the manhole cover, I climbed the iron ladder and we went down narrow alleys of Stare Miasto, the old town. There, in a different house every time, I met men of the Armia Ludowa, partisans from the Witold group, and obtained arms. Then I made contact with the more secret groups in the Armia Krajowa. Sometimes Mokotow the Tomb would contrive to buy a weapon for me and we'd celebrate by drinking vodka in his Praga apartment. I'd leave under cover of night and Mokotow would always insist on accompanying me, keeping watch as I raised the manhole cover and vanished into the familiar canals.

I went out again into the ghetto, into the silence broken by the clanging of tools, because everyone was getting ready to go to ground, to hide beneath the earth, protected by concrete walls. I didn't like those caves, those priest's holes: some had water, electricity, telephones, even separate toilets; but to me they were sealed tombs. When the battle came, I'd make for the streets, the rooftops and the sewers, not those deep bunkers.

Sometimes as I returned, crossing streets, dashing from one building to the next, stealing into attics, I actually brought weapons — sometimes just a single revolver — to 32 Swientojerska Street. This was the Organization's military headquarters, with two rooms and a kitchen into which were crammed a dozen permanently armed fighters. A few yards away, in the same block, were the "brush factories," which turned out all sorts of objects for the Germans. I'd make my way to the military headquarters by attic and rooftop, girls would serve me a meal, then I'd set off happily for Mila Street. I'd switch from the streets to the rooftops. We were going to fight, fight at last, spurred on by the fresh air of spring. I hadn't survived in vain.

I used to meet my father at Mila Street. The command bunker was almost opposite 23 Mila, at No. 18. My father would wait for me, or I for him. After a long talk, we'd sleep side by side on mattresses. We had stopped mentioning Mother and my brothers. They were all around us, in us, alive through our struggle. Father talked to me as if he wanted me to pass on everything he had thought and learned. In spite of war and death, he talked of a society in which men would be rid of such evils as poverty and injustice, of a world in which man's only concern would be his relationships with others and with himself, freed from the curse of self-interest. He talked about all that our people had given to mankind, and about how they had paid in suffering in order to survive, in spite of everything.

"It's life that's sacred, Martin. We have to kill today, but remember life, Martin, life. You must give life. It's difficult being a father, but when you decide, choose to be a man. Survive, Martin. I'd like you to have children later on, when it's over, when we men have won. And then give them your whole self. They're sacred."

I would listen to his voice, firm and gentle. Sometimes he'd talk about his childhood, how he'd started his factory, met my mother. Then he'd break off.

"Go to sleep, Martin, maybe I'll tell you more tomorrow."

Tomorrow would soon be there and I'd leave by way of the rooftops and sewers, waiting for the evening and more such conversations. If he didn't come, I couldn't get to sleep. One night he came later than usual, towards dawn.

"Julek Feld is dead."

He'd been shot by an SS patrol during a raid. I didn't know Julek very well but I liked his lean, intelligent face, his eager, ringing voice.

"He always sought the good. He believed in ideas. Julek was a man."

Father told me about my grandmother, Julek's aunt, a stubborn old lady who sent long letters, in the days when people wrote to us, asking for photos of her grandson.

"You'll have to go over there to New York one day, and bring her a bit of life. She was fond of you. The only time she saw you, you were just starting to walk. You were clenching your little fists."

I was listening, drinking in those words, his voice. That night, when he told me about my cousin's death, Father said, "Julek always stuck it out. A man always sticks it out, Martin."

He was near the window. The moon was lighting up the room and I could see the tears running freely down his cheeks.

"I wonder why I'm saying that to you. You've already stuck it out, Martin. Several times. You're a man, a real man, and have been for a long time."

Thank you, Father, for those words.

That was all the time we had for talking.

On Saturday, April 18, the Organization proclaimed a state of emergency. I dashed about the streets with the others, sticking up posters and handing out leaflets with our slogan:

"Death with honor! Men to arms, women and children to the shelters!"

This was the test. I was with my people, armed, we were about to start making *them* pay, and their debt was huge. I tramped the ghetto until late into the night, wanting to be everywhere, going from one bunker to another, carrying bottles filled with gasoline and messages from the brush-factory sector in Swientojerska and

Walowa streets to the workshop sector in Leszno and Nowolipie streets. I went from courtyards to attics, from streets to rooftops, from level to level: every cobble, every step, every chimney had a meaning for my eyes, my hands. I was at home here, the heart of my life was here, I was invincible here.

I met my father in the building on the corner of Mila and Zamenhofa.

"The Blues have encircled the ghetto," he said. "Tomorrow will be the day. You must get some rest, Martin. Who knows when we'll be able to sleep again."

I lay down and slept peacefully, without nightmares, until my father grabbed me by the hand.

"They're here!"

It was a clear, limpid night. Nearby, over by the wall, possibly in the brush-factory sector, I heard some grenades bursting, a few shots. Then silence. I went to a window. There they were, advancing cautiously, single file, along the fronts of the houses. They came down Zamenhofa; behind them, in the distance, I could make out some vehicles, possibly tanks. Then I was ordered to the Kupiecka and Nalewki bunkers to tell them to wait for the signal to fire. I leaped from roof to roof, a revolver stuck in my belt. I crept into attics, dived down stairs. In those days of battle, the ground, the steps, the rooftops, propelled me higher, faster.

From time to time isolated bursts of fire, a grenade exploding; probably the Germans machine-gunning a window or mopping up a cellar as they went.

At 6 A.M., under a clear sky, the SS reached the Mila-Zamenhofa intersection; we finally received the order, the liberating order: "Attack!"

Explosions! I carried gasoline bombs, then went upstairs again loaded with explosives manufactured in the ghetto and saw a soldier take a gasoline bottle on his helmet, catch fire and roll over in a sheet of flame; others were fleeing.

Someone shouted, "They're running away, they're getting out!"

I climbed to the rooftops, went to the corner of Kupiecka and Zamenhofa and leaned over; the streets were deserted; they'd fled, those iron butchers, Zamenhofa was ours. Elsewhere, from the brush-factory sector near Nalewki and Gesia, the sound of grenades, then silence. They must have been routed there, too. I came down again. We all embraced and shouted for joy. Then we ran down the street with others, looking for arms. Three bodies were stretched there, within a few yards. One was lying on his back, his face burned, groaning, horribly mutilated. I finished him off. Elsewhere I helped comrades drag the dead into a yard and strip them of their uniforms, helmets to boots. I had a complete SS uniform. Then we waited, resting. They were sure to come back. They'd probably win but for us victory was their retreat, our fight, the duration of our resistance. No longer were we animals being driven to the slaughterhouse, rushing towards it with our heads down.

"There they are!"

They returned cautiously, spraying the fronts of the houses with machine-gun fire, dodging from doorway to doorway. Then we heard staccato exhausts, and the clatter of caterpillar tracks on the cobblestones. I ran to my observation post on the rooftops. At the corner of Gesia and Zamenhofa, I saw the gray silhouettes of tanks. Two of them entered Zamenhofa, firing at the buildings.

It was about midday, April 19. I remember the sky, the sun, the lightness of the air, the throb of the engines, the grinding sound of the tracks. I was reminded of the panting of the excavator back there in the lower camp. Here, in the ghetto, we were about to destroy some of those death engines. The tanks moved forward, went past our positions at 29 and 50 Zamenhofa and reached the Mila Street intersection. At 28 Mila I was waiting with my father, a gasoline bomb in each hand. Infantrymen were following two tanks. I saw a soldier crouching, frightened and wary. Your turn, butcher! I threw my bombs: fire, explosions, the tanks were enveloped in flames. They turned back swathed in black smoke, and the infantry took to its heels. I saw a frenzied soldier running along the road before he slumped, clutching his belly. Beyond Zamenhofa our fighters were taking the Germans in the rear: they were on the run. I dashed into the street and collected arms and helmets. I dragged a soldier into the courtyard, another fighter stripped him. Those uniforms could prove invaluable. If one day we had to run away, run away to survive and fight elsewhere, those uniforms could save our lives.

The day passed: I felt at peace. I was fighting. In the evening, I went, first by rooftops then by the streets to the "workshop" sector, to the Schultz factory, at 76 Leszno Street. They hadn't been attacked, but had seen the Germans pass and make for our sector. Schultz, the director, was indignant, appalled; he kept saying, "The Jews are behaving monstrously." Schultz, fat Schultz, you were in for a few more surprises.

I dashed from attic to attic, avoiding the streets whenever I could. I wanted to see, know. Nalewki Street was enveloped in black smoke: our men had set fire to the big German shop, *Werterfassung,* at No. 33. I couldn't get close, the Germans were still there, blocking Gesia, firing on sight. The rest of the ghetto was calm. I went back to Mila by way of the rooftops. In one room a man was sitting talking, his head down, his hands in his lap, to a silent audience: he'd seen the Germans set fire to 6 Gesia, which was serving as a hospital for the ghetto, he'd seen them dash out the brains of newborn babies against the walls, rip open the bellies of pregnant women, and throw casualties into the flames. He'd seen them.

In spite of that I slept. Tomorrow would be tougher. I woke at dawn: the weather was fine. It was Tuesday, April 20, the first day of Passover. Father was there, near me, waving good morning; so what if we didn't speak, we were side by side: so what if we were separated, we both knew that nothing would divide us. I went into the brush-factory sector, calm the previous day. Toebbens had even asked the workers to return to work. I went into the attics. About three in the afternoon, the Germans arrived, entered the courtyard and there was an enormous explosion. The fighters from the Organization had placed a mine in the yard of the building. It shattered the German patrol. Bodies were flung into the air: survivors fled. Then they returned, single file, hugging the walls and firing toward my attic. I hurled gasoline bombs. Noise and smoke enveloped us. I went onto the roof and lay down; in the yard I could see the director of the brush factory accompanied by two officers who were asking us to surrender, after which we'd

REVENGE

A Soviet officer at nineteen, Martin was decorated with the most prestigious orders of the Red Army: the Order of the Red Star, the Patriotic War Order, and the Alexander Nevski Order.

"Suddenly, behind me, a cheeful voice. 'Greetings, comrade!' I'd joined the partisans." Martin Gray is in the center foreground. Standing against a tree, second from the left, is Mieczylaw Moczar, now a general, who played a prominent part in Polish political life, especially after 1956. After the partisans, Martin Gray joined the Red Army.

A NEW WORLD

Yesterday a Soviet officer; now a waiter and live wire at a Borsch
Belt hotel in the Catskills. At the end of the season the waiters put
on a revue for the guests. Martin Gray is between the two girls. PHOTO
BY NORMAN RAGAN

HAPPINESS

Dina

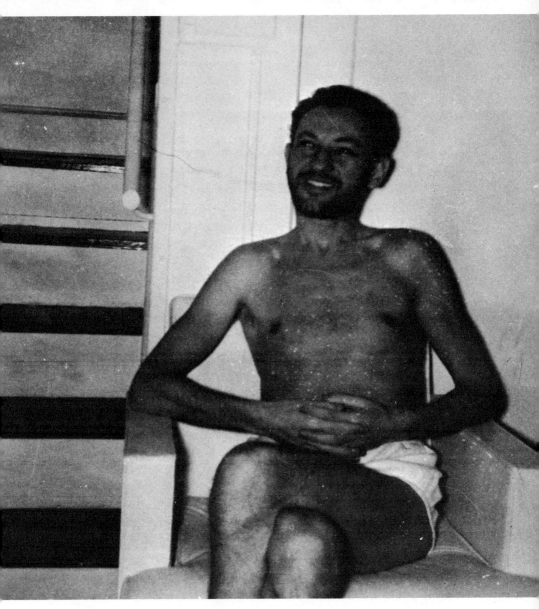

"I began a long fast . . . I was being reborn." Martin Gray lost thirty-eight pounds during his fast.

"Our Fortress." The estate of Les Barons, above Cannes, in the Tanneron mountains. "Here" said Dina, art must reign. It must be noble, spacious, like a castle, a chapel. We'll listen to the giants here." PHOTO BY D. D. DUNCAN

leave, without further ado, for the camps of Poniatow and Trawniki. We had a quarter of an hour to consider it. Shots replied
from all directions. Surrender? We, who'd seen mothers flung into
graves, brothers' heads blown to bits, fathers shot? Surrender!
Trust the butchers!

They returned in force. They shelled the ghetto from Krasinski
Gardens: from the streets they were firing with heavy machine
guns; at our buildings with tanks. I withdrew, leaping from roof
to roof. On the stairs, I heard a group of Germans approaching. I
threw my last bomb and fled. Sudden heat, shrieks and thick eddies of smoke whirling around me; it was like being smothered
with hot cloths.

This was a time of flames, one day much like the next. The
Germans set fire to the brush-factory sector. The tarmac melted.
On two or three occasions flames surrounded me. I touched my
hair to find it singed: the soles of shoes caught fire on the scorching ground and glass melted. The houses caught fire, flames
spreading from district to district.

Men and women, fleeing the flames, threw themselves from
windows to their deaths. From the roof I saw a frenzied woman,
her hair streaming, in the blast of that inferno, holding her child
over the street, ready to throw it. I shouted, "I'll take it to safety
over the roofs. I'll take it!" But how could she hear me? She'd already let go and with a piercing scream jumped after it.

I ran through the flames, between crumbling walls and over
rubble, while planes with the black crosses which I'd seen in that
far-distant September of 1939 at the time of my birth, hovered
over the ghetto and dropped incendiary bombs. They sometimes
lay unexploded in the middle of the street, black and
frightening — some tried to dismantle them for their explosives.

Then people went down into the bunkers, burying themselves
under the ruins. I kept on the move, preferring death in the
smoke under the sky, to suffocation beneath a slab of concrete. I
wrapped rags around my feet to stop my shoes catching fire and to
muffle my footsteps in the rubble when I went from bunker to
bunker, dodging German patrols.

The days went by under a blue sky often concealed by smoke. I was hungry, thirsty; but water mains had burst, so I drank from dark pools in which there could have been men's bodies. Sometimes, behind a fragment of wall, I would come across a sobbing woman, her arms in the air, kneeling by a corpse, one of her family whom she was mourning; to her the only dead person in a city that once had at least half a million inhabitants and of which nothing remained but corpses, ruins and a few buried survivors.

This was a time of heroism. I saw a young woman douse herself with gasoline, set fire to herself and fling herself on a tank; I saw men surrender to the Germans, their arms in the air, and then charge at them and snatch weapons from them.

We used every form of warfare to keep going. Hidden in the ruins, I would call to a German in the guttural tones of one of them, then we would cut his throat in the night. Some of us put on the SS uniforms we'd taken the first day. I remember looking at myself in a fragment of mirror: me, Mietek, in that helmet and those boots, those butchers' insignia! We marched through the streets to a barricade manned by a dozen soldiers; we went calmly up to them and opened fire. Three of them ran off so we gave chase and shot them in a courtyard. But they killed four of our men. We came back loaded with arms. I decided to rule out that sort of fighting: if we wanted to be effective it meant that we would leave no witnesses. We had to walk in the middle of the road so that our men would realize we weren't real SS men, yet we still risked being shot by one of our own. I didn't want to die in SS uniform.

I began again to run through the sea of flames which was now the ghetto, firing at Germans when I could, carrying ammunition from bunker to bunker, covering the two bunkers in Kupiecka Street from the upper floors. I saw General Stroop's soldiers force women and children out of a bunker, make them lie down on the ground amidst the rubble and shoot them. I saw more women jumping from blazing buildings, and others fling themselves at soldiers and get shot.

Yet sometimes a column of prisoners formed, women and children with arms raised in surrender, allowing themselves to be taken off to the cattle cars. Men, too, yesterday fighters; today exhausted, broken, like overstretched springs. Watching their columns, swathed in the thick black smoke of the fires, I swore to fight on, to survive even if we were defeated here, until Berlin one day became a furnace too, a field of ruins. We had to make up our minds to go right into the butchers' lair and return blow for blow. Dying, clutching our weapons, wasn't enough. We had to win, crush them beneath our heels.

The smoke was so dense you could hardly tell day from night: the flames lit up areas already illuminated by their searchlights. On April 27, I went down into the sewers. The Germans were only beginning to realize that arms and men of the Armia Ludowa and the Armia Krajowa, were passing through them. Women, children and old men, and fighters too, whom I was taking to the Aryan zone, waited hours there in the muddy water for the trucks that would drive them to the forest just outside Warsaw. The old men, the wounded, walked along, stooping, and sometimes some of them refused to go on, rejecting life, burying their heads in the slime and vomiting. I dragged them out, pulled them up, and carried them to the iron ladders. Then I went back again, this time leading underground fighters carrying munitions, who were astonished by my knowledge of the maze of sewers. We surfaced in the ghetto, amidst the smoke and ruins, and I led the Polish fighters to Parysowski Square, a devastated area. The German tanks moved in, firing their machine guns, and we hid behind bits of wall, covered in rubble and plaster. I managed to get to Mila Street, was spotted by the Germans when I dashed from one building to another, and found my father. He embraced me.

"You're alive, Mietek, alive."

He hugged me.

"You're not to die. Not to die."

Days went by: the Germans systematically infiltrated the ruins of the ghetto, shooting, blowing up the bunkers, firing gas into the sewers, explosives into what was little more than a furnace anyway. Picking my way through the flames, wandering in search of shelter among the ruins, I'd come across women and children, men hoping in vain for arms. Sometimes I'd take them along my routes, skirting fires, and crossing sections of roof still intact.

More often I'd leave them after a few words of advice: what could I do for them? I had to fight.

On May 1, I joined some comrades in one of the bunkers, the one at 74 Leszno Street. They were gathered under the low ceiling, one of them talking in the heavy and, to me, almost unbreathable air. He was celebrating the First of May.

"Our struggle," he said, "will undoubtedly have great historic significance, not only for the Jewish people but also for resistance movements which are fighting Hitler throughout Europe."

Among those men, who were about to die covered with soot and with only a few weapons, I felt convinced of our victory. We decided to attack the Germans in broad daylight, to celebrate the day. I dashed from ruin to ruin through the smoke, crawling across rubble, avoiding the German positions. The ghetto was a field of gray stones, blackened walls and crumbling buildings. My father wasn't at Mila Street, he'd gone to the brush-factory sector. I left, I wanted to be near him. Everywhere the fire was raging, to the dull pounding of the German guns; there had never been so many explosions. The streets were obscured, flames were leaping from windows. As I ran, I saw a man, bare-chested, arms raised, throw himself from a fourth-floor window without a murmur. I made my way through the ruins to the brush-factory area; I passed the building at 6 Walowa Street and reached the Swientojerska Street area. There was firing over towards Franciszkanska Street: I knew that the bunker at No. 30 had also decided on an attack for the First of May.

Then came a series of bursts of fire. I buried my head in the plaster; I heard orders in German. Then I saw a dozen men who had emerged, covered with dust, arms up, walking towards the SS.

I saw Father, head up, hands raised to the level of his forehead. He was walking forward with the rest. I saw him. I was waiting for a miracle. I would have liked to bury my head in the plaster again, not to see. But I had to stare death in the face, so that I could speak out later on, for his sake, for all those I loved.

They gave a shout. I yelled at the same time. They flung themselves on the SS; two or three fell, their steel- and leather-encased shapes rolling in the dust. There were bursts of fire. More bursts,

shouted orders, soldiers retreating and throwing grenades among
the bodies, kicking up clouds of white smoke. Then silence: explosions in the distance. Father lay among the ghetto stones, a
stone of the ghetto. Goodbye, Father. Goodbye to your thick gray
beard against my cheek, your firm and gentle voice; goodbye to
your hands on my shoulders, goodbye to your talk, goodbye.
You'll never see that just society; or man rid of his afflictions.
Goodbye to you who made me a man. Goodbye, Father.

I remained motionless, myself a stone, staring into the grayness,
broken only by a few black lumps. Then I crawled backwards,
sliding into holes. I found a bunker split open, like a cracked nut,
inside it rats were swarming over corpses. I crawled, not so much
because I had to, but to press myself to the earth, my earth, which
had taken my people. I was alone. Mother, Father, my brothers,
Julek Feld, around me stretched a desert not unlike the ghetto,
but I swore in those ruins, my face against those burning stones,
that every morning, as long as I lived, my people, all my people,
my family and all those in Treblinka and Zambrow and Bialystok, my people, all of you, those here, every morning, as long as
I had strength to think, I'd bring you back to life again for my
sake, with the dawn, every morning, so that you'd be a part of me,
sharing my life. I swore it among the ruins.

I went back to the bunker in Mila Street. I sang with the others the song of the ghetto, *Es brennt,* then I slipped off again into
the ruins. Now, the whole ghetto was on fire. A building at 7
Mila was apparently the only one still intact. Groups kept arriving there; fighters, women and children. There was a shortage of
food, water and ammunition; some considered escaping through
the sewers but the Germans had discovered the main network:
they were firing in gas and sealing the exits with cement, attach-
ing grenades that went off at a mere touch.

I could feel the tomb being sealed. For more than two weeks
we'd kept it open, almost with our bare hands; for two weeks
we'd been crying out to the world that a people was being slaughtered here. To no avail. There had been a few attacks by partisans on the outskirts of the ghetto, a few brave men had come to
die with us; but there were idle spectators too, standing around

outside the ghetto wall, staring at the fire, counting the shots fired by the German batteries and watching our bodies plunge into the flames.

Now the tomb was sealed: it was only a question of hours.

I fought on, around the bunkers in Kupiecka Street, meeting comrades who'd managed to escape from the bunker in Smocza. The Germans were using tear gas, fire, grenades. No one surrendered. Some killed themselves: others let themselves be killed where they stood. Ammunition was in short supply everywhere: at the Leszno Street bunker, there were only a few bottles of sulphuric acid left. Should I die with the rest or try and fight on elsewhere? In Leszno Street they were ready to leave the ghetto, to try and reach the forest and fight from there; but they didn't have time. The Germans massacred them. From a balcony in Zamenhofa I threw my last two grenades at a patrol; then I managed to make my way through cellars and yards to the bunker at 18 Mila. It was suffocating. More than a hundred fighters were there. I didn't want to die here, I wanted the sky above the ghetto. I wanted to see the man who killed me.

I went out, dashed across the street, and was back home at 23 Mila Street. As I climbed the wreckage of the stairs to the upper floors, I heard the vehicles, orders and shouts. There they were, surrounding the 18 Mila Street bunker I'd just left; dozens of SS men in armored cars. Over their loudspeaker they gave orders to come out and surrender. Maybe my comrades would try a counterattack! Silence. Then explosions, gas fumes, followed by a deeper silence; then sharp, isolated detonations. They were killing themselves. I lay down in the rubble listening to the butchers' voices, the stench of tear gas in my nostrils.

Goodbye, Mordekai Anielewicz, goodbye, my comrades, goodbye, men among men.

So I lay there until night, half buried in the plaster, concrete and stones. My mind was a blank, I was a part of the ghetto, neither dead nor alive. At night I began to crawl: I passed figures which resembled men, with torn clothes, covered with mud, looking for a candle, shelter, food. They were no longer even survivors. I crept towards Muranowski Square, at the end of Mila.

There, near the square, you could reach the sewers through a cellar tunnel.

I picked my way through the rubble, working myself forward to the cellar on my elbows, and found the exit leading to the sewer. I was alone in the narrow duct stinking of gas and dirty water. I walked doubled over in the light of a candle. I skirted the grenades dangling from wires near the entrances: Go on, Mietek, go on. You've known worse: Pawiak, Treblinka, the graves. Go on, now you know that men will triumph because, at last, a battle cry has rung out in the too-long silent ghetto.

I walked. I was unfamiliar with the route, having only used it once or twice because it was made up of minor sewers, today the only ones open. I was walking under Przebieg Street. When I came to the first exit without any grenades, I reached for the iron ladder. Water and excrement were running down my legs, I was worn out, sweating. I was thirsty, almost sick with hunger. I cleaned myself as best I could, then pushed with the back of my neck against the iron manhole cover. Outside, night; explosions, shots; lights a few hundred yards off. I had to gamble. I climbed out and lay flat on my belly in the road. Around me, and over in their sheds, were stationary streetcars: I was in a depot, hidden from view. I replaced the manhole cover. Down there they were still fighting, but I wanted to survive and win, and down there now meant the end. The struggle had to go on elsewhere. Death hadn't claimed me; I'd done nothing to avoid it, but I didn't want to meet it halfway.

I looked at the glow above the ghetto, listened to the firing. Goodbye, Father. Goodbye, fallen comrades. Farewell, ghetto.

I climbed over the wall of the depot. Aryan Warsaw was calm. A blackout was in effect, but I knew the city, so the night was my ally. I stayed hidden from patrols, skirted suspicious groups, and hid in a cellar entrance. Then I crossed the Vistula, to the Praga area. From across the street, I scanned Mokotow the Tomb's apartment. All was silent, deserted. I ran up the stairs and gave a tap, just one. The door opened instantly. I stumbled against Mokotow.

"I've been expecting you every night," he said.

I clasped his hands.

"They didn't get me, Mokotow, because I still want to fight, avenge my people. All my people."

"I know. You're stubborn, Mietek."

I clung on to his hands. A live man's a fine thing, a good thing.

II

Revenge

8

Greetings, Comrade

THEY were still fighting. Every day Mokotow went roaming, quite near the ghetto; when he returned in the evening, I could sense that he was of two minds. He wanted to tell me about the shots, the grenades bursting, the trucks crammed with soldiers, the smoke. But he was afraid that I might want to go back there, with the hard core of fighters, the men of the ruins, who would have to be killed off one by one, I knew, because they wouldn't surrender. Mokotow was wrong to worry: as I saw it, the front was elsewhere now. I'd helped my comrades erect this monument made from our brothers' bodies and standing in the heart of the ghetto. My father was there. Since his death, I didn't want just to fight, I'd done that, we'd done that. I didn't want just to live. I was alive. I now wanted to win. If we won, the butchers were mortal. I'd seen them run, seen them become corpses drained of blood. I wanted to win: I wouldn't go back to the ghetto, now.

Staying with Mokotow the Tomb, I built up my strength again. I had more money than I needed: it had come from the ghetto.

One evening, Marie whispered, "You should wait in a small town somewhere. The Germans must leave one day. With your money you could . . . you've done your share. You . . ."

She hardly dared speak but she meant to go on. Mokotow glanced at her, pursing his lips as if about to spit.

"Women don't talk," he said. "They keep their traps shut."

Marie burst into tears and buried her face in her hands. I had to tell her about Rivka, Sonia, my mother and the two little girls my comrades had seen crawl out of a pile of corpses near a ghetto wall, holding hands; two little girls covered with blood who'd escaped execution by a miracle. One kept saying, "Mummy's dead. They took Daddy away. I don't want to live anymore, I don't want to live anymore." How could you remain passive after that? How could you wait just to save your own skin? What would your life be worth?

"I know. I know. You're right, Mietek."

She put her arms around my neck.

"I don't want you to die, Mietek. You mustn't!"

"Don't worry, they've missed their chance. They won't get me now."

I was sure, sure I'd come through, as if everything I'd experienced until then had been a long climb full of terrible obstacles; as if I'd reached the summit now. I could picture their defeat; our victory and our revenge.

On May 16, Mokotow took me into the old town to his comrades in the Armia Ludowa. I described our battles, Treblinka again, Zambrow, and the attitudes of certain peasants, of the fighters in the Armia Krajowa.

"We'll create another Poland," said Witold, leader of the group.

"I want to fight with you as a Jew," I said. "A Jew *and* a Pole!"

They agreed, but I had to wait a few more days for false papers. I had money, so I paid to hurry things. As I returned to Praga with Mokotow, an explosion from the ghetto shook the glass in windows around us. It was followed by two lesser blasts. People in the street stopped, exchanged words, carried on with their lives. The next day, we heard that the Germans had dynamited the great Tlomackie synagogue. They even wanted to crush the stones, but they wouldn't succeed: our lives had the resistance of eternity.

A few days later Mokotow brought me two passports: one Polish in the name of Zamojski, and one a *Volksdeutscher* in the name of Krause.

"I'm going to start again."

I had to go to Lublin, to a street in Srodmiescie, the central district, from which I was directed to the partisans who were in control of the forest. At last I was going to fight in the open. Mokotow came with me to the train; there were very few, full of peasants going home and refugees leaving Warsaw for the country. Mokotow stayed till the last moment. We embraced twice; who knew if our paths would cross again?

"Make them pay, Mietek."

"It'll be thanks to you."

He shrugged.

"Marie and I are fond of you."

He laughed.

"You know women. Goodbye, Mietek."

He turned. I jumped onto the footboard and stayed there watching the last houses of Warsaw flash by.

There were detours to avoid demolished bridges and delays to let through convoys of matériel and troops for the East. At checkpoints, I handed my *Volksdeutscher* passport to the Polish police, my Polish passport to the Germans. With the first I looked disdainful; with the latter I adopted the meek, innocent expression of a young man of inferior race. I reached Lublin. It was dawn and the town was covered in a light, bluish mist. I walked through the old town, drank with peasants, waited for night, having found, near the cathedral, the low-roofed house where I was expected. An old Polish couple: the woman gray-haired, thin and straight-backed; the man, stooped but energetic, tight-jawed. Later, by candlelight, we talked.

"You have to be ruthless with the Nazis. The Nazis, not the Germans," said the man.

The old woman had made up a bed for me on a studio couch in a small room.

"Our son slept here," she said. "The Germans took him that first September. Long ago, 1939. Yesterday!"

I embraced her. I wanted to call her Mother, tell her that I hated this madness that left us, everywhere, parted forever. In the morning the old man left me near the suburbs. He nodded to a peasant leaning patiently against his cart.

"Get on."

The country around us was beautiful, green with patches of yellow. The wagon sank into potholes full of muddy water and I got down to shove. The space, trees huddled together like friendly folk, the gentle breeze: everything delighted me. We entered the forest, stopped, and the peasant hooted like an owl. He was answered by another cry.

"Walk straight ahead. They're here."

He turned his wagon and I walked in the cool shade of the forest. I didn't see them coming: suddenly, behind me, a cheerful voice. "Greetings, comrade."

I'd joined the partisans.

There were three of them, peasant types, with coarse jackets and caps, and the heavy faces and bodies of men of the soil. We walked for a day in single file, skirting bogs, roads and villages, plunging into the forest. Sometimes Sacha, the youngest, fair hair sticking out from under his cap, would attach to his shoes the curved irons which hung from his belt. Then he climbed to a height of sixty or seventy feet, vanishing among the branches. A few minutes later he would reappear, his hands covered with resin, and we'd head for a nearby open road, dash across it and enter another forest.

By nightfall we reached the Janow woods. We halted in the darkness. It had been raining, the wind blew off the drops; from nearby came the sound of a stream. One of our men gave a cry; a similar cry rang out very close by, then a lamp shone. We started walking again and soon emerged into a clearing with huts, a huge fire and men singing. I was greeted with friendly slaps on the back and scores of questions about Warsaw and the ghetto. The partisans never stopped questioning me or cursing themselves for not having been there, with their people.

"Brothers, the main thing is to fight."

I had a long talk with Gustav Alef, known as Bolek, a Jew from Lomza, a town in the Zambrow area. Huddled by the fire, squatting on the ground, he looked away and scratched the earth with a branch. He wanted to know everything about the Zambrow camp where his people had been interned. When I tried to offer him a ray of hope, he shook his head.

"I hope they didn't suffer too much," he said.

That's all you could ask for; brief suffering for your people. We stayed by the fire, not speaking, while others clasped each other by the shoulders and sang. They put potatoes in the ashes, raked them out with branches and burned themselves as they juggled them. They tossed me a few; then someone came with an accordion and the songs grew louder. Bolek started singing alongside me. I joined in the chorus. It was the dead of night, chilly, with trees around us like the walls of some fortress. We sang and life erupted in our singing; in my chest my voice rose like cheerful sap. Some peasants brought a huge metal pot, with a black crust on it from having been in the fire, filled with potatoes and chunks of bacon. They made a kind of stew into which we plunged our wooden spoons, sitting in a ring, our faces red from being so near the flames. Then a bottle of *Bimber,* the peasants' rough vodka, was handed around. There were shouts when anyone kept it too long.

"This is a celebration, for Mietek."

Some Russians, escaped prisoners turned partisan, began to dance as we clapped time with our hands. I laughed when one of them, in his enthusiasm, fell over and jumped up again, wilder than ever. I laughed and laughed, clapped my hands and sang, I, Mietek! For centuries I'd forgotten that life was joy too. I'd forgotten the silence of a forest, the rustling of leaves when a bird flies off the sound of the wind. In my head there was only the crackle of fires, bursting grenades, crumbling walls, shouts of the butchers; and the engine of the excavator always inside me. I had to reaccustom myself to men's songs, to men's health, to these trees, kin of those in the forests of Zambrow and the vast Puszcza Bialowieska. But here I wasn't alone or on the run. I had comrades.

"Mietek, we don't make distinctions. All Poles. All partisans. All comrades."

Gregor Korczynski was sitting in his hut, talking slowly the way you soothe a nervous animal. He was the leader of the Taddeus Kosciuszko group, more than four hundred men.

"I want to fight my revenge."

Those were the only two words, the rails, on which my life ran. I was surviving for them.

"You'll fight, Mietek, you'll fight. We all want to fight."

Around the fire, in the forests, I got to know the partisans: Jews, Poles, escaped Russians, Frenchmen, Czechs, a whole people; a Poland of forests and shadows; the Poland and Europe of revenge. The Jews were survivors of the ghettos, eyes glazed with horror; the Russians had seen tens of millions beaten and starved to death; the Poles told of burned villages, hostages, men and women, shot in public squares, in front of a silent crowd. The witnesses had gone up to them and found faces disfigured by torture, mouths full of hardened plaster. Mieczyslaw Moczar, who'd arrived from Warsaw after traveling the country, was speaking quietly: the butchers wanted to destroy a whole people. "They won't succeed," he said. I clenched my fist: we all wanted to fight, we were the Poland of revenge, we dwelt in the forests, the forests of Parczew and Chelm, Borow and Lubartow. There, in the clearings, I met men: Kot, Kruk, Kolka, Slavinski the Typhus, Franek, Ianek the Long. I sang and drank with them. I fought with the men of the Mickiewicz group led by Jan Holod, known as Kirpiczny.

"You fight well, Mietek," Moczar said.

He sent me on reconnaissance and in the evening we drank.

"The two Mieteks fight on vodka," Bolek yelled.

Often Gregor would call us together and start talking. He'd pace in the warm glow of the fire:

"Comrades, the Nazis, the Fascists . . ."

Everything was simple. I listened: the U.S.S.R. was our great ally. Hitler was Fascist capitalism. Socialist Poland would soon emerge and we were her Red Army. I listened. It was as if I were listening to echoes of Julek Feld's words and my father's hopes. I thought I understood the injustices of the ghetto. I was on the side of the poor, the starving, the beggars, the victims. I listened but I hardly had time to think: I wanted to fight; win! I'd do the thinking later.

Gregor, Moczar, and Slavinski the Typhus who talked about the Spanish Civil War and never tired of reminiscing about Marseilles with Maurice the Frenchman, an escaped prisoner; Typhus, for whom Warsaw wasn't Barcelona; Theodor Albert, a Soviet officer, another escapee: all fought well. I trusted them. Like me, they wanted to destroy the butchers. For that, I was with them.

Sometimes we crossed the Bug and headed east, forest after forest. Yesterday it was Poland, tomorrow Germany: today the Ukrainian *Banderowcy,* looters in the pay of the butchers, who spied on us. The countryside and the men changed but the forests remained. I trudged on, often wading through marshes, passing through villages at night; sleeping in the daytime; carrying mail for General Alexis Feodorovitch Feodorov, in command of the Soviet partisans in Bielorussia. The Russians' camp was vast, with uniformed officers making speeches to attentive young partisans. For the first time I saw a plane come down on an improvised landing strip. The Russians were rich partisans whereas we were poor, watching for parachute drops that never came. The fires in the clearing would go out. Dawn would arrive. I still watched an empty sky.

Eventually, one night, we heard a single engine and threw gasoline on nine fires forming the letter M. The plane turned, skimmed the treetops dropping two envoys from Moscow; a Czech and a German woman who were returning to Warsaw; and, arms, *Pepechas,* those automatic rifles with circular magazines which I'd seen on General Feodorovitch Feodorov's partisans.

In the morning, Moczar lined us up in the clearing. The automatic rifles lay in open crates. He stopped in front of each of us, took a *Pepecha* and held it out. He paused in front of me and winked.

"Make good use of it."

Then we left the forests. I went on reconnaissance. I spoke Polish, German; carried my forged papers. I entered villages, spoke to the peasants, reconnoitered German sentry posts, rubbed shoulders with soldiers in the streets, soldiers I'd be shooting at hours later. In one village, a huge fellow smiled and grabbed me by the arm.

"Eggs, eggs."

Laughing, he mimicked a hen. I shook my head: that butcher resembled a man. I went back into the forest: war was savage. That soldier would kill and be killed. It was the law. Moczar listened to my conclusions.

"Mietek, you've a memory of steel," he said.

Some of us went off again. I learned about tree ambushes: we were keeping watch on the road from Wlodawa to Sosnowiets. German trucks kicked up clouds of dust. We let the convoys roll by; but when I spotted a truck alone, I signaled. We dragged a tree trunk across the road. The truck approached, my *Pepecha* jumped, bodies slumped. Sometimes I'd dash out and chase a fugitive. We had to remove all evidence to prevent the Germans from tracking down our bands. I'd sweep the blood from the road with branches; grunting, we'd push the truck into the forest, strip the bodies and throw them into the marshes. Less than an hour after an ambush the road would look peaceful again, winding among the trees as if the earth and the forest had suddenly opened up under the trucks, and immediately closed again.

I volunteered for such operations: I'd think about my people, their faces on the platform at Treblinka or in the brush-factory sector in Swientojerska Street; my father. Every morning, in my hut, the forest still heavy with dew, I'd relive my past.

Moczar tried to stop me from taking part in minor operations. "I'd prefer to keep you as courier."

I wanted my place alongside fighters. Moczar would shrug.

"Go on then, but come back alive. I need you."

"Why should I die, I want to go to Berlin!"

There were many raids. We blew up the Wlodawa-Chelm railway. When the dynamite was in place the rest of them took cover; but I remained behind ignoring their whistles. I wanted to see the rails, the bridge, the train go up; to see my revenge. I learned to fell telegraph poles with a few hatchet blows: the steel sank into the wood and my ax sliced into the wound I'd opened. Go on, Mietek, go on: remember Ivan on the edge of the graves. I ran to another pole and struck it until my arms were exhausted, I carried on beyond tiredness.

I went around the villages, handing out leaflets and newspapers which Bolek had edited, asking the peasants not to deliver milk or grain to the Germans. I blew up dairies so that the Germans couldn't obtain any more butter: let them drown in milk! I set fire to sawmills. I linked up with Janusz and his men; he was a woodcutter's son who led about a hundred men in the forests around Lubartow and Ostrow. The Germans were everywhere, occupying the smallest of villages: I wanted to be among them. At night, with two or three men, I'd creep to a village, attack the German guard post, terrorize the local tax collector and stampede the police. Whole forested areas passed into our hands.

Then I asked to be assigned to the towns, where I saw the enemy marching peacefully in the streets, the *Kommandantur*, with vehicles parked outside. But I'd stopped being Mietek the quarry, Mietek the peasant's man, denounced by the thieving in-former-mayor of Zaremby. I was Mietek the partisan, spying on traitors, devising punishments for them. In broad daylight with a comrade, both wearing German uniforms, I knocked at the door of a man who'd denounced a group of partisans, and we stabbed him to death; then strolled out through the town. I was Mietek the avenger. I scrutinized houses, the countryside, men, memoriz-ing details.

The ghetto and its geography, streets, rooftops, sewers had been my kingdom: now the forest lay open before me. I could sense hostile villages, the presence of Germans, a peasant's attitude. I'd set off by myself after learning by heart a coded message which I didn't understand, then go from forest to forest, from one group leader to another. I too learned how to make bird calls, be recog-nized by sentries: I had become a courier. I repeated my message, slept, and then set off again through familiar trees, dashing across the roads. I slept in barns; when it got cold I dug into the hay, making a hole in it and burying myself in its warmth. Sometimes I'd enter peasants' houses to sit on one of the benches around the tall earthenware stove and warm myself. But I seldom agreed to sleep on the hearth as some did. I trusted my caution first: I wanted to live and see victory. I accepted being cold.

One day, Moczar and Janusz called me over. Moczar was

wrapped in a rough blanket. Janusz didn't know what discomfort was, he was a man of the forests.

"You know about Treblinka, Mietek. Explain."

I talked all night, I could have talked for centuries.

"South of Lublin," said Moczar, "there's Majdanek."

It was another Treblinka, with its "factory" and graves.

"It's just possible, Mietek, that we could attack it."

I dreamed of punishing the butchers and of the attack, of the prisoners coming towards me, fear banished from their faces. I dreamed.

A few days later we found Janusz's mutilated body, his ears cut off. Janusz, victim of the N.S.Z., *Nesezowcy,* militiamen who fought against us "bandits" for another Poland and handed over Jews to the Germans, for ten pounds of sugar a head. They were ruthless, fanatical; to them, we were "Reds," "Russians." Only they could save "Catholic and eternal Poland."

We dug Janusz's grave in the black soil, all of us standing around our comrade. Then we remained in front of the displaced earth, listening to Moczar and Gregor, who'd known him.

"We need someone to infiltrate the N.S.Z.," said Moczar.

I was a comrade of Janusz, who'd wanted to attack Majdanek. I was a brother of Jews hounded in villages by the men of the N.S.Z. I liked fighting clutching an automatic rifle, and the strength others gave me when they reassured me with a wave or a whistle, and Bolek humming beside me as we waited for a German truck. I preferred not to be alone. But I wasn't in the forest to do the work I preferred. I handed in my *Pepecha,* left my comrades and took to the roads, my Polish passport in my pocket; dispatched to the enemy.

Once again I began asking the peasants for work. In one of the villages which the N.S.Z. held, around which they mounted constant guard to protect themselves from our attacks. I saw them, grenades with wooden handles stuck in their belts, fur caps pulled down. They had watched me arrive. There were two of them, I gave them a wave and they let me through. I was alone, unarmed, no risk. I went straight to the church and explained to the priest how I'd escaped from a labor camp in Germany, why I wanted to live in the country. The priest listened to me in silence, then gave me the name of a peasant, and I began anew the endless days that I'd spent before the uprising in the ghetto in Zaremby. I forked hay, cleaned out the stable, and in the evenings talked, saying I wanted to fight.

The peasant, arms folded, shook his head. Then one evening he said, "Maybe Major Zemba can use you. Go, say I sent you."

Major Zemba held court in a peasant's house on the edge of the village, an automatic rifle and grenades on the table, a silver crucifix hanging on the wall. He looked me up and down. I recognized those pale eyes, that shallow smile, that sarcastic voice: Zemba was a beast, with a man's face. He questioned me, flipped through my passport with his ringed peasant's fingers, then poured me a drink: my head stayed clear.

"If you want to fight, come tomorrow," he said.

In the morning, twenty of us set off for a village that had been found guilty of helping the partisans. I stayed at the side of the road with a few others, keeping watch; I heard women's screams, explosions. I saw the peasants run into the forest, saw some brought down by an exploding grenade. Then we returned to base, and that evening I joined in the drinking. I drank myself sick and threw up. I remembered my forest marches with Bolek whistling our Jewish songs; yet here I was, among these bandits, laughing with them. My torment lasted weeks. One night I slipped out of the village to the forest: a comrade was awaiting me. I passed on the names of the N.S.Z., I identified the villages loyal to them, the peasants who were helping them. Later, on two or three occasions, I managed to send word about one of their operations, and when we got near the village which Zemba wanted to attack and loot, the partisans were there, forcing us to run away. I swore with the others, drank with the others, played my role. Yet I gradually sensed their suspicion mounting. Zemba called me in and began an interrogation meant to be friendly, bland, intimate; asked me to talk about my parents, why I was here, in this village. His pale eyes never left me. His ringed hands fondled a dagger. I was reminded of Pawiak, of the Gestapo in Szucha Alley; I wasn't going to be afraid.

"You know," he said. "I always keep the spies to myself. Eyes, ears, snip! We've crucified some of them. There's no lack of trees. It's easy to make a cross."

I laughed and drank with him. I kept a grenade in my boot.

A few days later, after a successful operation, we began drinking as usual in the house on the outskirts of the village. Zemba was clutching a bottle of vodka.

"There are spies," he was saying, "the bandits of the Armia Ludowa have spies everywhere. Snip, and off with their ears!"

All of them laughed at Zemba's gesture. I felt he was looking at me. I wanted to live, win, not die there in that Polish hut, from the knives of those drunken bandits. Win. Live. I owed it to my people. I got up as if to ask for a drink, made a dash for the door and, turning, threw the grenade into the room and ran for the forest.

They looked for me all night, searching the outskirts of the village, probing the forest. I climbed a tree and clung to its trunk as if it might imbue me with strength. The N.S.Z. fired blindly, threw a few grenades, but they were frightened of the forest, our world. I waited until my arms ached. At dawn, I ran through the forest, slept in a ditch and eventually joined Moczar, Gregor and the rest. That was the end of Mietek, counterspy. That evening, around the fire, I sat near Bolek and dipped my spoon into the large black pot. I was a man among men, without a mask, silent and at peace among their friendly voices. In the morning the first snow fell, followed by more white and frozen dawns. The forest became hostile; damp logs were slow to kindle; fires went out; food was scare.

"Comrades, the Red Army . . . "

Moczar and Gregor announced future triumphs, but our lot was cold, mist and sabotage. Lying on the ice, I counted trucks; with frozen fingers attached explosives to railway lines. I saw trains loaded with tanks blow up. I drank brandy and champagne "requisitioned" from the cellars of a country mansion whose owner was collaborating with the Germans. I walked in snowdrifts deep as the ocean and lived for days with only fiery *Bimber* for rations. I dug graves in frozen earth for dead comrades. I am-

bushed, killed, watched men die. The war was a ritualistic nightmare. Sometimes I slept in peasant huts. Late one morning, I was
caught off guard by dogs barking. German soldiers were there,
smashing doors, looking for a family of Jews some informer must
have denounced for a few bank notes. I was hidden in the hay
when the soldiers were laughing in front of the church, handing
around a bottle of vodka; before them, three children, arms in
the air, and a man and woman on their knees. I was unarmed.
Everything I'd seen since 1939 caught up with me: I shut my
eyes. Later I ran away, wept, and returned to our clearing. For a
day, Bolek at my side, I lay prostrate. Those children, my mother
kneeling, my father mortified, my brothers earmarked for death:
bound for Majdanek or Treblinka.

We laid a trap. Bolek wrote the Germans one of those anonymous letters they no doubt were accustomed to receiving: there
were some Jews hiding; Bolek mentioned the village. We kept
watch for days, the snow covering us. I lived on snow and vodka,
refusing to be relieved.

They came at last. SS men; arrogant. They advanced to the
middle of the village, rifles slung. Nadia, a young Russian girl
from the group, was with us. She and I got up and went towards
the SS men. When they saw us, we ran for the forest.

They fired, yelled, *"Halt, Juden, halt!"*

Ahead of us were the trees, and Bolek, Gregor, Kot and Kruk.
We didn't leave a German alive. Only their black bodies red-
dened the snow. I stared at each of them in turn: I prized their
stiffening fingers from their weapons. Bolek came up to me.

"We've avenged them, Mietek."

I shook my head. We'd never be avenged. The deaths of butchers didn't restore life, revenge was always bitter.

"Even if we kill them all, Bolek, my brothers won't come back
to life again."

I sat in the snow. How many dead lay in the graves at Treblinka? What madness! So I had to kill, too, to stop them slaughtering any more of us. Kill those beasts with men's faces.

"We're killing too, Bolek. We're killing."

"But then what? The choice is up to you, Mietek."

I knew. We left them half-naked on the edge of the forest.

By the end of winter, the front was drawing closer. I crawled through the mud towards roads carrying trucks full of wounded Germans back from Russia. The convoys were heading for Lublin.

"They're pulling out, Mietek."

Bolek was jubilant. We made lightning attacks, then disappeared into the forest. One day, early in the morning, a plane flew over our camp in the Ramblow woods, skimming the trees. Several of us climbed to the tops of pines and when the plane returned we fired. It plunged into the forest, exploding in a column of black smoke and leaping flames. I gave a yell of triumph but then our lookouts arrived.

"They're here in force."

Moczar called us together. There were several hundred of us in the forest. I saw Soviet partisans around Captain Czepiga.

I dug a foxhole behind a tree; others hid among the branches. We waited in silence; then I saw them, dodging from tree to tree. They were SS men of the Viking Division. Live, Mietek, so you've got to kill, that's the law. I took aim and fired, along with the rest. No quarter, no pity. Kill to live. The bark exploded, the trees screamed as they were ripped apart, men were yelling. Kill to live. Moczar gave the word:

"On your feet, comrades!"

I left my foxhole, yelled, and charged through the trees. I yelled in order to kill. All those from Treblinka and the ghetto, Zambrow and Bialystok, were yelling along with me. Come on, Father, on your feet, sing out! On your feet, Rivka, on your feet, you too, Pavel, and you, my red-haired friend, and you, Sonia! On your feet! It's them or us. Beasts or men. Kill to live.

We drove them out of the forest but they were still in the fields and on the road, and when night fell, their flares lit up the darkness. I looked for Bolek: he was alive, Moczar and Gregor, too.

"We must move," said Moczar, "before tomorrow."

I helped bury the dead under a thin layer of earth.

We carried our wounded into another forest, slipping through Viking patrols.

Every day now brought news. They were on the run, no longer

even trying to attack us, concerned only with staying away from the forests. Our strength grew. We became an army. I was now entitled to a uniform, and one day General Rola, arriving from Warsaw, called us together in the clearing. He took a step forward, his cap pulled down over his fleshy face, huddled in a white greatcoat.

"Partisans, comrades, victory . . ."

I stopped listening. It was the end of an era. The escaped Russians would rejoin their army, the Poles would return to their towns and villages where their families were waiting for them. Where was my town, where were my people? A grandmother in New York? I couldn't even remember what she looked like. All else was desert. The butchers had left me like a solitary tree in a felled, burned, ravaged forest. I couldn't just stand there, I had to do something.

General Rola passed through our ranks, dishing out promotions. Moczar took two steps forward: lieutenant colonel. Bolek and some others stepped out of the ranks, and so did I: lieutenant. The general clasped me to him, and that evening, Mieczyslaw Moczar and I clinked glasses.

"The two Mieteks, the two lieutenants," said Bolek.

"Cheer up, Mietek," said Moczar.

How could you be cheerful remembering all your massacred people. Bolek gripped me by the shoulder and gave me a shake.

"Don't forget, Mietek, our victory is being here, still being here."

I shook off my depression by drinking vodka. Bolek was right. One tree was enough to reforest a mountain. I drank. I sang with the rest. We embraced Moczar who was leaving for Warsaw and the Kielce area. There were partisans there too.

A few days later, we saw long columns of Russian soldiers; rolled blankets across their chests, dragging behind them machine guns mounted on wheels, like those of General Feodorov's partisans. So we dashed out of the forest, waving our arms: the Russian partisans ran even faster. "*Tovarishch,*" they shouted. On the road, the soldiers had halted, some replying, "*Na Berlin! Na Berlin!*" To Berlin!

I ran to the road, too. *Victory* was the face of that soldier, younger than myself, who looked at me in astonishment as I cavorted around him. Gregor called us together and we advanced with the Soviet troops. On July 21 I entered Chelm; Lublin on the twenty-second. It was summer, blue, green and yellow; the Germans weren't resisting, they were pulling out. In Lublin I went back to the house where I'd been given shelter; the old lady wept and the old man clasped me in his arms.

"We must make them pay, we must hang Hitler," he said.

"*Na Berlin,*" the soldiers shouted in the streets, and the Poles took it up: "*Na Berlin!*" I, too, started shouting, "*Na Berlin!*"

They'd entered our ghetto, *they'd* left our bodies and streets in ruins, *they'd* burned us, ravaged us, reduced us to ashes. But I'd survived them and I wanted to shout in Berlin, in the name of all my people, that I was still alive, I, the fugitive from the ghetto, I, the witness of Treblinka. Alive and victorious!

I drank with the soldiers. "*Na Berlin, na Berlin!*" In Bernardynska Street, at the headquarters of the Polish Committee for National Liberation, I idly roamed the corridors; what was I going to do? I rejoined Gregor and the partisans. They were discussing governments, publishing newspapers. Gregor looked up.

"Mietek, I was thinking about you. Do you want to give the Soviet Army a hand?"

I clicked my heels.

"*Na Berlin!*"

9

Here I Am, Father, Here I Am, Brothers

So, you were born in Warsaw? How about your father?"
I was sitting in a small office at the Soviet *Kommandantura*
in Lublin. On the floor, files, helmets, bottles, an automatic rifle,
and already hanging on the wall, a portrait of Stalin. It was hot;
the officer who was questioning me had unbuttoned his tunic and
was sweating, cursing the Polish climate. I'd been sitting opposite
him since morning, answering questions which probed into my
life and that of my family.

At regular intervals, the officer kept saying, "You understand,
Tovarishch, serving in the Red Army is an honor."

He removed his glasses and mopped his brow. I nodded: the
Red Army was going to Berlin, I had to join the Red Army.
When the officer asked me my father's profession, I promptly
said, "Mechanic," and added that he was of Russian origin. I
wanted to get to Berlin, and I'd gathered from Gregor and Moczar that it was better to be the son of a proletarian than of a
small-time private manufacturer. I tried to speak Russian with almost no Polish accent, but several months as a partisan with escaped Soviet prisoners hadn't been enough.

At the end of the morning, the officer read me back every page:
the interrogation had produced a sizable dossier.

"Do you agree, *Tovarishch?*" he said after each page.

I nodded: the Red Army was going to Berlin and I signed at
the bottom of each page, amazed at all these precautions. I

wanted to fight, I'd escaped the butchers; were so many questions, so many signatures necessary, for the right to risk your life?

"Come back tomorrow morning, Mischa."

Once again I'd changed my name, I wasn't Martin or Mietek anymore but Mischa: it didn't really matter, I remained myself and only myself, with all that I'd been through, and which no one would ever remove from my mind, with my determination to stick it out. "That's what a man is, Martin," Father, back there in the ghetto, had said it on one of our last nights, I could still hear his voice, see his face. For me he'd always be alive. Sticking it out meant Berlin. How about afterwards? The streets of Lublin were decked out. One day all the streets would be decked out and the age of true peace would have arrived. Even when General Rola had mentioned victory back in that forest clearing, I'd become aware of the desert they'd left around me. Now, because I'd nothing to do but march on, without fear but without any plans for the future, my sole aim to get through to the next morning, I once again began to wonder what it would be like afterwards, afterwards, when the others, those who weren't alone, had put their arms around their wives and children again. What would they leave me? What would I have left?

I went to the edge of the river which flowed down to the town. I found a spot between two large stones and dozed in the sun all afternoon, my feet in the water. Maybe, afterwards, I'd have children too. Father had said back there that a man becomes a man when he decides to start a family. I dreamed. I'd reforest the desert with them, my sons. Through them, my people would go on living. Later on I'd tell them about my mother and my brothers, about my father's courage in Swientojerska Street. Later, much later. When they were strong enough to understand and endure.

The following morning, in the *Kommandantura*, I waited in a corridor. Men came and went, ignoring me. Eventually the officer who had interrogated me called my name.

"I've been looking for you for hours," he shouted. "The colonel's expecting you."

In another office, the same confusion. A gray-haired, heavily built officer was striding up and down. He was holding sheets of paper, my interrogation.

"Ah, it's you. You seem to have done quite a lot. How old are you?"

"Nineteen."

He gave a whistle.

"Do you still want to fight?"

I merely nodded. Could he doubt it?

"There are a hundred different ways of fighting, you know. Sit down."

He threw me his pack of cigarettes across the desk, then a box of matches.

"Here," he said, "we're a kind of police force. Do you know the N.K.V.D.?"

All I knew was the butchers, my loathing for them, my desire to fight to avenge my people.

"We need people like you, able to weed out the bandits. You've seen the N.S.Z. at close quarters. You've been to Zambrow and Bialystok. If you want, you can start there. Do your best, find us the N.S.Z., the informers, the denouncers, the collaborators, the people who don't like us."

"I wanted to fight in another way. Get to Berlin."

"You'll go to Berlin afterwards. First we have to mop up our rear. Here. Well?"

The colonel cracked his knuckles.

"Well?" he repeated.

They'd traded my people for ten pounds of sugar; *they'd* tortured Janusz; *they'd* denounced those three Jewish children whom I'd seen, their arms in the air, in a village square one morning. The mayor of Zaremby had aimed his finger at me, pointing me out to the German police. *They* were butchers. I accepted.

I arrived in Zambrow one morning in civilian clothes, a peasant. I recognized the streets, the store in front of which the police had arrested me. The German *Kommandantur* had become the Soviet *Kommandantura*. Different soldiers were patroling the town where nothing had changed: death had merely seized several thousands of my people, and Sonia.

I went from village to village, and mingled with the peasants as they gathered to set up illicit stills for making their *Bimber*. I started them talking. I knew those peasants well, I'd suffered, thanks to them, and survived, thanks to them. I visited barns, sensing if someone was sleeping where I once hid, someone who, like me, might have unnailed the boards at the far end so that he could escape into the forest. I found some N.S.Z. men, and an N.K.V.D. car came and picked them up in the morning. The butchers had calculated one Jew for ten pounds of sugar. I counted my arrests. They were paying.

In one village, a few miles from Zambrow, I noticed a new house, a country lodge for the rich. A woman was living there alone. I offered to work for her. She refused awkwardly, giving unconvincing reasons, making a fuss over me and rousing my suspicions. How did she manage to fill her barn and her sheds, clean out the stable and tend the animals alone? I discussed it with the peasants. They shrugged. I gambled on their envy.

"The house must be well insulated against cold, with two thicknesses of wood."

I spoke like them, slowly and deliberately.

One of them grumbled, "At a hundred marks a Jew, they can afford it."

I returned by night despite the dogs. Someone was in the stable, a man raking the earth. I went closer. His wife was sitting next to him. Suddenly he looked up and saw me in the shadows. He came for me with his pitchfork, pinning me against the wall.

"What the hell are you doing here?"

I didn't move, the steel points on my chest. I stared at those mad bulging eyes, and was filled with terror and rage.

"What the hell are you doing here?"

"Looking for work. I can't stay in town. I need work."

His wife got up.

"He came this afternoon. Leave him alone," she pleaded.

He lowered the pitchfork.

"No work," he said. "Off you go."

I went off slowly to reassure him, but I returned the next day through the forest with three Soviet soldiers. We approached the barn where he was hiding. He was asleep, half drunk. I gave him a shake. He saw the soldiers.

"Bastard! Informer!" he shouted.

"How many Jewish children have you betrayed?"

He mopped his forehead.

"Bastard!" he repeated.

I grabbed him by the shirt: he was enormous, a head taller. I butted him on the chin.

"I'm a Jew, a Jew, do you hear? I was at Zambrow and Treblinka."

I could feel him trembling against me. His wife came up, screaming, "I didn't want to, it was him, for drink, for drink."

When they saw us pass by, on our way to the army truck waiting on the outskirts of the village, the peasants began to talk. There had been five families and a dozen children hidden in the forest. The man had begun by selling them food in order to get all they possessed; then, when they were destitute, he betrayed them and collected the reward. Here, as in Warsaw, there were men who hounded "Bedouins" and "cats": every village had its Ptaszek the Bird and Pila the Saw. We had to purge the countryside; it was their turn to pay. I went from village to village, tracking them down in a pitiless, bitter spirit of revenge. There was no choice, I had to think of the future, of the evil that men could still do: they were like a poison. I had to stick it out.

I went back to Zaremby. The peasants were returning from the fields. The torrid heat had left the air scorched and lifeless, though the sun had already set. In Zaremba's farmyard all was quiet, the cart had been put away. At the church a different priest was kneeling at the altar. I waited in the cool shade until he got up and passed close to me.

"A calamity," he mourned in reply to my questions.

The Germans had come and killed the priest in front of the church. The mayor had been shot one night by the partisans and many peasants had vanished in the forests, Zaremba among them. I went back to Zaremba's farm. The old mother was praying in front of the crucifix in the darkened room. Maybe I'd been the cause of the war coming to Zaremby. I left.

In Zambrow they were waiting for me. Some men appeared before me where the streets began, where the houses were scattered and separated by fields. Three of them were barring my way, arms outstretched, faces invisible, the sunset behind them. I leaped aside and made off through a cornfield, crossing a stream and managing to reach the forest. They were behind me, I ran through the forest looking for a way to double back to the town, crashing into tree trunks. They were calling to each other, swearing. Yet I gradually outstripped them. I wasn't going to let myself be killed now. Idioten at Treblinka, so many others, in Pawiak, in the ghetto, had tried and failed. Not now, bandits! I ran on and reached the scrub at the edge of the forest, then a field. They'd given up the chase but the warning was clear: I was no further use in the Zambrow area. The N.S.Z. had spotted me. I slept in the *Kommandantura,* revolver at hand, and the next day the captain in charge at Zambrow decided to send me back to Lublin.

"You've done your stuff, Mischa: they're after you, that's a compliment."

It must have been late September. I traveled with some truckloads of soldiers. They drove fast, smothering us in warm white dust. The young, fair-haired soldiers were singing: I was the same age as they were, yet I was old, I'd lived through centuries, I was carrying so many vanished dreams. They passed me cigarettes, laughed at my Polish accent, shared their black bread, their mess cans full of fresh cream or gruel, and slapped me heartily on the back.

"Tovarishch, Tovarishch."

It was their password. I tried to get them to talk about their country, that great fatherland of a new world, as Gregor called it. They shrugged. They were interested in vodka, Polish women and peace. They laughed like children, their ruddy faces glowing; they knew nothing. One of the trucks dropped me off on a Sunday at the Capuchin church in Lublin. There was a meeting in the square opposite the church. I mingled with the crowd.

"Comrades . . ."

I saw the stand decked out in red, flags hanging from the trees. "We want to be rid of Germany, that nation of looters and aggressors."

The voice over the loudspeakers was distorted and hard to understand, but the crowd applauded. Then the speaker announced that the courts were going to try the butchers of Majdanek. I shouted with the crowd. All Lublin must have been there on that square listening to Wladyslaw Gomulka. Only a few months earlier, the inhabitants of Aryan Warsaw had looked on as we died, and those in Lublin had gone peacefully about their lives, leaving the butchers unmolested. For every partisan, for every Janusz, for every Julek Feld, for every man like my father, how many were there who had cringed and wilted in front of *them*.

I went back towards the river, well away from the area where the loudspeakers were blaring. So many men in the ghetto, in Warsaw, in Lublin, had submitted to the crimes of the butchers, so many had believed them. Those men were like bits of wood swept by the current, nothing stopping them but the rocks in the river. Father, Julek Feld, Janusz, those who refused, who knew, had made a stand. We were the rocks, we had to stick it out. A life is always an example: without my father, without his strength, I wouldn't have been anything, just a bit of wood floating with the crowd towards death.

At the *Kommandantura,* the gray-haired colonel called me. His office was now in order. Around a large portrait of Stalin, photographs of generals, well-known persons. The colonel had been reading my file. I stood stiffly in front of him.

"Sit down. You've done good work. They wanted to make you pay for it."

"They're the ones who'll pay."

"They're paying, they're paying."

Then he got me to talk, at length. I talked, watching his face, choosing my words carefully, telling the truth, but using my discretion. He listened to me, chain-smoking. Then, after a long silence, he said, "I gather you want to go to Berlin?"

"Na Berlin, Tovarishch Colonel."

"Na Berlin. You'll be hearing the *Katioucha* sing. I'm going to hold onto you."

He had me attached to an N.K.V.D. unit that followed up the front-line troops and moved in, behind the rocket batteries, purg-

ing Russian-occupied territory of suspicious elements. I spoke
Polish, German, a smattering of Russian. I knew the N.S.Z. I was
a Jew with a private score to be settled. To the colonel, I was a
good recruit. That same evening I was given a uniform and a cap
with green N.K.V.D. trimmings. This time I'd earned my ticket
to Berlin.

For weeks I scoured the countryside around Lublin, sometimes
in uniform, sometimes in civilian clothes, collaborating with the
Polish police of which I had officially become a member. Mietek
the Snip, Mietek the boss of hoodlums, Mietek the smuggler, was
a policeman! I was amazed, myself: yesterday still seemed so near,
and yet the face of the world had changed.

Then we drove north to Warsaw. There was nothing left of it.
Arriving in Praga, I slipped away from my comrades and walked
to the Vistula. The snow, whipped up by a violent wind, blocked
the horizon. I looked for Poniatowski Bridge, the other bridges,
my bridges. I found only a few broken arches and temporary
foot-planks thrown across from bank to bank. I went to the left
bank. A column of people was moving along, hunched, laden
with bundles, lashed by the wind. I stopped at the end of a foot-
bridge: before me was nothing but a plain of stones from which
rose traces of towers, fragments of wall, as if the disemboweled
ghetto had caused an infectious sore that had spread unchecked,
poisoning a whole city, leaving nothing. Warsaw! My Warsaw!
Warsaw of the ghetto and Zofia, of Dluga Street and Senatorska
Street, Mila and Leszno had ceased to exist. I returned to Praga;
my Russian comrades laughed.

"You're home, Mischa."

I'd hoped to find Mokotow the Tomb. Nothing had changed
along his street; I recognized, in front of the door, the cart belonging to the tradesman who lived in the yard. But the apartment was occupied by other people. Nothing was known of Mokotow or his sister; they had vanished, like thousands of others, in
the Warsaw uprising.

That same evening I began to search. I walked the streets of
Praga in civilian clothes, recognizing every street: here in this
shop near the market I had put down a parcel and the shop-

keeper had shouted "Swine" when I'd come and collected it after the raid; there was the East Station where Wacek the Peasant used to go and buy goods for me. But I wasn't in Praga to revive memories. I walked on, scrutinizing the passersby, hoping to recognize one of the Blues who'd killed the children caught crossing the wall. A Jewish committee had been set up in Praga, in Targowa Street. There were a few men there, lonely and wretched, looking for their families, hanging on in the hope of finding them, and avenging them too.

They only spoke to each other now and then, exchanging names, dates and places. I arrived one evening in uniform. These men, like me, were alone in the middle of the desert: we had to work together.

"Who wants to come with me and look for them in the Praga prisons?"

Two of them got up. One, who looked quite old, Joseph Rochmann; the other, younger, thin, sorrow written in his face, like me in Red Army uniform: Jurek. We went from prison to prison, I had the cells opened: perhaps a Blue had been picked up by Soviet troops in the early days. It was up to us to expose him. I stared at dozens of men, trying to recall the hours, all the hours, all my crossings of the wall, trying to picture the Blue whom I'd seen take aim at a child, the one who'd refused to "cooperate," all those who'd beaten me, denounced me to the butchers. I'd always wanted to look, in the days of the ghetto, to memorize faces, but all I saw now were lowered eyes, faces that all looked alike. It was Rochmann who found one: as soon as he entered one of the last few cells, he caught me by the arm.

"Mietek, that's Pchla the Flea. He betrayed us."

We faced an elderly, innocent-looking man who gave us an ironic stare. I took over an office in the prison.

"You denounced Jews."

He didn't even answer. I saw a trace of contempt on his face. I repeated the question.

"I did as I was told. I carried out orders. I always did, I always have."

"Answer yes or no."

"I obeyed the law."

Jurek took a step forward, his fists clenched, his jaw tight. The other spat on the ground.

"You can hit me," he said. "You're Jews."

Jurek let fly with his fist, the man's lip split open, spurting blood. I shouted, "Jurek!" then pushed him outside, asking Rochmann to stay with him. I ordered the man to sit down and I sat opposite him. He was holding a handkerchief to his lip, proud of his easy martyrdom.

"Look, I'm not going to hit you, I'm not going to kill you. The Russians can do what they like with you and you can do what you like with yourself. Just listen to me. So you obeyed the law? The law which ordered you to kill children?"

He shook his head: he hadn't killed anyone.

"Listen to me."

I forced him to look at me.

"Listen to me, you're not a martyr, you're a coward. I've the right to kill you a thousand times over. Listen, I'm going to tell you about a camp where you sent the children. Listen carefully."

A few hours later, Jurek, Rochmann and I took him through the streets of Praga to the *Kommandantura.* He was walking with his head down. Maybe my words had sowed a seed of doubt which would gnaw him all his life, slowly; as the memories gnaw us, Jurek, Rochmann, me, the old lady in Lublin, millions of others. Jurek was walking behind him and I was watching him. As we were nearing the *Kommandantura,* Jurek wanted to fling himself at the policeman. I stopped him, gripped his arm, and felt him gradually simmer down.

"Let justice take its course," I said. "We're not beasts."

"But they . . ."

"We're not the same."

We talked on and on into the freezing night, unable to part company. Jurek was, like myself, from the ghetto; he'd known the *Umschlagplatz,* the streets transformed into a furnace, the sewers in which the feeble drowned. And he'd known Majdanek. He was also alone but determined to avenge himself. Like me, he wanted to get to Berlin.

Jurek and I met again a few days later in the same unit. Soon we and Wladek, a partisan from the Lublin forest and a veteran of the ghetto, were inseparable: Wladek, Jurek, Mietek, the ghetto three. In our uniforms with green trimmings we were carrying on the fight.

Shortly afterwards we left for the north, keeping to the Vistula: the trucks drove along slippery roads, passing ambulances and peasant carts returning to Warsaw. Sometimes we pulled in to let tanks and truckloads of *Katioucha* pass. I crossed a Poland strange to me, everywhere finding ruins, death, children roaming in search of their parents. I would go into an official building, meet partisans, refugees, the few surviving Jews: I learned of fresh horrors, of men who had been tortured and hanged. I tried to find the guilty; but I began to understand that revenge can be madness.

Our convoy pulled up in a field at the side of the road. Near us was a group of prisoners: SS men, thin, arrogant, shielding their faces from the blows they were receiving. They were surrounded by tormenting Soviet troops. I looked at the victors and the vanquished. An old bus was stuck, half capsized, in the ditch beside the road. A Russian soldier ran up, shouting something to his comrades that I didn't understand: then, with kicks and rifle butts, the soldiers drove the prisoners towards the bus. I understood the looks the SS men were exchanging, I could imagine their terror. I was seized by fear too, an anguish, in my throat. I could have ordered my driver to leave and avoided looking. But I wanted to see, see how far men can go when war deforms them.

The soldiers forced the SS men to crawl into the bus. Some rebelled. They were shot and their bodies shoved in through the rusty doors. On the road, convoys rolled by, tanks and heavy guns: we were near the German frontier and resistance was stiffening. One of the SS men tried to address the soldiers in Russian, another was screaming. Most of them just stood there in a huddle. But when a soldier poured gasoline over the bus, when the blue-and-yellow flames leaped up, when the prisoners began to shriek and shove against the metal sides, then the soldiers suddenly fell silent as they watched the other men die, I sprang forward and began to wave my arms about, shaking one young gaping Russian after another, feeling that they were about to be contaminated by the war too. The bus was a mass of flames and smoke. The soldiers didn't resist me but then they began shooting into the blaze. By the time we left, the bus had finished burning.

That evening we entered Germany. We passed through devastated villages, old men and dogs wandering through the flames and charred timbers. Our truck pulled up in front of what must have been a town hall. An old woman was sitting on a stone, clasping her head. When we climbed out she stood and raised her hands.

"Hitler kaput."

I was reminded of the old women in the ghetto, their hands raised too, in front of the SS.

"Drop your arms."

But she shook her head, keeping her hands open.

"The men are restless," warned the driver. "They've seen too much. They've been waiting for Germany a long time."

I was waiting for Germany too, but not the Germany which wore a mother's face. I was waiting for the Germany of the butchers; that was what I'd come to seek out and destroy.

We pushed on deep into that terror-stricken country. The master race wasn't proud. Everywhere all of them were shouting, *"Hitler kaput."* What would they have done, what would they have said, if we'd shut them up in a ghetto? They'd have accepted everything, denied everything.

As soon as we arrived in Dramburg, I looked for a printer. Jurek was walking beside me in the rubble-strewn streets.

"What do you want to do, Mietek?"

I entered shops with smashed doors, all looted. In what must have been a small perfume factory, among some broken bottles on the ground, in a tank filled with liquid to floor level, three Soviet soldiers floated face down and motionless. I gave them a shake. They were dead: they had drunk raw alcohol and had drowned in it. I picked up a container, filled it with alcohol and handed it to Jurek.

"For our canteen. We'll make vodka with it."

I wanted to be alone. I looked at those three soldiers, pointlessly dead. In a narrow street I eventually found a printer, hiding at the back of his workroom.

"Can you print posters?"

He shook his head, pointed at the machines.

"I need some posters for tomorrow morning. And you can stick them up yourself. The whole population has to read them. Start writing."

He tried to speak, then took some paper and I dictated. Where did those words come from, which I hadn't given a thought to, which flowed as if I'd been pondering on them since the ghetto? *"All inhabitants of German race of more than sixteen years of age circulating in the town are ordered to wear an armband with a swastika on their right arm. This armband is compulsory."*

The printer looked at me.

"Large white posters, tomorrow. Sign it 'The Soviet Authority.'"

Then I went back. Jurek had mixed alcohol and water to produce a whitish liquid that looked like milk, but burned the throat and stomach like cheap vodka. A few comrades turned up and we drank in defiance of Red Army regulations, which banned alcohol, leaving the bottle on the table instead of hiding it down by our feet. Alcohol was our milk. We drank and drank until we rolled on top of each other. In the morning, a soldier came and woke me.

"Lieutenant, Lieutenant, it's urgent."

My neck was stiff, my legs racked with cramps. I went down into our office. Men of all ages were there, arms raised, pinned to the wall, two Soviet soldiers pointing machine-pistols at them. All were wearing swastika armbands on their right arms. The soldiers were outraged. They'd already beaten them and were talking of shooting them. Luckily, we were quite a distance from the front. I called off the soldiers, freed the civilians, and then Jurek and I made the printer tear down the posters. Jurek laughed.

"You copied the ghetto, and they wore them. Like us, they wore them."

I wandered all day through the town to make sure that the

printer had definitely removed all the posters, to forestall violence by the soldiers against civilians who ventured into the streets. Armbands or not, the soldiers weren't gentle. They were interested in watches, fountain pens and a good many other things. The women made themselves scarce. I didn't meet a single victim of my joke. That evening Jurek and I, not drinking this time, talked about Warsaw and the uprising.

"We've got to be careful, Jurek, now we're the stronger. We've got to be men twice over."

All night I lay awake: I could see the civilians, their faces covered with welts from the soldiers' blows. They had the look of men who didn't understand what was happening to them, victims of their obedience. Mietek, Mietek, be careful! It's easy to become a butcher.

So I tried to be careful. My war wasn't with a people, only with the butchers. I remembered the elderly German soldier who·hadn't wanted to give me away in the streetcar; the officer-interpreter who led me to the Zambrow camp after saving my life, taking my hand in his and muttering, "Run away." I wasn't hounding a whole people, only the butchers.

On our arrival in a town, I got in touch with the burgomaster — I needed informers. Sometimes my men gave me the names of former Communists, sometimes I made the burgomaster point out those who had suffered persecution from the Nazis. In Reppen I was confronted with a gray-haired, toothless woman, just released from prison. Her son had been hanged from the girder of a bridge, sentenced to death by a mobile military court that tried deserters.

"He was seventeen, he didn't know anything."

She showed me over the town, pointing out those she suspected of being Nazis. I questioned them, trying to assess their degree of guilt.

"Then there was the Ukrainian," she said. I recalled Ivan.

"He always wore his armband and gave the Fascist salute, shouting 'Heil Hitler.' A Nazi, a real one."

We looked for him. He had already gotten himself a job at the

Soviet *Kommandantura,* working as a mechanic. I caught him as he was bending over the engine of a car.

"Turn around."

I didn't know him, that would have taken a miracle. There were groups of Soviet soldiers around us. He looked at them, terrified, his face flushed, his hands trembling. The man did not impress me.

"He was a Nazi," I said.

The soldiers began knocking him about. "Traitor!" they shouted. "Vlassov soldier, *Vlasovietz!*"

"I'm a Jew, I'm a Jew, Lieutenant."

"Speak to me in Yiddish."

He couldn't. He'd forgotten, he said. "We must liquidate him at once," the soldiers insisted. I protected him, and went to search his place. The small room was decorated with a huge portrait of Hitler, covering an entire wall.

"Some Jew," I thought.

He was still talking as I took him back to our offices, but I wasn't listening. Our captain questioned him. The man cried and kept saying that he was a Ukrainian Jew, that he'd hidden in Germany, acted the part of a Nazi as a blind. I listened, my doubts growing. Careful, Mietek. The captain shrugged when I asked to see if the Ukrainian was circumcised.

"Look, Mischa, even if he is a Jew, all the good Jews are dead," he said.

Even so, I checked: the man was circumcised. He wiped his eyes with the back of his hand, humiliated, terrified.

"It was hell," he explained. "I had to raise my arm, salute, keep remembering to lie."

I had to persuade the captain to release him. He hesitated.

"There are such things as Nazi Jews, Mischa. You mustn't let yourself be blinded. The Jews are like everyone else."

I listened to him. How could he imagine what it meant to be a Jew under the Nazis? Moreover, to him, as to many Soviet officers, Jews were not quite like everyone else, but a notch below. I knew it: I'd gradually realized it from the jokes they exchanged with winks, jokes in which rapacious Jews judged everything by the yardstick of profit. One evening, a Russian friend and I got angry. A giant, he grabbed a slender captain by his leather jacket and held him across a windowsill, high above a courtyard.

"*Nie Budu, nie Budu,*" yelled the captain. "I won't start again."

The giant, a black-haired Caucasian with a steely grip, and half drunk that night, threatened, "Will you leave the Jews alone? Will you?" The other promised, again.

The Red Army was going to Berlin.

I insisted that the captain release Moniek the Ukrainian and he left with me. When we set off for the west, Moniek became a driver in our unit.

We pushed on towards Berlin, I was near my goal. On the banks of the Oder, which was in full flood, our truck had to stop. Two columns were crossing a temporary bridge made from broad boats. The soldiers returning from the front raised their arms in greeting; I saw arms covered with watches up to the elbows. The two columns were almost stationary, barter was going on between those "going up" and those "coming down." Suddenly, three German planes, the first I'd seen since Warsaw, emerged from the low cloud and began to machine-gun the bridge. They flew over once, their bullets ripping the water, but the trucks on the bridge didn't accelerate and the barter continued. I dashed over to an officer with the trucks, shouting, pointing to the sky and the planes, which were getting louder and louder. The columns barely moved. I flung myself under my truck. I didn't want to die here. My goal was Berlin. The planes flew over twice more. There were shouts and explosions, spurts of water; then silence from the sky. I crawled out: on the riverbank a truck was blazing, soldiers were attending to the wounded; others went on trading watches. I caught one of the soldiers by the arm, yelling, pointing to the wounded on the ground. He pulled away roughly, shrugging, carrying on his discussion. Jurek came up. "Forget it," he said. "Forget it."

We eventually set off again for Berlin. We passed columns of refugees; passed prisoners moving forward in ranks of three, silent, bowed down with tiredness and despair. On we drove, the sound of gunfire getting nearer, tanks more numerous. Here and there large placards had been placed on the side of the road: "Forward, men of Stalingrad, victory is ours." I was not from Stalingrad but from the ghetto, and victory belonged to us too: to us who had survived, to us who had known the graves; it belonged to our dead back in Treblinka and in the sewers. I'm about to reach my goal, Father.

It was my birthday. Friday, April 27, 1945. At the age of nineteen, I entered Berlin.

How long a road it was to these ruins, these stones; but here I am, Father, on my feet, here I am, brothers, on my feet, and you, all my comrades from the ghetto and the forest, you, Zofia, you, Janusz, and you, my red-haired friend beaten to death for a herring, I remember you, all of you, naked men at the sorting lot, old men in the *Lazarett* still pulsing with life, whom I laid out on the yellow sand. Here is Berlin in ruins, here is Berlin also a skeleton, a dead butcher with gaping sockets and bare, scattered bones.

For you, Father, for Julek, for you too, Mokotow, here is Berlin.

On Friday, April 27, 1945, we were flung into the battle too. *Na Berlin!* I marched with Jurek, Wladek and Moniek, leaping from wall to wall. Just as in the ghetto: but this was the ghetto's victory, we were marching *behind* tanks. In the streets with us were soldiers of all units, as if the Red Army had sent representatives of all its members to take part in the final battle. On I went, blazing away. I had to live: I was there, I didn't want to die, I wasn't taking any risks. I waited until the guns had razed the barricades of streetcars and vehicles filled with stones. The streets were clogged with guns and *Katioucha,* wheel to wheel, firing continuously. On the first night, fires lit up the central districts of Berlin. Berlin was burning! Jurek, Moniek, Wladek and I took up positions in the garden of a house. In the middle of the night some soldiers arrived, asking us if there were any women in the house. We didn't look. They smashed in the doors and only emerged next morning, waving to us, laughing together. The battle recommenced. I saw children in uniform, clinging to their *panzersfaust* and getting killed. I saw red flags hanging from the windows in some quarters and white flags everywhere. I saw looting, the lunacy of war, innumerable dead and wounded.

The second night the fires redoubled, lighting up the ruins, the devastated streets. I slept in a cellar with a group of soldiers. One of them stepped outside, a shot rang out and he fell back in.

"The partisans," the soldiers shouted.

We crawled out and tried to dislodge isolated snipers who were firing at us from the ruins. You mustn't die here, Mietek, you mustn't. But there were snipers to silence. Jurek, Moniek and I went to their rear, hugging walls, stumbling over soldiers, our comrades just fallen. I dashed forward and pushed open a cellar door. There were people in there, snipers perhaps: it would have been easy to fire a burst without danger. I shouted.

"Outside!"

There was noise: women came out, arms raised, a thin young man with them, his black hair over his eyes. Maybe he was the sniper? The soldiers with us came out, manhandling the women, shoving the young man against a wall.

"Partisan," a soldier shouted. "He fired."

They were already taking aim. I stood in front of the German.

"We must try him, comrades. We can't kill him just like that."

Other snipers, the "werewolves" of the *Wehrwolf,* harried us. Crouching, we advanced along streets, guided by soldiers. My teeth clenched, I was kicking myself. You mustn't die, Mietek, die here before the end! What lunacy to protect a German! Remember Treblinka! You're taking risks. Leave him, Mietek. Did *they* hesitate?

We arrived at a water tower, its battered dome lit by the fires. Sentries had set up a machine gun in front of the steel door. I gave the door a shove. There were four of our officers behind a table, the air heavy with smoke, candles stuck in bottles on a long table.

"He fired," said one of the soldiers.

"He was arrested in a cellar, the shots came from elsewhere," I said.

The officers looked at me, trying to understand.

"I don't think this fellow was involved, Colonel; the soldiers wanted to execute him there and then, so I thought . . ."

"That'll do, Lieutenant, don't waste our time."

The officers hesitated. They stared at the silent young man, his black hair obscuring part of his face.

"Treat him as a prisoner of war," said the colonel.

The young man was taken away. Back there, in front of a cell in the Zambrow *Kommandantur,* an officer-interpreter, with a few words, had saved me from summary execution. I'd repaid that debt.

The next day I advanced behind tanks towards the center of Berlin. Their shells reduced the walls to clouds of gray dust rising in a low sky, where it thickened the smoke from the fires. I saw Russian soldiers fighting floor to floor eliminating pockets of resistance, others going from cellar to cellar in pursuit of girls, others in search of souvenirs. I rejoined Moniek, Wladek and Jurek and we slept together rolled in our blankets, one of us standing guard.

Our war was almost a partisans' war; I came across Mongols, Cossacks on horseback and soldiers in fur caps. The Red Army, with its tanks, its *Katioucha,* was also that vast heterogeneous troop which had just crossed the whole of Europe and finished up here. Here I was, fugitive from the ghetto, from the forests of Poland, running behind the tanks all the way down the broad Unter den Linden. At the end was the Brandenburg Gate, that proud edifice which I'd seen on posters proclaiming: "Forward, men of Stalingrad, victory is ours." In the middle of the avenue the trees had been razed, and soldiers charged forward, yelling. They sprayed the gaping fronts of houses with automatic rifle fire. Now and then, a louder explosion made the earth shudder: an ammunition depot or bridge must have gone up.

Another night began, with isolated snipers, "werewolves," shooting from the ruins. The tanks reached the Brandenburg Gate. I saw soldiers climb out onto the highest arch and plant the red Soviet flag there. Wall by wall, I advanced on the Reichstag with the others behind the tanks, and in the smoke of the fires and explosions, I saw some men, brandishing a red flag, run towards the shell-scarred building. They disappeared in the ruins, to the stutter of automatic rifles and the bursting of grenades. Then they charged up to the top of the building waving their flag. From down below I shouted with the rest, letting off a burst of automatic rifle fire in the air, I yelled, "Hurrah! Hurrah!" I had come such a long way. Jurek rushed over to me and we did a dance.

Here we are! We breached the wall they built around us: we cut the barbed wire they wound around our tombs: we smashed open the doors of the cattle cars and scattered that thick layer of yellow sand they pushed over us: here we are in their ruined capital: here we are, alive.

Here I am, Father.

10

Revenge Is Bitter

Down streets full of rubble, between the shattered fronts of houses, they filed past: some bareheaded, others still wearing their helmets, most of them a cap or forage cap; they were loaded with equipment, their mess cans clanking against their sides. They were marching silently, soldiers of the defeated Reich. I stood there with Jurek, watching them pass: they didn't look like our butchers, arrogant and invincible, when they'd entered Warsaw on a September morning. These were too old, too young, they already had the downcast eyes of victims. So were there only victorious butchers? Could the vanquished become innocent so quickly? I almost wanted the fight to continue: everything had been so simple. Now, truth was blurred. This was a dead city, women fighting around the corpse of a horse to tear off its flesh, old women, children and the disabled crowding around a pump for water, bowed men picking up bits of wood from the ruins; and soldiers jostling the people, making cyclists get off their bikes and commandeering them, patrols stopping passersby and making them clear the street. I'd seen it all, centuries before, back there. This time I was the victor.

I walked about, exploring the dead city, both to learn my way around and to comprehend the meaning of my revenge. There, in front of the entrance to the Chancellery, their lair, a soldier was sitting, his rifle across his knees, in a large green silk upholstered armchair. My revenge, my victory. Further along, civilians, watched by a soldier, were wandering in the Tiergarten strewn with felled trees and corpses covered with a thin layer of soil. The stench was unbearable. The men flung the dead on carts, the corpses were covered with black camouflage paper. On the pavements were bodies concealed beneath sheets of white paper, like the marked bodies which used to be removed by Pinkert's men. All along the Charlottenburger Chaussee, dead horses were rotting away, partly dismembered by the starving. It had been a September day when they'd bombed Warsaw and I'd seen that dead horse lying in the ruins still harnessed to his *droshka*.

My revenge was bitter. I could sense the fear around me, I recognized those lowered eyes watching me, those lines of men and women waiting for a little water, and who suddenly froze, went silent, because I was passing. I too had lined up for a little water on the banks of the Vistula; I too had seen a uniformed stranger, who was absolute power and the new law, walk up to me. Old women in black, motionless, holding containers, men stooping over ruins, I know you. I know you, dead city, hungry and frightened, I know how to tell the victims from the butchers. They hit us first, and you let it happen, then they pushed you in front, like a shield. Today it's your turn. And we have butchers too.

I tried to pick them out in the *Kommandantura*. Members of the Nazi party had to appear each morning: they came along, well disciplined, and lined up in front of the old employment offices. Some had certificates proving their good faith, they'd helped Jews, prisoners and anti-Nazis. Others kept silent, endured. They went off in groups to clear streets, to disinter corpses and give them proper burial, to clean the sewers. Our revenge was mild. There was no wall or *Umschlagplatz* here, they were working for their own city. Then one morning the order came for me to interrogate members of the *Wehrwolf*. They assembled in a building which was serving as a prison, in the Pankow quarter. I wandered through the corridors, glanced into the rooms where they were waiting: there they were, sitting on the floor, thin young men, some of whom didn't even look fifteen. When I opened the door they looked up, watched me in silence, elbows propped on knees. Some, leaning against a wall, stared at me ironically; most of them just looked exhausted.

"They're partisans," one of the guards told me.

He raised his automatic rifle.

"No need for a sentence."

He sprayed an imaginary group.

I moved into a small room. I had a long list of questions to which they had to reply yes or no. Sometimes it was assumed that they could provide certain details. I read them out. I remembered the officer who'd interrogated me in Lublin: the Red Army was the army of interrogation. But for these men, some of them still children, their lives were at stake. The first one came in, small, dark and sickly looking, absent-mindedly wiping his nose.

"Did you swear absolute loyalty to Hitler of your own free will?"

He looked down.

"Did you swear to fight the enemies of the Führer with every means, even after the capitulation?"

He said yes, again and again: question followed question. I stood up. At night in the battle of Berlin, some "werewolves" had fired at us. I'd seen my comrades fall. But who'd fired? He answered yes, yes.

At the end I shouted, "But did *you* do anything, can you handle a gun?"

His eyes were bright with candor and innocence.

"Nothing, nothing. I stayed in our cellar with my mother."

I added my question and his answer, and then made him sign. They were all like him, picked up off the streets by patrols when the battle was over, suspects, guilty to others. They passed through one by one: they'd all sworn the oath of absolute loyalty to the Führer, they'd all volunteered for the *Wehrwolf,* they'd all joined the resistance, they were all war criminals; and they were all innocent. A colonel looked in. I tried to explain to him but he shrugged.

"Guilty, innocent, they'd have finished us off with a bullet. Did you get your medals in action, Lieutenant?"

He flipped my decorations.

"You know you can't make war with lambs. Or make peace. You have to make them realize they're beaten, Lieutenant, get rid of their urge to start again, forever. We'll train them."

In the evening, when I left the building, groups of women
were waiting some distance from the door: silent women holding
small packages. Had I come all this way just for that? I tried to
forget and returned to Berlin, but the roads were clogged with
refugees coming from the East, Silesia and Pomerania. I recognized peasants from their corduroys, their hats; often the old
women were lying on bales of hay in the carts, the men in harness, heaving, pushing blindly on, the children in their wake.
What turmoil! What madness! The poison that the butchers had
brought into the world kept spreading: interrogations, refugees,
executions, would there never be peace, happiness around me?

It was the beginning of July. Berlin was still under curfew; yet
in the evening, at the end of a scorching day, you began to see
groups of cyclists apparently returning from rides in the countryside. Electricity, too, had been restored in certain areas. Then
suddenly, at a street corner, you'd see the wounded returning,
ragged soldiers who'd lost their arms and legs, being pulled along,
sitting on wooden boxes. I didn't go out much. I drank by candlelight, then by a small electric bulb. One evening, Moniek the
Ukrainian caught me by the arm.

"Come on," he said.

He kept on. We walked through the deserted streets and occasionally ran into marauding soldiers.

"The Americans have arrived," he said. "I've seen them."

What did I care!

"I'm going to see them tonight, Mischa. I'm going there."

We talked as we walked, long after curfew, in the sweltering
night, our footsteps echoing in the street. He hadn't anyone left
in the Ukraine, all his family were lying, with thousands of others, in the graves.

"I know Russia, I know the Russians, Mischa. They don't like
us."

"But who saved me? Who?" They had walked onto the road, on
the edge of the forest, their rolled blankets across their chests,
they had been General Alexis Feodorovitch Feodorov's partisans,
and they had hoisted the red flag over the Reichstag.

"But the war's over, Mischa. I want to live. I don't like uniforms. Russia's full of uniforms."

I walked off abruptly, without a word, leaving him in the middle of the street, hearing only my footsteps, not his. We'd saved him from the butchers and he was leaving us.

I wanted to live too, I didn't like uniforms or interrogations either, I too had discovered that many Russians didn't have much of an opinion of us. Over in New York was the last tree in my forest, my mother's mother, Julek's aunt, my family. But I didn't like owing anything and I had debts to repay to the army and the country that had brought me to Berlin. All the debts had to be squared. A man has to stick it out. But Wladek disappeared too, like Moniek.

A few days later, I left Pankow for Potsdam. The town was already in a state of siege. The Big Three were about to hold their meeting and they were waiting for Churchill and Truman. I kept running into soldiers, filling the huge parks, the mansions and the long, straight avenues. I questioned suspects and arrested former Nazis, like one SS man denounced by his wife and hiding in a cellar, where we found him surrounded by bottles of brandy, swimming in alcohol, a revolver at hand, and all around him dog-eared photos of gallows, with their clusters of bodies, and morgues. He was a butcher, a real one, with a long scar across his cheek and bulging eyes, insolent even after he'd sobered up in his cell. He had debts to pay and it was up to me to collect them. Moniek and Wladek had left that task unfinished. That was another reason why I wanted to stick it out. Then one morning we were posted along an avenue in the park: an officer every ten yards. Stalin was coming. I saw his black limousine, a vague shape, a swiftly vanishing profile. So that's what one of the Big Three was. Standing for hours alongside that avenue, I dreamed of a world where, as in the forests of Poland, among the partisans, or as in the ghetto, in the bunker at 18 Mila Street, leaders were ordinary men like the rest, mingling with their comrades.

After Potsdam, my unit went to Leipzig. On the roads I passed columns of trucks loaded with equipment, machines, prisoners and still more prisoners. A whole people seemed to be on the move, ants, as we'd been, trying to find their way again to some sort of life. The towns were in ruins, the railways out of action. In Leipzig a whole sector had been evacuated for us, in the Golis

district, opposite a huge park. Back there had been the district of
Zoliborz, where I'd cleared snow from in front of the villas occupied by the Germans, for the officer with the pale eyes. The villa
which I occupied in Leipzig was vast, with heavy, carved wooden
furniture. I had two floors to myself, an officer's privilege; but I
was prisoner to that alien decor, prey to my nightmares. I moved
into a small room by the stairs, sleeping on a mattress, amidst a
confusion of bottles on the floor and uniforms thrown on chairs.
I'd cross the hall, run up the stairs, shut myself in, drink and try
to sleep. But my people were always there. In the mornings I
evoked them, in the evenings they came of their own free will. I
could picture Senatorska Street, our house. I was the victor, alone,
dispossessed and vanquished.

One day the owners of the villa turned up. The wife first, a
heavy, overobliging middle-class woman, who wanted to collect
some linen; then her elderly crippled husband, who flaunted his
empty sleeve like a manifesto; a daughter too, bringing up the
parents' rear. They knocked at their door, looked at their house,
reclaimed it with their eyes.

"We really don't know where to go," said the man. "Leipzig's
full of refugees."

"They're afraid to stay in the country," added his wife.

"Some are from Poland. They chased them out," the man went
on, waving his empty sleeve.

They were cornering me: I could have hit back with so many
words, so many facts steeped in blood and horror. I could have
mentioned the plaster forced into the mouths of the Poles executed on the square, the three children, arms raised, who were
crying in the middle of the village, and Warsaw, the whole of
Warsaw reduced to a desert. My house, all the houses, and all my
people. They were forcing me to be brutal, violent, they wanted
to make a butcher of me.

"Move in here," I said, "I'm only using one room. No one else
will come."

I'd given in. I was a dupe. They were jubilant, contemptuous.
"We're home," said their faces. "It's ours by right." Did you have
to choose between being a dupe and a butcher?

I avoided them, came home late at night, left early in the morning and buried myself in my work.

In Leipzig I was after big game. The town was on the road to the south, Austria, the Alps, Italy, freedom. We often found out, too late, that high-up SS officers had just escaped, towards the mountains. The informers turned up after the event, Nazis who wanted to atone for a murky past by a belated, worthless denunciation. They pestered me for petty privileges, wheedled me with their "Tovarishch Lieutenant." They swore on their children, their mothers. They were hungry and scared. They were servile.

But Walter didn't cringe, and from the first morning I trusted him. Tall, thin, with short gray hair, he was a man of few words.

"I'm not asking you anything for myself," he said. "I don't need anything. I'm used to it."

He slowly unwrapped a handkerchief in which he kept a piece of brown cardboard that smelled of earth.

"My first," he said.

It was a Communist Party card, dated 1921. I held that small, innocuous bit of cardboard which represented his honor. I handed it back to him and he wrapped it up again.

"We're onto a trail," he said. "Someone important. Are you interested?"

Through a whole network of contacts he knew that a suspect was hiding in the old town and was trying to get to the south, possibly Czechoslovakia.

"What do you need?"

All he wanted was a few cigarettes, to use to obtain information. At that time, in Germany, you could buy a woman with half a cigarette. I gave him what I had.

"I'll be back."

A few days later, I saw Walter again. He was no longer alone; and his companion, a small man and thin like Walter, also belonged to that race of indestructible men that I'd met in the ghetto, the camps and the forest. Beaten to death, they rose to their feet. I'd seen them beside the graves. I could pick them out.

"It could be Martin Bormann," said Walter. "He's heading for Grimma."

I wasn't too clear about Bormann's importance, but the radio had mentioned him on several occasions.

"He looks suspicious," said Walter's companion.

He smiled.

"It'd be a fine catch, but the people here are scared."

I collected my cigarettes and obtained some from my comrades. I tried to get a *Kommandirovka,* a permit to go to Grimma. No luck. I badgered the captain, the colonel. Both of them laughed. The colonel, who always had a bottle by the foot of his desk, banged the table with his fist.

"Mischa, Mischa, if you've ferreted out Bormann, why not Hitler? Bormann!"

He looked at me and laughed.

Walter returned. The suspect had moved again, this time for Chemnitz. I looked at a map: he wanted to melt away in the mountain villages, reach the forests. Walter explained in great detail how he'd had to spend hours with the peasants, and I knew from Zambrow those endless conversations before tongues wagged. I knew how stubborn and cautious peasants could be. "What are you going to do?" Walter asked me. "It'd take a long time to find him in Chemnitz. You'd want to be able to pay."

Jurek gave me his cigarette ration; they were scarce, precious; they were the only sound currency. Walter found the man in Chemnitz. I went back to the colonel, and asked him to agree to see Walter, a German Communist.

"Did he live here in Germany, under the Nazis?"

Yes, Walter had survived.

"Impossible, Mischa, impossible. You'll make fools of us. Drop the whole thing. If Bormann's around, there'll be others on his trail. Do your work, stick to your own territory."

I persisted.

"Stick to your territory," the colonel shouted.

Out in the corridor, a lieutenant grasped me by the shoulder.

"Forget it, Mischa. What can you do about it? *Malchi,* keep quiet."

Walter followed the suspect to Aue, at the foot of the Erzgebirge. That was where the mountains and forests began. Czechoslovakia and Austria weren't far away. There Walter lost him.

"I think we've missed him," he said. "If it was Bormann, it's a pity. Good day, comrade lieutenant."

I shut myself in my office and drank. They'd deprived me of my revenge through stupidity and indifference. Bormann! The colonel laughed. "Mischa! Bormann? Why not Hitler?" he said. To the feeble everything's impossible. Impossible the plans for the extermination of an entire people, impossible the ghetto, impossible the *Umschlagplatz*, impossible Treblinka, impossible to escape from Treblinka, impossible the deportations to Zambrow camp, impossible to get through the sewers. My life echoed with their choruses: everywhere I'd gone I'd met the flock bleating, "impossible." Yet here I was alive, and they were dead. I'd always believed the impossible possible. I believed Walter. Why shouldn't that suspect really have been Martin Bormann, as Walter thought. Why not? It was an age of the truly incredible. Yet all the colonel and his like, narrow-minded and conceited, could do was parrot and obey.

They sent me to Rosswein, to Doebeln: there the prisons were full of young men from the *Wehrwolf,* innocent as those in Berlin. But we had our orders and we carried them out to the letter. Once again I had to pace up and down the corridors of prisons, endure the stares of youths who didn't understand why they'd been rounded up, thrown there. A colonel arrived from Berlin, one of those fleshy, pink-faced officers who drop in when the fighting's over; there were two young secretaries with him.

"Lieutenant, you're to be my interpreter."

The prisoners filed past him, bewildered, with their childish looks and movements, and the colonel, self-important, his hands resting on the table, smiled.

"Did you swear loyalty to Hitler?" he kept on saying.

With every yes, his face glowed, he rapped the table.

"Good, good. You'll have to pay for all that. Fair enough?"

If the young prisoner refused to answer, he got up and shouted, "I asked you a question, pig! Fair enough?"

He had bulging eyes, too. I couldn't sleep. I lived on vodka. I was in the butchers' camp, again I tried to reject such a conclusion: justice is difficult, Mietek; but I quickly stopped reasoning. For years, my reason had been my instinct. I'd learned how to know without needing to think. I knew that those young men were victims. I knew that, in Doebeln Prison, I was in the camp of other butchers. I drank, I had to escape, but why escape? Every morning I went to see the colonel, clicked my heels in front of him, his secretaries took up their stand behind him and another day began. I was in the grave, as at Treblinka, trapped, I'd have liked to swap skins, become one of those young prisoners, regain the feeling of standing up against injustice, the strength that a struggle gives you. But I was interpreter to the officer with the bulging eyes.

One evening, Jurek, who'd stayed in Leipzig, came and saw me. We talked, walked along the river. It was raining, our greatcoats became heavy.

"Maybe we ought to leave, it's not our army," he said.

I listened. If I left those men in whom I believed, what would I have left? I'd lived for revenge, but they were mutilating it, they weren't letting me have it. They were perverting it. What was there to live for?

"You can't just live for yourself, Jurek, you can't."

There was Palestine, the *kibbutzim,* he said.

"And anyway you've got someone," Jurek finished.

Jurek went off and I walked all night in the rain, striding on into the dark, wet countryside. The cold, the rain, the walk: I became myself again, by testing myself against things, through tiredness.

Gradually, with each step, I was climbing out of the grave, I was refusing to lie in it. Gradually, with each step, I was climbing out of Doebeln. Yes, I had someone, and even if there were butchers in every camp, I'd never be one of them. If none of the systems organized by men and run by the Big Three sweeping by in black limousines suited me, I'd start my own system, my organization, my family, a wife, sons around me, grouped together as in a fortress, bound by blood and love. I'd build my fortress, my castle, for them.

I lay down in the grass, I was soaked with rain, but what did I care about the rain? I'd found my path. In the ghetto, I'd worked out my own system, in Treblinka I'd discovered my own way of leaving the lower camp, and I'd build my own fortress. For them, my family, that wife, those children. I had someone over there in New York, a tree in my forest. I'd build my fortress there. Avenging my people, all my people, meant producing another family, scattering fresh seed on the ground and nurturing it.

I slept in the grass, at peace, in the rain, then later in sunshine. Late that afternoon, I turned up at the barracks. One of the colonel's secretaries was waiting for me, supercilious, hostile.

"He's very angry," she said.

"I'm ill, I'm going to Leipzig hospital."

I lingered in the hospital, going from consultation to consultation. Lying in a huge room among the convalescent wounded who were playing chess, I dreamed away. I let myself be borne away by time, as I'd never done before, I let my imagination run riot; those children, my children, looked like my brothers; that woman was my mother, Rivka, Zofia, Sonia, she was all women. There were trees around us, patches of green. I dreamed on: my father, my mother, all my comrades, they were there with us, amidst the trees.

One morning, the major pronounced me cured. A general from Leipzig asked for a German-speaking officer: a few hours later, I was having a meal with him, his wife and his children, drinking his vodka.

"Another glass, Mischa?" he asked.

He took the bottle from under the table as if he were afraid of an inspection in his own home, like some little second lieutenant in a canteen. What a strange mixture, the Russian people and that army of theirs! The general seemed concerned with only one thing: procuring coats, furs and clothes of all sorts for his friends at home.

"You're a Jew, Mischa. Jews are smart. You're to find me all these things."

It was nothing, just a friendly remark. I explored the old town in Leipzig, discovered some stalls, used my authority as an N.K.V.D. officer and requisitioned things.

"Do you know the color of my cap?"

They knew it. They accepted what I offered. I bought away, I became the man the Russians couldn't do without.

"Mischa is unique," said the general. "Unique."

The senior officers' wives pursued me.

"Mischa, Mischa, we don't have anything."

The inspecting generals, who had left their wives in the U.S.S.R., sent for me and handed me long lists of "presents" to be found the same day. I played along with them. Time passed, I waited, observing my own actions: had I come through the ghetto, Treblinka, the uprising, just to procure fur coats for officers' wives? Me, Mietek, me, who'd thrown sacks of smuggled grain, me, had they reduced me to this? It was lunacy. Had we fought the war just for this? I listened to them, watched them: decorated men who had led others into battle, leaders whom you saluted and who had the power of life and death. How pathetic to see them hankering after a few skins stitched together. To create an image different from theirs, I left off my badges of rank and wore a long leather greatcoat concealing my insignia and my decorations. I was Mietek the indomitable, Mietek the nonconformist.

The political commissar, a young, dark, nervous man, who seemed to have the same opinion of the military officers as I did, often called me aside.

"Mischa, your place is with the Party. You're good material. If you join the Party, you'll have a great future. A military academy."

With a wave of his hand, he opened up new horizons to me. I listened to him. But I didn't believe him; by now I had another dream ripening inside me. But I didn't do anything, I let myself be swept along by time. I'd met a Polish girl who was about to return to Warsaw, and spent some happy hours with her. I was like a runner relaxing before a sprint.

The evening my girl left, Jurek joined me on the platform of the railway station. He seemed excited.

"Mietek, I've caught Schultz."

I gripped him by the shoulder. Schultz from the ghetto, the

boss who spoke from the balcony, promising the workers a safe
life in his camps at Poniatow and Trawniki. Schultz, for whom
we'd been slaves. I ran with Jurek to the prison. I remembered
the ghetto, Leszno Street; and Father's cry, his last cry, in Swientojerska Street. We were from the N.K.V.D. so they let us in, and
a soldier took us to Schultz's cell. He was sitting on a high stool,
Schultz the profiteer, the cajoler, the accomplice. He looked up.
Jurek and I had our faces up against the bars. He stood up.

"What do you want?"

I could see the beads of sweat on his face. We didn't move.

"What do you want with me?"

His voice had gotten shriller.

"To see you again, Schultz. I saw you, back there, near Leszno
Street."

"I want to be tried, you've no right to judge me without a
trial."

A frightened beast, backing against the wall of that icy cell,
sweating.

"This isn't Treblinka, Schultz. I just want to look at you. To
show you we're here."

Jurek spat first.

"I always protected you," Schultz exclaimed. "I always tried
to."

Then I spat.

That night, Jurek and I drank silently in my room until we
passed out, slumped over the table. The days went by, I bought
more fur coats for the generals' wives. I dreamed on. Often, as I
listened to programs in German on the American radio, I tried to
understand the world in which that old lady, from whom I was
descended, lived. She was over there, on the other side of life. A
few more weeks, then Jurek came into my office one morning.

"They've let Schultz go," he said. "Let him go. They're even
planning to use him, make him talk. He keeps saying he wants to
help them."

You had to take things coolly, try and change them, listen and
learn. The general was friendly, even paternal.

"Basically, Mischa, Schultz was just an opportunist, not a war criminal. Maybe he was a criminal for you Jews, but we Russians, you understand, Mischa, have to make distinctions. He can be useful to us here. That's life, Mischa. That's politics."

I didn't argue. What was the point? The general was from a country where deep graves had been dug by the butchers. Kiev, Kharkov, Smolensk, Leningrad, so many towns razed, millions of dead. There was no point in talking to him about Warsaw or Treblinka. None. I recalled the arrogant Schultz, passing through the streets of the ghetto, dispensing life or death by granting or refusing a permit to work in his factories; King Schultz, slave master of the Warsaw ghetto, making gold from the failing strength of starving men and women. Well, my brothers, I'll never succeed in avenging you completely; and even if I did, it wouldn't restore you to life again. That's my failure. Death can't be redeemed. Only another life can efface it. Other lives.

One day Jurek disappeared. "I'm off," he had told me. We had embraced. Good luck, brother. I waited a few more weeks: some investigations to finish off. I had to stick it out. The Soviet army had brought me to Berlin, I'd fought with it, served it. At first it had fed my revenge, but then it had twisted it, made nonsense of it. We were quits.

Thank you, soldiers who appeared on a Polish road one July day shouting, *"Na Berlin!"* Thank you, fighters in the streets of Berlin, so close to victory, shot on the road by the butchers. I was off. Our ways were parting. To each his own life, to each his own way. Your dream wasn't mine.

Thank you, fighters, comrades.

It was months since I'd had a rest. When I was promoted to captain, the political commissar called me in.

"Look at this, Mischa, what do you think?"

He showed me a bulky envelope covered with seals.

"The Poles are very keen to have you with them. They've got problems. The Fascists are resisting. They've held out in the forests, in the mountains. You're Polish, so if you like you can go back there, help your comrades."

He stood up.

"But think about it, you're one of us too. I value you. So it's us or the Poles. Choose."

He granted me a long leave. I drove to Berlin. I wasn't Russian, I was Polish, but what good was a deserted country, or soil on which none of your people were living? My native land, my only native land, meant those I loved, those for whom I'd lived, the people of the ghetto and Treblinka: my people were my native land of blood and suffering. For those I loved, there was only one choice I could make.

I'm going, comrades in arms. The time for revenge is over and a new era is beginning, a new order, all right for you perhaps, but not for me.

I'm going, comrades in arms, our ways are parting. What future would I have with you? Policeman, soldier? That's not what I survived for.

There was only one choice. I'd often discussed ways of leaving with Jurek. Once in Berlin, all I had to do was take the subway from the Russian sector to the Western sector.

When I arrived in the former capital of the Reich, the city was still dark, sinister, with ruined fragments of wall framed against the sky like part of a stage set. I slipped away into a deserted yard, changed into civilian clothes and mingled with the crowd in the subway. I had difficulty pushing my way into one of the cars. I got off at the first station in the American sector.

Outside was a deafening sound of car horns, scurrying Jeeps. The crowd was swarming on the pavements, the shop windows, with their red and yellow lights, glowed brightly. I leaned against a wall. No one was taking any notice of me. I looked at those men, those women, those soldiers. A news vendor was running along shouting. I was surrounded by noise, plunged into a new world where it was up to me to build my fortress.

III

A New World

11

One Day, I'll Build My Fortress

So you were born in Warsaw. How about your father?"
A Soviet officer had asked me the same question in Lublin.
I'd changed worlds and there was an officer questioning me here
too. He was kind, weary, rather bored. In front of me, behind me,
so many faces, the whole of stricken Europe, Jews on their way to
a fatherland, Silesians, Hungarians, Czechs, Sudetens, Poles, survivors of the horror, haunted by fear, exhausted, destitute, with a
single hope: America. That officer was America, already within
sight and earshot. It was America in him that you had to convince. I was watching him, trying to make out what was going on
behind those eyes, inside that round head.

"How did you get to Berlin?"

He spoke Polish, he was barely looking at me, his hands resting
on his typewriter.

"On foot, alone, I walked."

The Red Army, my revenge, that was my business, over and
done with. They didn't need to know, maybe they wouldn't have
understood, they'd be binding me to the past, whereas I wanted
to be reborn, start afresh, to be free, over there.

"I have a grandmother in New York. All my family are dead."

He looked up. The man was a man.

"I want to see her, make a life for myself, raise a family. I'm
alone, there's only her."

He gave little nods of approval, jotting down the information that I gave him, the name Feld, the district in New York which my father had told me about.

"We'll see," he said. "You'll have to wait."

I didn't know how to wait, I'd learned that waiting meant dying. Now that I'd decided to go over there, I wouldn't let myself be stuck in Berlin. I started to badger him.

"I'm alone," I repeated. "She doesn't even know I'm alive. She could die. We'll have to move fast."

I was saying things that I'd never said before, which came to the surface as if they'd been quietly deposited there, deep inside me, day by day.

"I must get there, I can bring her a bit of life. She's only seen me once. I'm the sole survivor."

My voice was breaking, my words derived from a night in the ghetto, the night when my father broke the news of Julek Feld's death to me. The words were his. The officer looked at me, went on shaking his head.

"You're all the same," he said, "you all think . . ."

I almost screamed: yes, I thought I was entitled to push it, to reveal the scars that they'd inflicted on us, that they'd been allowed to inflict on us, I thought I was entitled to be impatient.

"I don't know about the others," I said. "You must appreciate my case."

"I don't have a lot of time," he said.

I was aware of that. In the corridor, sitting on benches, standing, they, the wanderers, the displaced persons, were waiting to be seen.

"It won't take very long."

He lit a cigarette, pushed back his chair. He was stocky, almost fat, his uniform well pressed.

"I'll give you five minutes," he said, "I can't spare you more."

Five minutes, that's what they're offering you, Mother, that's what they're offering you, brothers, Rivka, all of you. Five minutes to recount your deaths and my suffering and my rights. I talked, not looking at him, talked for their sakes, I was their spokesman in this life, and I had to go there, for them as well. He didn't interrupt me, and when I'd finished, there was a long pause.

"You're so young," he said. "Come back tomorrow, ask for me directly."

Now I was sure he'd do his best for me. The man was a *man*. In this new world where I was still hesitating like a blind man at the curb, I resolved to go ahead despite everything. That man gave me a hand.

Thanks to him, I got a place in a D.P. camp and I was able to get out and around the divided city, its ruins tidied up and concealed behind fences or neatly arranged in piles, like toy bricks. Thanks to him, I met up with Jurek and found out that Wladek had made the West, too.

The first night, we wanted to celebrate our reunion. The bar sign was flashing above the ruins, and we plunged into the murk, music, shouts and laughter. Soldiers were drinking, dancing, changing dollars. The butchers' daughters brushed against us with their bare legs. I shunned their eyes, their ardent flesh, and looked at the cheerful barman with the frostbitten ears; he too must have dashed from tree to tree in a Polish or Russian forest, yelling away like the SS men of the Viking Division, which had mounted the attack in the Ramblow woods.

We drank a strong light beer laced with spirits, the *Weisse mit Schuss.*

"This is peace," Jurek kept saying, "peace. We've got to get used to it."

I'd never get used to those wasteful, aimless, pointless lives going on around us, life was precious.

"Don't let's stay here, Jurek."

Jurek went ahead of me; suddenly the barman rushed out, winking and gesturing, in an attempt to detain us. I butted him violently in the chest, he crashed into the coats in the cloakroom, and we ran and disappeared into the ruins. A chill wind was whistling down the empty, gleaming avenues.

"You're on edge, comrade," Jurek said with a laugh.

I burst out laughing too, and we walked on, in friendly silence. I was accountable to the dead, the best of us, Father, Julek and Mordekai. They'd made a success of their lives, crowning it with sacrifice. I had to make a success of life, too; to try and be like them. That night we talked about Israel where Jurek was hesitating to go because he'd discovered an uncle in London. He described the age-old barren, arid, dead soil, and how we'd return to it and instill fresh life into it. I listened to him, saw my people standing in that desert, a desert waiting to be conquered and transformed, my people for whom I'd fought, with whom I'd suffered. Because I'd suffered, I felt a Jew to my very bones. Proud and happy to be a Jew because we were still alive despite the butchers' fury and the world's indifference. One day, I'd go to Israel but I had other commitments, too.

"I've got a plan, Jurek."

"You've always got a plan."

We laughed, slapped each other on the back, and ran through the deserted streets, suddenly cheerful. It was true, ever since the bad times began, I'd always been working out schemes, trying to think one move ahead of the rest, so as to get things going, not to be led by them, but to make use of them. I told Jurek all about my dreams, the plan I had to carry out, my Jerusalem.

"My grandmother, America, work and then more work, and when I've gotten enough, a wife, children, my family, then we'll go somewhere, all of us."

My silent, speechless brothers, shut up in that room, condemned not to be able to go out, who yearned for the sun, my brothers, hidden behind the false cupboard, who clung to me in the evenings when I finally returned to you. My brothers, who knew only walls, cement, cattle cars, death, I'll bring you back to life.

One morning the American officer came in person to find me in the corridor of the hut: he was waving a letter.

"You didn't have to wait long. Things happen here, we're not brutes. Here's your grandmother."

I sat down on a bench. Around me a hotchpotch of languages, Polish, German, Yiddish, Russian, Czech, a child crying, names being called out, typewriters chattering. But I was deaf to them, I had eyes only for those words written by her, my mother's mother, a frail, distant voice, in a shaky handwriting with ill-formed letters, repeating in a hundred different ways, "Come, Martin, come."

Shortly afterwards I left Berlin for Bremerhaven. On the dock, beside the *Marin-Marlyn,* a squat Liberty ship, a crowd of us stood lashed by the spray, weighed down with suitcases tied with string or belts, and bags, a calm, passive crowd, as if it had spent all its energy getting as far as it had. Then when word came to board ship, there was a sudden mad rush for the gangway, violence, the fear of being left on that soil which held prisoner so many cherished bodies. Jurek embraced me.

"You're leaping another wall," he said. "You always have to run."

I gripped him once again by the shoulders. I'd return one day to that soil on which I'd suffered: I was bound to it by blood and death, hope and struggle. I was of that soil, old, ravaged, full of graves; I realized that, even as I was leaving it. I'd never forget the soil where my people lay sleeping.

"See you soon, Jurek."

I stayed on deck but fog swiftly enveloped us. I could hardly see the flat, gray banks as we slipped between them. In front of us lay the greenish, undulating expanse on which we were to languish for days on end. I lived in a corner, sleeping, retching; sometimes, when I went up on deck, I'd be drenched by a heavy sea, so I'd go back down to the stench of sweat and vomit. I was immersed in nightmares: I woke up in a cattle car bound for Treblinka, the pitching was my body held out at arm's length, which they were going to throw into a grave along with the rest, the ocean was a stretch of yellow sand. I scarcely drank, or ate, sinking into despair: why had I left them back there, why was I still alive, on the move, why, as Jurek said, did I always have to run? I threw up; the sea never stopped moving. Inactivity paralyzed me, left me to grapple with the past, clammy with horror and misery, and sucked me down like a whirlpool. The others around me took the line of least resistance. The war had cut our moorings and set us adrift.

Then the seas calmed and at last I was able to stay on deck, breathe fresh air and spray, and study the coastline of the new world, the end of my long journey. Others gradually came up on deck and we all stood shoulder to shoulder, straining towards our future, silent, watching those ramparts of concrete, steel and glass, that powerful, lofty forest, which we were about to enter, draw near. The boat glided across the gray water with its patches of blue. On the wooden dock for which we were heading, I could see some cars, a few figures. Suddenly there was a light bump: the *Marin-Marlyn* had stopped moving. Policemen came aboard and we slowly lined up. I'd arrived, I started looking. Another struggle had begun: I had to remain myself, not be influenced, keep faith. Win again, survive in a different way, keep alive in myself the memory; keep alive the will to build my fortress, to deserve your trust, you who were no more.

I showed my papers, emptied out my small canvas bag in front of a customs officer. I owned nothing. The past had left me with only nightmares, and a few photos in which I appeared as a Red Army officer, fighting the Nazis, which I'd kept to explain later on to my children how I'd avenged my people. We crossed the dock, were subjected to another inspection, then walked along between two metal barriers forming a long corridor. Here and there, leaning over the barriers, men and women scrutinized us. Sometimes there was a hysterical cry, a raised arm, hands linking and staying linked, being clutched across the barriers, or someone would start running. I walked blindly towards the end of the corridor, my mind numb, aware of the questions in those eyes, the agonizing wait; I threw my bag over my shoulder. She can't be there, Mietek, you'll have to take a taxi there, to 567 West 186th Street. I walked on.

Erect, her nervous white hands clutching her purse, she was at the end of the corridor, dressed in black; she was in front of me and I'd been walking towards her ever since I'd dived into the cellar, near Muranowski Square, ever since I'd run through the sewer, tearing myself from the devasted ghetto, from my dead father: I'd been walking towards her ever since I had been alone. She was at the end of the corridor, thin and erect; in her I recognized Mother, Julek Feld, their eyes, that smile. I stopped in front of her and she clasped me, imprisoned me in her arms: she was trembling, weeping. I could feel her bony shoulders beneath my hand, the frailty of her life. We stood there, in the middle of the disembarking crowd, clutching each other. A policeman gave us a push to one side, still linked.

"Please, please," he said.

We stayed there, she murmured my name.

"I knew it," she kept saying. "I knew it, you're so like your mother, in those photos she sent me."

She held my face and stroked my cheeks. I was speechless: one word would have opened a yawning gap, the walls would have collapsed, and I would have cried, sobbed with joy and despair, and I would have huddled against her, calling her Mother, asking her to clasp me still more tightly, to hide me in her arms. For so many years I'd restrained that torrent of fear and sorrow, the need for those soft, maternal hands, Mother, Mother. But I kept silent, stifling my emotions, she was so frail, straining towards me, she would have been drowned in my anguish, shattered by my unhappiness, my memories. It was I who had to protect her, bring her some of my life. She was there, still alive, what more could I ask of her? I pulled her to me, enfolding her in my arms.

"Mama, Mama."

I comforted her, finding that word deep down inside me: "Mama, Mama."

"They killed them," she kept saying. "Your mother, Julek, Fela, all of them . . ."

She was engulfed in her despair, sobbing, leaning on me, and it was as if there were something miraculous about her life; she was so thin, her bones seemed so brittle. Protect her, protect her.

"Mama, Mama, I'm here."

We left, she wanted to carry my canvas bag, her tears interspersed with comments on my size, my strength.

"You're a man, Martin."

Suddenly she said, "You're going to get married, have children. I want to see your children, be a great-grandmother."

She laughed, I clasped her to me, then she burst into sobs.

"I didn't see your brothers, they killed them."

I felt sick; I had to keep going, not talk, help her recover, I was much further gone than she was. In the taxi, she talked to me about Warsaw, the old houses, the cobbled streets, the market stalls.

"Everything's too large here, too new."

I looked, tried to grasp the laws of this world surging around me in long lines of cars, in vertical walls which imprisoned the sky, in an explosion of lights. Everything seemed to be movement, a maelstrom of lives, streets, noise and color. I had to understand so as not to be overwhelmed. Here, too, some would let themselves be led and others would choose their way, blazing a trail towards their goal. As in the ghetto, as in Pawiak and Treblinka, some fell in line submissively while others stole a march on fate and grasped it.

My grandmother opened the door. She went in first, busy, overjoyed, all aflutter. "You're hungry," she kept saying. There before me was a house, with its gentle warmth; I went in slowly, I wanted to explore this kingdom, bit by bit.

"Your room's there," my grandmother called from the kitchen.

I could hear the clanking of saucepans, butter sizzling, I saw a table laid out, a white tablecloth.

"I'm going to wash," I said.

I locked myself in the bathroom, turned on the taps and sobbed, my head in my hands. Then I washed my eyes thoroughly.

For several days I scarcely left the apartment. I ate, slept and talked. My grandmother was at the stove, getting the cholent ready: I watched her sew up one of the ends of the goose's neck, chop up the meat and the garlic, crack the egg neatly and beat it. Her precise, assured movements seemed to date back centuries, filling me with a calm, serene joy. Sitting by her, I felt time cease to exist: nothing had happened, that kitchen was our kitchen, my brothers were coming, Father would give two quick rings. Mother was there ladling small spoonfuls of stuffing, which I'd have sampled, into the neck. That evening, my uncle came. When he had left Poland, my grandmother had followed him intending to return to Warsaw, but time had passed and then the war had come.

After supper they got me talking. My grandmother, clutching her handkerchief, kept asking the same question:

"Did they suffer? Did they suffer?"

I shook my head. I blotted out the screams, the children with shattered heads, from my memory; I described a life that was merely difficult, which she could understand, without realizing the true horror of it. Even so, she kept breaking into sobs and saying, "But why, why?"

I clasped her to me, hugging her by the shoulders.

"I'm here, Mama, I'm here."

She got up and offered me a slice of vermicelli cake, smelling of cinnamon.

"Eat," she said, "you must eat."

Sometimes, without telling me, she made me fritters after we had eaten. I could hear her beating the eggs. I wasn't hungry anymore but why deny her the pleasure of giving? She'd come in with the plate of hot fritters, strips of rich, sweet dough which crunched between my teeth. I'd kiss her.

"I'll teach your wife," she said. "You'll remember your mama later on."

I never tired of seeing her, listening to her, living with her. I'd been persecuted, I'd known hatred, misery. There, in that Washington Heights kitchen, I could at last lay down my sword and shield. In the morning she got up before I did, I listened to her, smiled to myself, eyes closed, allowed myself one more day's respite, and gave her the joy, the great joy, the only joy, which is giving happiness. But it was drawing near the time when I'd have to begin again.

"America's tough," said my uncle. "You'll have to fight."

I wasn't afraid of America, I knew countries where there was killing, where you paid for carelessness or exhaustion with your life, where any slip meant death. I wasn't afraid of this country. I'd figure out my route here, build my fortress.

"I'm ready," I told my uncle.

The peace and quiet lasted for a few days, many of my people had never experienced such luxuries. Then I came to grips with America. We left one morning. I spoke no English; I explored the city, the subway, the scurrying pedestrians, I had so much to learn. But there were no SS men, no Ukrainians, no graves, no wall: America lay open before me. My uncle was manager of one of a chain of stores. He introduced me to the purchasing agent. I listened to them talking: the purchasing agent smiled at my uncle, he smiled at me. I didn't understand a thing. My uncle translated: I'd open packing cases; then later, when I'd learned the language, I could become a buyer, salesman, head of a branch, go even higher perhaps, later on. I listened: later on? That was a dimension of time I didn't know. I saw the young men in white jackets opening parcels with a neat flick of a curved knife.

"I'll stay here one or two days," I told my uncle. "To get the hang of things, make a few dollars."

He shook his head. The purchasing agent had moved away, was giving brisk orders.

"It's a good job for a start," my uncle kept saying. "You'll do fine."

I couldn't explain to him why I had to move fast, not get bogged down in a routine, why I wanted to dodge from one activity to another, to get to know America, try one thing then another until I found the compartment which would provide the key, the means of being independent as I had been in the ghetto, with money in my pockets, dollars, which I'd known back there gave you the freedom to be what you wanted. I'd build my fortress, so that I wouldn't have the curt tones of the purchasing agent ringing in my ears.

I spent two days in the shop, drew a few dollars, learned a few words. In the evening I went home with cakes and flowers. My uncle didn't say anything but shrugged his disapproval. I lifted my grandmother in the air.

"My first few dollars," I said. "Tomorrow I'll double them."

I left early, in the gray, misty dawn, the streets lay open, empty, straight, endless: walking and space were like alcohol to me: I was Mietek the adventurer, at large in a world to be explored and conquered. I'd leave my mark here. I walked for hours, tirelessly, across Central Park, along Broadway. My uncle had given me a few addresses, a letter of recommendation explaining my position. At the end of Varick Street, near West Broadway, I went into a tailor's workroom. I handed my letter to a young girl who started laughing because I didn't understand what she replied.

"Chief, Chief Goldman," I kept saying.

I wanted to see the director, the boss. Goldman finally turned up, a small, bald, waistcoated man who spoke German. He wanted to know all about the war, back in what had been his Europe. He listened, solemn, distressed: of course he'd give me work. I followed him: he kicked open the double doors which opened on some rooms bathed in bluish lighting, men and women bent over sewing machines.

"Have a try," he said, showing me a machine. "You'll soon pick it up."

I shook my head. I wanted air, movement, activity. I knew quite well that you couldn't make your mark behind a sewing machine, like thousands of others, for a few dollars. To carry out my plan, I'd have to take risks as I had in the ghetto, leap walls, find out what was in demand, choose something that others couldn't or wouldn't do.

I took a cleaning job, in the evenings. In the day I walked around the city, getting to know the streets. I investigated the subway, went down into a station at random, headed uptown, explored a district, then ran down the steps of a station, and back downtown again. The city was my freedom, vast and savage as a forest. I observed the passersby, the passengers on the subway, saw the attitudes, the weariness and exhaustion in their eyes. They allowed themselves to be led from the beginning of their lives to the end, they were chained to timetables, to places; but I wouldn't let myself get caught, I'd make my own laws, my own maps, I'd be an urban partisan, turning up where I was least expected. I could only live free, only with those fetters which I myself chose to take on.

Never give in, Mietek.

I worked as a messenger; then I spent some weeks in the kitchens of a restaurant, washing dishes, learning more words, listening, asking questions, getting to know the Negroes. Gradually I became familiar with the city. In the evenings, my uncle used to look at me.

"If you decide to come back, Mietek, there's still a place for you at the store."

I shook my head. He wanted to restrict me. I wanted to explore, understand. I walked whole nights, repeating the words I'd learned, as wary as if the SS men of the Viking Division might suddenly show up. I let the city, America, become part of me, I opened myself to it, so as to feel it better. I worked for a butcher on 110th Street, I learned how to cut meat, and how to press a pedal which falsified the weight when you threw the package on the scales. The butcher paid well — he didn't want to be given away — but I only stayed with him a few days: there the women were, smiling at me, often talking German, Yiddish or Russian. When I pressed the pedal underneath the scales, I knew I was robbing them and I couldn't face their smiles, their trust. So I often gave them the correct weight. One day at closing time I went to see my boss.

"Pay me," I said, "I won't be coming back."

He swore in German, cursing the man who'd recommended me.

"If you say a word . . ." he began.

I grabbed him by the apron and shook him.

"You're a thief, a petty thief, but I'm not a squealer."

Some of his assistants came up, laid into me and shoved me out onto the pavement. I fought back but there were four of them, hitting me with their massive fists used to handling great hunks of red meat. I had to run, wiping the blood from my lips: then I walked in order to cool off. They were cowards. Here, in the heart of New York, they were perpetuating the race of butchers I knew so well: it was everywhere, in Warsaw, Zambrow, Zaremby, it wore the mask of an SS man, the mayor of a Polish village, a Soviet colonel, or a thieving American butcher. You had to avoid dealing with them, whatever the cost, even learn to stop your campaign to survive and build your fortress, rather than be their accomplice. With them, whoever they were, it would always be war. There was a frontier running through the heart of every city, everywhere, through the heart of every people, separating the men from the butchers.

I did scores of jobs, switching from workshops to restaurant kitchens, carrying packages, hoisting crates in warehouses. In the evenings I came home exhausted, slept a little, then went out, walking along Broadway, immersing myself in the bright lights. I had to understand this city, this country. I saw men in dinner jackets and women in shimmering dresses getting out of cars, flash-bulbs going off, chauffeurs bowing and scraping and doffing their caps. I returned to see the long empty streets, the down-and-out-ers, the Negroes, Puerto Ricans, those whom the city was oppress-ing. Here too you had to fight not to succumb, not to be chained to a machine, you had to fight and win, to be able to choose your life, to flee those gloomy workshops, those dusty warehouses. You had to make your way fast, build up a fortune, not so as to have chauffeurs doffing their caps to you, but to have the right to give life and to be able to protect your family.

When I came home one evening, my grandmother showed me a whole batch of handkerchiefs and shirts which she'd bought that afternoon from a peddler.

"And you let him in here!" my uncle protested.

"It was a young man," she said. "He looked like Martin."

He examined the articles, criticizing their quality and compar-ing the prices with those in the shops. In the end my grand-mother started crying.

My uncle shrugged, I caught hold of my grandmother, spun her around and lifted her up, as I often did. I was going to be an urban partisan, free.

"Thank you, Mama, thank you, Mama," I said. "I'll buy these handkerchiefs and shirts from you."

She laughed happily, bewildered, adjusting a hairpin.

I didn't sleep much that night: I felt that my time of discover-ing America was over, the moment had come for action.

I left at the crack of dawn for Seventh Avenue. I went back to the tailor's workroom, but the young girl didn't laugh as she let me in this time: I jabbered away in English, I'd bought an American-style suit, I was wearing a white shirt and a tie with big blue spots. Once again I passed through the rooms with the bluish lighting and pushed open the double doors. Goldman was waiting for me, his thumbs stuck in his vest. I wanted the addresses of some handkerchief manufacturers. I wanted to buy some women's clothes Goldman had on hand. I found I still enjoyed persuading people, getting what I wanted from my audience. In the rooms, bent over the machines, the men and women were still sewing away. They weren't free anymore, perhaps because they had children, because they'd had to stop taking risks. I paid cash for part of the goods and obtained a week's credit for the rest.

"You've got to give people a chance," said Goldman.

He wasn't risking more than a few dollars, but I appreciated his hand on my shoulder, his wink. I came home with two bulging suitcases: my alarmed grandmother watched me unpack piles of brightly colored blouses and printed scarves.

"But what are they, Martin?"

"I'm going to sell them to all the little mamas in New York."

I raced from factory to factory, mentioning Goldman, buying pink and blue handkerchiefs. That evening my bedroom was piled high. Grandmother laughed, carried away by my enthusiasm. She put on the blouse I'd given her and a scarf on her head, and looked at herself in a mirror.

"You've put new life in me, Martin," she said, suddenly catching my hand. "Thank you for coming."

Then she started crying and I was unable to comfort her, overcome myself by a wave of infinite sadness. But I had to clench my teeth, use the past and not let it suffocate me, move on. By morning I'd packed my two suitcases, with the various articles neatly arranged, the prices, a few phrases learned by heart. My uncle had helped me, shaking his head and warning me. I didn't have a license, the police didn't play around.

"The Blues didn't play around either."

He shrugged: who were the Blues?

"Polish police."

"New York isn't Warsaw," he said solemnly.

I knew. Grandmother came up to the door as I was leaving.

"You're bound to succeed, Martin," she said. "You deserve it."

I bit my lip; stupidly, I wanted to cry. I didn't deserve to live any more than had all those of my people who'd succumbed, who'd disappeared in the graves, under the yellow sand. But I had stayed alive and I was fighting. I walked the streets of the Bronx, all the way down Webster Avenue. The big buildings formed massive blocks, dotted with thousands of windows, crammed with thousands of lives, like a city within a city. I looked at those gray façades, with their blackish streaks, I went into squares dominated by still more façades. I couldn't fail to sell the contents of my suitcases. The customers were there behind their doors; they had to open up; all I needed was for them to open up. I started off: the stairs were dark, bottomless wells, the dusty landings opened onto endless mazes. On every floor, there were hundreds of doors along the corridors. Behind each door was a client; each handkerchief sold was a stone for my fortress, a step towards freedom and happiness. I rang, registered the suspicious glances of lonely women, managed to jam in a foot, get talking. Sometimes I was answered in Italian, Polish, Russian, German or Yiddish. Then the doors opened, I displayed my goods. Sometimes I was offered a chair, I talked about Warsaw, old women burst into tears. I climbed thousands of stairs, rang hundreds of bells. In two days I'd sold everything I had bought. I came back covered with dust and sweat, with grimy hands: my grandmother had already run my bath. When she saw the suitcases lying open, empty on the bed, she rushed over to me.

"You've done it, Martin."

I did my accounts. I hadn't made much. Too many refusals: the women in the Bronx were afraid of being attacked. I went back there, spent hours copying down the names of the tenants, then addressed dozens of envelopes on the kitchen table. Grandmother folded the handkerchiefs and the circulars which I'd had printed. I sent a sample, announced when I'd be calling. Sales multiplied: I had my password, "I wrote to you," I had an excuse for going in. "All right, so you don't want to buy from me, but give me back the handkerchief I sent you." The doors opened up, they went to fetch the sample but I'd already have my suitcases open

in the entrance, my prices were low, my wares good quality. I
gave credit.

"I'll be back in two weeks, you can pay me then."

In a few weeks, I'd acquired a clientele, dealers who trusted
me, and enemies. A janitor cornered me in a stairwell and
shouted, "He's here, here!"

A policeman came and took my name, and led me off. I looked
at the man with his shaven neck, his stick at his side, a new kind
of policeman that I was encountering after so many others. The
janitor was waving his arms close by him, I couldn't quite follow
his torrent of words.

"The tenants are complaining," he said as he poured out his
speech of hate.

I recognized him, he belonged to the race of informers, those
who bark with those in authority, like those repentant Nazis who
came over to me in my office in the *Kommandantura* in Leipzig,
in Rosswein, and who'd tried to smile and create an intimacy
which I'd rejected with a single word. New York had its informers too.

The policeman took me to the courtroom, I waited, my suitcases by me. The judge, towering above me on his dais, shook his
head at my approach.

"You've no right to be selling," he began.

"I don't even have the right to live," I broke in, "and yet I'm
alive."

I hadn't stopped to think, the words had slipped out involun-
tarily: did the world have the right to let our throats be slit? The
judge didn't reply but stared at me, caught off guard.

"Explain yourself," he finally said. "What do you mean?"

I didn't speak for long, a few words were enough.

"All right, all right, but don't start peddling again."

I left with my two suitcases. I had to begin again, perfect my
system: I was back in the days of the ghetto, caught up in activity,
the joy of selling, which was to me also the joy of finishing what
I'd started, sticking it out. I already had a few hundred dollars. I
decided to buy a car, my suitcases were heavy. I spent whole evenings saying the highway code over to my grandmother, learning

it by heart, because my knowledge of English was still imperfect. Yet I got my license, answering the examiner very quickly, disconcerting him by asking questions myself and immediately answering them.

"You've got a good memory," he said.

I came from a place where a slip of the tongue meant death. I took the paper he handed me.

One Sunday morning, I pulled up outside 567 West 186th Street: I'd told my grandmother to be ready. She was outside the door, a wide-brimmed hat over her gray hair, her bag clutched under her arm. I opened the door of the blue 1940 Plymouth I'd bought the previous day for four hundred dollars.

"There you are," I said, "there you are, Mama."

She kissed me.

"You're an American now."

I was just a man reaching higher, with a goal to achieve, a man for whom that gentle old lady was his only joy, and his only audience. I was lucky that she existed, that she'd extended her hand and invited me to America, which had welcomed me and left me free to act, to work out my life as I thought fit.

I drove slowly across the Hudson River into New Jersey and along the white sand of the Atlantic. It was a fine day, I was seeing pine forests, meadows and sky again, I could breathe. The trees were tall, proud and noble: I was rediscovering nature. My grandmother didn't say a word, sitting very straight, her bag on her knees. I listened to the songs which were welling up inside me, from the clearings of Poland in the evenings when we gathered around the fire to the lingering notes of an accordion. That was friendship, men like the fingers of one hand; the days of a just and common task to which we all dedicated our lives. Why had my hopes narrowed, why had Gregor's speech remained a daydream? Why did you have to decide to build a fortress for your family alone when there were men all around? But that seemed to be the law.

We reached Atlantic City and had lunch there in a restaurant near the jetty.

"You're crazy, Martin."

What was crazy was not to give everything you could to your people while they were alive, what was crazy was not understanding that death can snatch them away and leave you with nothing. I drove off again towards the country of forests and lakes, choosing roads that followed the riverbanks. That was how we came to Lakewood. I pulled up and we took a walk, finding more forests, a string of lakes, and wooden buildings. The hotels were full. When we entered the foyer of the Post Hotel, the residents were playing cards and chatting, we could hear snatches of Yiddish, Polish and German. I'd found a new clientele.

I worked out my plan all the way back on the return journey as the winter sun shone on the ocean. That week I sold furiously, and on Saturday I set off for Lakewood, my car full of suitcases. Back in the Bronx the weekend was sacred, selling was impossible, husbands slept late at home. I parked my car some distance from the Post Hotel, entered the hotel, observing the layout, the porter, the manager's office and the large room full of yawning guests. It was cold and gray, the weather was on my side. I had a suitcase, and in I went, an anonymous guest directing me to the main room. I opened my suitcase in a corner—so far no one had noticed me—and displayed my scarves, blouses and handkerchiefs; suddenly, I lifted handfuls of scarves and waved them above my head. There was an astonished silence, then sympathetic laughter, as I talked in my shaky English, spiced with Polish and Russian, German and Yiddish; I had to move fast, get the guests on my side before *they* intervened. I could sense *them* around me, on both sides of me. I kept going, clowning, the laughter redoubled.

"Buy, buy, I've come a long way, buy, buy!"

Then the proprietor grabbed me by the arm and tried to drag me away, and the porter shoved me.

"Anti-Semite!" I joked.

The room broke into spontaneous laughter. The two men hesitated, not knowing how to react. Then some of the guests came over to me and I was surrounded by respectable old gentlemen remonstrating with the manager; and my stock was exhausted in about half an hour. But I had plenty more in my car.

Now I knew how to spend my weekends. I would speed to Lakewood, set up shop in the foyers of hotels, play the fool; the guests were on my side and the managers were forced to accept me. At Lakewood I sold not only handkerchiefs and scarves but my own personality, and I raised my prices. During the week I continued to cover the Bronx, always the same two or three blocks, where I now had a routine worked out. I parked my car, I kept an eye open for janitors, and I kept running. One day, one of them, an Italian, came over to my car before I'd even gotten out. He leaned over towards me, wearily shaking his head.

"Hey, move along now, I'm going to have to get you arrested."

He gave me a wink.

"I don't want to, only the others pay and pay well. Leave your stuff, come on, I'll explain."

Near the building was an Italian restaurant. We drank some red wine. The janitor explained.

"You see, the licensed salesmen have spotted you. They're paying me, they're paying the others. One day it'll come to blows. Got it?"

It was he who paid for the bottle of wine.

"It's a matter of principle," he said. "I'm telling you this because I'm for the little man."

I didn't do much selling that day: they'd declared war on me. The janitors, the police, the prices. I wasn't risking my life, as in the ghetto, but the same rules applied. So I dug in my toes. I had to run away, losing a suitcase of goods; some policemen were watching me, I shook them off; one day I found my car with a puncture; the next day, all four wheels were damaged. Before long it would come to blows. They didn't frighten me but I could see my profits diminishing. So what was the point? Hanging on in the Bronx wasn't any good. I gazed at those vast, gloomy apartments, those thousands of cells where lives were being lived: I could have spent years wandering up and down those corridors, I could have built up my business, I could envision a whole mail-order system; but it would have been a long haul. So now it was war. At least America wasn't the ghetto, I could shift my ground, as in Poland with the partisans, when we moved from forest to forest. The main thing was to find something better, to pile up a few hundred dollars more and then gamble everything. I decided to pull out of the Bronx.

Summer was on the way, the heat was beginning to bear down on New York, my thoughts turned to trees and lakes. I set off, driving steadily along the Hudson into the lofty forests dominated by the Catskill Mountains. Between the trees I could see white houses, a horse trotting along by a cottage, fair-haired children running after it. I was only a few hours from the Bronx, the bleak, uncompromising streets, dark corridors plunging between lines of doors into the depths of buildings, staircases winding upwards among the hurly-burly of lives. I drove on: my fortress would be like this place, isolated, surrounded by trees. There, far away from man, my children would become men.

I arrived in Fallsburg: it was the start of the season. The decorators were still busy, on scaffolds hanging from the fronts of the hotels. Goldman had told me about this resort in the Borsch Belt, frequented by Jews from Russia and Central Europe, the borsch eaters who came and occupied the hotels for a few weeks. I knew those bald men with craggy faces, fleshiness gradually ironing out their determined features. They'd made fortunes in the garment industry, like Goldman they worked on Seventh Avenue. They were manufacturers, clothiers, salesmen, tailors, antique dealers. With them I felt rather as if I were back in Poland. I pulled up in front of the Premier Hotel. My thinking was simple: they were on vacation, they had dollars to spend, they had to spend them with me. Their dollars had to pass from their pockets into mine.

I started by working in the kitchens. As I washed dishes, I watched the waiters scurrying around the dining room, snapping up tips. I had to get into the dining room with them. I laid siege to the proprietor, a well-built, gentle man, who'd been born in Warsaw.

"Give me a chance."

Mr. Berg hesitated: I had no experience, my English was poor.

"Wait and see," I said.

He saw. I started off as a busboy, serving desserts and side dishes, clearing the tables. I scurried between the customers, holding out plates, playing the fool, enjoying the laughter that greeted me. Order taken, order served, that was my motto. One week later, I was a proper waiter, with eight tables of my own. I shelled out tips in the kitchen and got my thirty-two dishes first: order taken, order served. The guests came to know me.

"A table with Mendle," they said.

Mendle: that was me. Once again I'd changed my name: Martin, Mietek, Mischa and now Mendle, but I was still myself, unchanged, on the move and with a plan to carry out. Another week and I was head waiter. Most of the waiters were students, who made fun of me, my impatience.

"Mendle, Mendle, you're cut out for America," they said. "You'll make a fortune; you want dollars, you'll get them. Don't get so worked up, you'll bust a gut."

What did the dollars matter? I had a fortress to build, and quickly, because I'd been waiting years and years for peace. I was in a hurry, condemned to be: they had their diplomas, their futures, they had time, they were soldiers in a regular army. They'd been protected, their moves had been worked out: they weren't journeying into the unknown. I was one of life's partisans. Between sittings, they read, played the piano; I thought about dollars. I had to: I'd have liked to take it easy, sit down, walk in the forest in the heat of the day when the guests were playing cards, walk with Margaret, a dark-haired student who smiled at me. But I didn't have time.

I returned to New York, loaded up my car with my remaining handkerchiefs, scarves and blouses, and started selling them in the Premier Hotel foyer. For the three sittings, I became Mendle the waiter again; and in the evening I was bellhop who dashed around with the suitcases. Then I bought the gaming concession: I hired out cards, sold delicacies and various little odds and ends.

"Mendle, Mendle." Berg now swore by me and only me: I brought along actors, handed out newspapers, livened up the evenings. On rainy days, I really came into my own: I added to my showcases. Postcards, ties, fountain pens: I sold, listened, told stories. The dollars were rolling in. But that didn't explain my euphoria: there were men and women around me who knew me

now, with whom I exchanged winks. And the dollars they gave
me, the objects I handed them, represented a kind of complicity,
a kind of friendship, too.

At the end of one season, the students put on a revue for the
guests: I took part in it, playing myself, Mendle, who got hold of
a couple of guests and emptied their pockets by offering them
stuff which they didn't want and which they bought in spite of
themselves. I sang, we linked arms and danced. *"Mendle, Mendle,
Mendle!"* the audience shouted my name and clapped. It was happiness of a kind. I wasn't alone; I was surrounded by friends,
guests, dollars, activity and work; they bombarded me with noise,
words and questions; and it was also a form of oblivion. I stayed
in the dining room until the last couple got up to leave. I was
there at dawn, even before breakfast was ready to be served, escaping from the silence of my room, the nightmares. If I hadn't scurried about enough, held out plates enough, waved my arms about
enough, I couldn't sleep: I'd lie still and try to calm down, but it
was no good, I had to get up, go to the window.

Sometimes, in that state, I'd pace the corridor, knock on a
woman's door and be let in; I drank and smoked too. But the past
came back, surging back in dark waves, Warsaw, Mila and Leszno
streets, my streets, the columns of children making their way to
the *Umschlagplatz,* the yellow sand. My people. At such times my
new life, my plans, all seemed futile. It was as if, by living and enjoying myself, I were insulting my people. So I'd collapse for a
few hours, and the despair those butchers still left in me, in my
mind, killing everything. They were grim nights.

During one of them I felt so lonely, shrouded in death, unable
to remain there in that faceless room, that I took my car and
drove to New York, windows open, breathing in the salty air that
blew up the Hudson valley. When I got to my grandmother's, I
was amazed to find the lights on and my uncle standing there.

"I was going to phone you," he said.

The earth gaped, sand filled my mouth.

"It's nothing, a little warning."

She was sitting in an armchair with a white lace cover, her
hands in her lap; she smiled at me.

"You were so quick, Martin, so quick."

In the middle of the night she'd felt as if she were suffocating and had managed to alert her son.

"It's age," she said. "Emotions."

I took her hands. I had to move fast, give her other pleasures; she'd live with me, with them, in my fortress among the trees. I sat up with her; then when dawn came, I drove quickly away. Life is a race, Mietek, you have to run. I stepped up my activities, games, sales, sittings and shows. I was raking in the dollars. In the evenings I fell on my bed exhausted. In the afternoons I was supposed to be carrying on an affair with a woman; but I often put off seeing her, worn out, only wanting to sleep, obliterating my nightmares with tiredness. Once a week I'd drive back to New York. I'd ring my grandmother from a phone booth on 186th Street, she'd answer promptly, I'd recognize her anxious voice, all the frailty of her life in that first word. I'd imitate one of the doctors who had seen her, a specialist who had come to examine her at my request.

"How are you, Mrs. Feld? This is Professor Waser."

She'd begin to complain a little.

"I think everything's fine, real fine, Mrs. Feld. Don't worry. I'll phone you regularly."

I'd hang up, dash across the street, and leaping up the stairs, open the door: she'd still be by the phone, radiant.

"Professor Waser just phoned me," she'd say. "He's worried about me, I'm not as well as you think."

She lied clumsily, making a play for my affection.

I'd kiss her, hug her, and curse the professor whom I always seemed to miss.

"It's me he wants to talk to," she'd say. "He hasn't forgotten me."

She was proud, happy, as forthright and open as a child. I'd watch her get the meal ready, repeating what Professor Waser had told her.

My lies were a fortress that I was building around her in order to protect her. I listened to her: she gave me confidence. If the jewel like the one in her sparkled in everyone, if everyone were as gentle as she was, then the days of the butchers were numbered.

The months went by at the hotel. I became general manager, Berg gave me a free hand. To honor the rebirth of Israel, I organized a wild party for the first guests of the new season. Never again would we be imprisoned within the walls of a ghetto: a fortress had emerged for a whole people. I shouted, joined in the crowd's applause, became a regular contributor to the United Jewish Appeal Fund; but I didn't leave for Israel. This was another nightmare for me, one over which I had little control, and which haunted me along with the rest. I mentioned it to Goldman: the director of the Seventh Avenue shop had been ill and had come to the hotel for a long stay. In the afternoons, he'd drag me off into the forest.

"I'll make it up to you," he'd laugh.

Sometimes we took a boat, and I rowed, while he talked about his youth and asked me questions. He kept his thumbs stuck in his vest.

"You're somebody, Mendle. You've made your mark quickly. I realized that the first day."

I told him about the ghetto, talked about Israel.

"I feel guilty, I'm letting them fight, but I haven't gone there."

"Live a little," he said, "you're always fighting. Learn how to live. You don't know yet."

I'd never had time. I still didn't.

"You like talking, taking chances. You like challenge. You wanted to survive, you survived. Now you want wealth."

I shook my head: the zlotys and dollars were only paper and metal, a dead thing.

"I want a family, for me, for them."

I was rowing. He lit a cigar.

"I'm not supposed to smoke but what the hell. A family? It's harder than dollars, Mendle. You need a wife."

One day he asked me to drive him to New York. We stopped on Third Avenue. The elevated train rattled along between the dingy buildings. I followed Goldman into a shop where there were huge piles of German porcelain and French china.

"My passion," said Goldman.

He sat down in an armchair, examined the marks on the bottoms of teacups, the borders of plates. I watched him write a check for five hundred dollars. With him, I discovered the gleam of crystal; I saw display cabinets lined with rare treasures. Then his daughter joined us: a thick-set smiling girl.

"This is Mendle," Goldman said.

I took her hand: it didn't feel alive, it lay there inert, like an inanimate object. In the late afternoon we returned to the hotel, alone and in silence.

"You could be a son to me," said Goldman just before we arrived. "I'm going to die."

He was offering me a ready-made fortress and a wife, and yet I knew I wouldn't accept. I had to build my walls, stone by stone, myself; I had to find the woman who would stand at my side, I could only be linked with someone whose hand felt alive in mine, as Zofia's and Rivka's had from the first day, back in Warsaw. I shook my head.

"I didn't really expect it, Mendle. You're the sort who has to find his own way. Like me, a long time ago."

The trees flashed by, behind them the sun seemed to set the sky aflame. Goldman was a man too.

"Five hundred dollars," I said, "for a few cups."

Goldman burst out laughing.

"Mendle! Surely you aren't planning to go into antiques?"

Among the guests in the hotel, I'd noticed a group of antique dealers, who kept themselves to themselves, kept their distance from the cloak-and-suiters. They booked the best rooms, gave generous tips. Some of them wore large rings on their fingers.

"You've got it in you to succeed," Goldman went on.

The first chance, my father used to say. That's the one to seize. Ideas are like luck: you have to grab them as they pass by. That evening, I stayed up talking for hours with two of our guests: Jack and Joe Ellis, Third Avenue antique dealers. To them I was just Mendle, a hotel employee. They were telling me about the goods arriving from Europe, about their customers' enthusiasm.

"They come to blows over a piece," said Jack. "Since the boys went overseas, it's all Europe, Europe. We're from Europe, aren't we, Mendle?"

I listened to them. The Atlantic was the new wall, Europe was Aryan Warsaw, America the ghetto, and in that ghetto were men, their pockets bulging with dollars, who wanted not grain but old china. I listened to Jack and Joe Ellis and saw myself crossing that new wall, buying overseas, selling objects over here more precious than grain. Nothing had changed: and I didn't even have to risk my life. I bought a book on china and learned it by heart: I counted and recounted my dollars: I had several thousand. I kept selling, worked so hard that Berg suggested my coming in with him in his hotel. I had no hesitation in refusing: I was holding a good card, my card, I had to play it.

One evening, at the end of the season, I received a phone call from New York. An unfamiliar voice.

"This is Shirley Goldman, Mr. Goldman's daughter. He's just died. You've got to come."

I'll never get used to death. I'll never accept the injustice of an end to a man's life. I drove to New York, thinking of Father, Goldman, Rivka, Janusz and thousands more: those torn up by the roots too young, still full of sap, with no idea how they might have flowered, how high they'd have grown; those who fell, struck down in their prime, like Janusz, unfulfilled; those who went to their deathbeds old, but with a world of memories and thoughts in their heads, a host of still-living creatures inside them, thanks to them, which would disappear with them, leaving the world in little pieces. Goldman had told me about the Berlin of 1920, as he sat in the boat smoking his cigar. Berlin, his parents, his youth, now were buried with him. Shirley let me in, her eyes red, she said the right things, but her hand still didn't feel alive. She handed me an envelope.

"For you," she said.

I left almost immediately, unable to bear the darkness of the living room in which I'd seen Goldman. I left my car and walked, holding the envelope. I came to the end of Manhattan, at Battery Park. I sat down. It was nearly two years since I'd landed on this now familiar soil. Hour by hour I had come to know it: I'd met informers and men who could have been butchers, if they'd been around, back in Poland. But lots of others too, Berg, Goldman, so many others, in a country which had welcomed me who arrived with nothing.

I tore open the envelope. There was a check in my name and a card in Goldman's shaky handwriting.

"From Joseph Goldman to Mendle, *antique dealer,* with luck."

The words "antique dealer" were underlined.

So long as I lived, Goldman would live on in me.

12

I Was Forging Ahead

I walked along Third Avenue. Step by step from the Bowery to Fifty-seventh Street, step by step from Fifty-seventh Street to the Bowery. The wind swept down the avenue, the long, straight, dirty gray avenue: it raised eddies of dust above the elevated train, it smelled of cheap coffee and grilled meat. I visited Joseph Goldman's antique dealer, a well-dressed old man, whom I remembered busy and friendly, dancing attendance on Goldman: "Of course, Mr. Goldman, of course." He barely looked at me and went on writing, concealed by objects, little white statuettes which he was examining in turn. From time to time he gave a bored, ironical glance through his spectacles.

"Buy? I buy everything and anything. You can't weigh art by the pound. Look . . ."

He showed me a statuette, asked me what I thought it was worth, kept me at a distance in amused contempt, but I wasn't there to listen to him: I had to find out what he sold, get to know the market through him, the Third Avenue customers who paid with five-hundred-dollar checks. I pointed to a cabinet, indicated one or two pieces.

"Would you be interested? Yes or no?"

He stopped writing.

"I've a whole lot in Europe, my father had a store back there. Goldman used to buy a good deal from us. He gave me your name."

He was old, shrewd and condescending, but I had the upper

At Les Barons, with Dina, Suzanne, Richard and Nicole: life and happiness.
"I'd gaze at Dina: she'd never looked more beautiful."

Suzanne and Nicole trying out dance steps to music at Les Barons. In the distance, the sea and the mimosa of Tanneron.

"They were fresh, sheltered, rejoicing in nature and the sun, nourished on vegetables and fruit."

Mingling with society at the Cannes Film Festrival. PHOTOS BY ALFIERI AND D. D. DUNCAN, PARIS-MATCH

News to Print"

The New York Times

..No.40,497 © 1968 The New York Times Company. **NEW YORK, MONDAY, DECEMBER 9, 1968**

MEET
ADERS
N KIEV

l to Have
Scope of
v Ties

'S TEAM

s Degree
rol That
: Soviet

Population explosion !!!! 1968

In France, by Americans

FOURTH EDITION
A male again

December 9 th

RICHARD the IV   Profession: **
                          Philanthropist

Delivery : by father
Labor : by mother
Cord cut : by Nicole Gray daughter
Qualified assistance : by son Charles
Witness : daughter Suzanne

            Weight : sorry no scale
            Height : too busy to measure
            Other details : comme and see
              in Tanneron

** Please no gifts.Send contributions to your
   favorite orphanage.

AS PER OUR PARIS CORRESPONDENT, JACK EISNER

U.S. Planes at Thai Bases Step Up Bombing in Laos

Con Ed and Union Announce Terms of $

Bernard E. Gallagher, left, senior vice president of Consolidated Edison
D. McDonnell, center, chairman of the State Mediation Board, and
business agent of Local 1-2, during yesterday's news conference at the

NEW POLICY URGED IN COMMUNICATION

U.S. Panel Asks Monopoly,
Backed by Government, to
Send Messages Abroad

By JOHN W. FINNEY
Special to The New York Times
WASHINGTON, Dec. 8—A
Presidential committee will
shortly recommend a drastic
reorganization of the nation's
communications industry in-

Union May Agree School Make-Up

By M. A. FARBER
The controversial rules gov-
erning the making up of school
time lost because of the teachers' strikes may be renegotiat-
ed to make them more respon-
sive to the needs of individual
communities.

"It could be done by mutual
agreement of the union and the
city board—it's negotiable,"
said Albert Shanker, president
of the United Federation of
Teachers.

Calif., on Friday, Mr. Laird
talked again with the President-
elect on the way from Palm
Springs to New York on Saturday.
Mr. Laird, whose constitu-

In the *New York Times,* the announcement of Richard's birth on Monday, December 9, 1968.

FATE

The fire, Saturday, October 3, 1970.

PHOTOS BY P. DOMENACH, PA
MATCH, AND D. D. DUNCAN, PARIS-MAT

FOR THOSE I LOVED

Martin Gray today is devoting his life to the Dina Gray Foundation, which is dedicated to the protection of human life. PHOTO BY CHRISTIAN BOUCHET, PROVENCE MAGAZINE

hand: I might know nothing about china but I knew how men were consumed with the lust for gold. He stood up.

"That depends on the pieces," he said.

"You'll see the goods. But tell me what you want."

"Very well. I think we'll get on."

He smiled, wandered about, placed some objects on a table.

"That's what they like. They want to astonish. They pay, you know. Often they're *nouveaux riches*. Oh, and I was forgetting the inkstands, the eighteenth-century inkstands."

I couldn't get away from him now: he kept telling me his phone number, mentioning his affection for Mr. Goldman.

"You'll call me as soon as you get back, won't you?"

I made promises to him and to many more on Third Avenue: word by word, they betrayed their customers' tastes, their secrets. Now I knew what to buy in Europe.

"I'm absolutely counting on you," said the last man I visited, a slim, scented young man in a pink shirt.

They could all trust me. Mietek would be back on Third Avenue again.

But there was the wall of the Atlantic to cross. I went from agency to official bureau: it was an expensive journey, I wasn't an American citizen, no one could guarantee me the right of exit and entry. In Korea, tanks from the north were driving towards the south; and Europe appeared to be Stalin's next victim. My grandmother wept.

"You'll find yourself in the middle of a war, you won't come back."

My uncle kept saying that there was still a place open for me at the store, now that I spoke English.

"You mustn't leave me," said my grandmother. "You've got everything here. I'll die before you get back."

Sometimes you had to keep even those you loved at a distance: like Father in the ghetto, they tried to envelop you in their love, in their desires, in their arms. They didn't understand.

"Mama, you'll wait for me," I said. "You don't want me to be unhappy, do you?"

She wiped her eyes. Why was it that every step you took cost so dear, why were you always tempted to stop fighting the current, to drift along with the rest, to accept the *Umschlagplatz* and the graves, a job as a salesclerk?

"I'm right, Mama, I'm right. I'm always right."

I wanted to convince myself too.

At the passport office, my application was turned down. The clerk shook his head smugly.

"I told you," he said, "you can't leave the United States. Do your military service first."

I walked blindly down the street: once again I was back in a cell; each time I surmounted an obstacle, another would surge up unexpectedly, higher still. You had to keep on fighting, cling onto the slippery wood as at Zambrow, try and reach the top of the wall, fall down again, climb up again, over and over again. I went back into action: I badgered politicians, recruiting offices, passport offices; submitted requests, petitions and protests; called for a meeting of a special commission; vowed that I'd sleep in the doorway, die there if necessary. They hadn't been able to hold me in the Treblinka lower camp from which there was no escape; I'd got through the wall, the barbed wire and the fences in the Zambrow camp; I'd got away from the Gestapo headquarters in Szucha Alley and Pawiak Prison. Were they hoping to keep me here? To send me to Korea to fight in a war that had nothing to do with me? They didn't know Mietek. If America had been attacked on her own soil, I'd have defended her. I knew what I owed her and I'd have sacrificed my life. But those distant battles didn't seem to me to threaten the country's future. I'd already paid for man's inhumanity. I had the right to carry out my own task. For my people.

I was eventually called before a commission. The three retired officers in civilian clothes who were on it seemed calm and understanding. I was sitting opposite them and observed their faces.

"I've got to go," I began.

I said that I had to find my family over there in the D.P. camps in Europe; I described a few episodes of my life in the ghetto.

"I've got to go."

One of the officers thumbed through my file, now and then

glancing up at me. Did he realize that I was gambling with my life? To them it was just a word on a form, to me it was opportunity, and at the end of it my peace, my fortress. I looked at the men as they exchanged whispers. So many times I'd risked everything like this, as if I knew only one way to play the game: all or nothing. One of them, with a gray crew cut, applied the stamp.

"At your risk and peril," he said, handing me the form.

I'd won. It always pays to fight, Mietek. All I had to do was wait for the day of my departure.

I went back to Fallsburg and Lakewood, drove through the forests, taking my grandmother with me on my expeditions.

"You want me to forgive you," she said. "But you're going. I knew you would."

I held her by the shoulders:

"You're going to wait for me, like a good girl. A few trips and I'll take you, you'll see."

"I shall be dead."

I protested loudly to conceal my anguish. I showed her photos of my young women, affairs of a night, sometimes of a few weeks. She made all sorts of comments, fascinated, delighted at suddenly being let in on my secrets.

"Which one are you going to marry?"

"My fortune first."

I drove, walked, unable to stay indoors. I went back to Third Avenue, sold off my last few articles of clothing in the Bronx, met the Italian janitor, all smiles at seeing me.

"They've forgotten you," he said. "Go ahead, go ahead."

He rubbed his hands together, gave me advice.

"You're stubborn," he said.

The stairs, the corridors, the doors, the same children, the same nervous women: nothing had changed. I rang, they hesitated, there they were, motionless, behind their doors, every day, year after year. Why? Why did they put up with it? I offered them my last few scarves, bullied them when they refused, kept on at them. There they were, motionless, was it tiredness, age or contentment? Maybe my gambles, my rule of take all or lose all, was my form of madness, my way of escape, an admission that I was doomed never to rest. They half-opened their doors: I could see the dark rooms, the children clinging to their legs. "Mendle, you don't know how to live," Goldman had said. I could sense the fear and sadness in their lackluster eyes, the resigned slope of their shoulders. What is life? Men herded back to these rooms for their weekend of freedom, then plunged again into their week, their life, then back to the Bronx. They didn't know, they couldn't stick it out any longer, bogged down in their quicksands. Life: life was dashing from tree to tree, sticking it out, taking risks, keeping moving, all or nothing, like an attack in the Ramblow woods.

But it wasn't easy. Often I had to accept being alone. Weariness and sorrow were constantly lying in wait for me. They had never left me; and they attacked me as soon as I set foot on the deck of the liner. The passengers were standing in animated groups all around me, laughing with the officers of the *Île-de-France*. I was already in a bad way, alone, seasick, and the crossing had only just begun. We'd left two or three hours earlier, in the fog, and had hit the heaving seas which I'd loathed on my journey by Liberty ship. Others were already dancing, singing songs, making up fours at bridge; I was alone, I was a man divorced from joy. I'd have traded my future for a woman from the Bronx, for the warmth of one of those depressing apartments, for Shirley Goldman, for a job as a salesclerk. I went up to a woman at the bar and started talking, if only to hear the sound of my own voice. She smiled and then went off with someone else. I was left to contend with loneliness and inactivity once again. I had to cope with the unanswered questions, the lost years, the faces, the nightmares. I drank, vomited and slept, to forget time, to escape.

At last, we entered Cherbourg harbor.

I was one of the first to set foot on the ancient earth, my soil; I walked over the cobbles, worn by the trampling of feet, like the ones in Mila Street, like the ones in the old town, Stare Miasto, back in Warsaw, like the ones in Lublin and Bialystok. I found alleyways, squat houses bulged by time, grubby cafés with cooking smells: I was in Dluga Street, it was my soil, my ancient earth, Europe. I felt despair and joy. Here were my people. Cherbourg,

Paris, Frankfurt: I was back in that countryside, I confused places with memories, the Seine was the Bug, the Rhine the Vistula. I recognized Europe, the peasants at their plows, the stone steeples, the cramped towns, I was plunged back into my past. I didn't sleep, thinking of the children I'd have one day, for whom I was here, preparing their fortress. Maybe I should rear them on the land where my family had been born and now lay dead, where they had suffered and where I had fought. So that on this ancient, glorious, humbled soil, pitted with graves, they would understand better what we had been.

In the morning I reached Frankfurt. Around the station they'd started rebuilding: broad avenues reminded me of distant fields of rubble. I hesitated, a stranger to the town, disconcerted by the German voices, memories of the war. A dark young man with hair falling over his eyes came up to me, he reminded me of the young man in Berlin whom the Russian soldiers had wanted to shoot and whom I'd saved.

"Change dollars?"

I hesitated again, torn between caution and greed.

"Six fifty," he said.

It was a very profitable rate. I looked at him: he flicked back his hair, staring me in the eyes. I pulled out twenty dollars.

"I'll go and fetch the marks."

He took the twenty dollars.

"I'm not a thief. Wait here."

I watched him stroll off and turn the corner of one of the streets opposite the station; and even before I lost sight of him, I realized that I'd been robbed. I waited for a few minutes but I wasn't trying to delude myself: I, Mietek from the ghetto and Treblinka, had been robbed like any tourist, swindled, and in Germany! I'd trusted him, I'd lowered my guard, I'd made a mistake. But I was stubborn. I walked along the Main, barely glancing at the river, in my indignation, my fury with myself and with them. Those twenty dollars were my entire life, my revenge, vanquished Berlin which they'd recovered at a stroke. I went back into the station and onto the platform and waited, long enough to convince them that I'd given up. Towards evening, I came out again among a group of passengers: there he was, standing at one side, sizing up another victim. I came at him from behind, gripping his neck, pulling him against a fence in the dark. I kept squeezing.

"My twenty dollars," I said in German.

He was suffocating, struggling. I eased off a bit.

"Hurry up."

He had nothing on him, the others had kept the money. We walked on, I held onto his wrist, he kept his head down. His sister, his mother, his father, he explained, trying to convince me. Finally we climbed the stairs of a gloomy-looking building: I grabbed his neck again.

"I'll kill you," I said, "if there's any trouble."

But they were just petty thieves: an old man with a shifty smile, half lying on a bed, and a skinny girl. I had the other fellow by the neck, in the crook of my arm.

"My twenty dollars."

They looked at each other, the old man stood up.

"I'll kill him," I said. "Here and now."

I didn't look as if I were joking. The old man searched under the mattress. There was a wad of dollars.

"Give me the whole thing."

I kicked him away, grabbing the notes with my free hand. I counted out four five-dollar bills and threw the rest of them into the room. Then I shoved the young man in their direction, made a dash for the door and ran into the street. I was still Mietek. I was going to win my war. I scoured Frankfurt but the shops were poorly stocked, all the goods came from Berlin. Two days later, I was flying to Tempelhof: always draw water from its source.

I felt at home in Berlin: the streets, the sky, everything had meaning for me. I found Jurek, who was barely getting by, doing odd jobs, thinking of Poland, of Israel, but stuck in Berlin because of family commitments.

"Work with me," I said.

I formed a gang again, just as in the days of Mokotow the Tomb. I visited the antique dealers, remembering the choice items on Third Avenue. There they were in front of me. I discussed prices, tried to understand, strove to find out how an antique dealer's mind works, how you can slow it down, get inside it. I moved cautiously: they were a shrewd, grasping race. I held back, let them make the first move, then I'd come up with a figure, well below their price.

"You're mad, my friend."

Then we'd start again. I was stubborn. I managed to get them to drop some of their demands. They weren't big enough to fight me: they talked about profits, but I was staking my life and years of work on this first trip. As in the ghetto in the old days, I had a wall to cross. And this one was easier. Everywhere I went I left my name and orders for future visits.

"I'll be back."

That was my password. Jurek was there to stand in for me. We stored our purchases at his place, every night we counted and packed. Jurek laughed to himself as he mopped his brow.

"Whether you're after Nazis or inkstands, you're still the same, Mietek, they'll never change you. You're raring to go."

"I'm behind time, I always am."

I was late for my childhood, my happiness; I was chasing after them. I couldn't stop myself.

Customs, forwarding agents, the boat: that first trip was soon over. I hadn't a dollar left when I arrived exhausted in New York. I took the subway home. The city was under snow, the buried cars white lumps. I felt as if I were drunk: I looked at the faces, as I passed the people walking calmly down 186th Street. Which was the real world? Theirs, motionless, or mine, shifting? I rang the bell. There was my grandmother, hugging me, clasping my cheeks in her warm hands.

"But you're frozen, Martin, frozen stiff."

I laughed wearily and happily: I was there, I'd crossed the wall, Father was waiting for me at the door, I was telling him about the bread I'd bought and sold, the cakes from Gogolewski's cake shop, the streetcar.

"I'm back," I said. "You see, Mama, I'm here."

I barely had time even for a bath. I was already pacing the docks, with no money to pay the customs duty on my goods, with no money to transport them. Yet I had to sell fast, so that I could go and buy again, come back, sell, buy. I asked to see the director of a shipping firm with its offices in Battery Park.

"But who are you, sir?" asked the secretary. "Mr. Clark sees people by appointment only."

"I'm not leaving. I'm an importer. Your firm will be losing an important deal, an important deal."

I was shown in to Mr. Clark.

"You'll be taking only a small risk with me," I said, even before I sat down. "Because I'll be giving you security and I'm going to be a good customer. I'm an importer."

I was an importer: the word echoed and reechoed in my head. Importer. You've made it. They didn't kill you and now here you are: an importer. . . .

The director looked me up and down, not quite knowing how to take me. I smiled.

"I'm not importing grain or potatoes but works of art."

I began talking, described my time in the ghetto: after an hour he agreed that in return for the security of my goods he would assume responsibility for customs clearance, transport and warehousing. I'd pay him on sale. It was my job to sell. I returned to Third Avenue and offered one or two objects; but the antique dealers had their claws out. The slim, scented, pink-shirted young man complained about my prices, one after another, thinking he'd get the better of me.

"Of course there are buyers, but it's a difficult time."

I didn't argue: sometimes you have to bypass obstacles. I gathered up my bits and pieces and made a deal with an official appraiser at a large auctioneer's: below a certain offer I'd buy the goods back without paying commission. I had to talk the appraiser into it, I kept at him, arguing.

"I'll be there, I'll raise the bids. You're not risking anything. Look at this china, they'll be fighting over it, I promise you."

He hesitated. They always hesitated, in the ghetto, in Zambrow, in New York, I always had to force men to act. Every time I had to extort decisions. In the end he said wearily, "O.K., we'll try it, just this once."

At the first auction, I sat in the middle of the hall, observing my customers: women in hats with wavy fair hair; antique dealers from the Midwest, the South and California to whom New York was like Berlin. I was the first to stick up my hand to get the bids moving. Then, from time to time, I sang out and raised them. There was a battle. My objects filed past. Three days, three lucky days: the dollars piled up, I made twice, sometimes three times my investment. I paid Clark. That evening, in the kitchen, in front of my grandmother, I made little piles on the table between the dishes: checks, dollars and more checks. She shook her head, delighted, worried, happy and anxious.

"You're not going away again?" she asked.

I left again two days later. I was finished with the boat: I leaped the wall. A dash by plane to Frankfurt, another to Berlin. Jurek was waiting for me at Tempelhof, we embraced.

"It works, Jurek, it works."

I went around to the antique dealers by taxi, Jurek had put some advertisements in the paper: various individuals phoned. I stopped haggling over prices. My principle was buy and sell quick. Small profits multiplied meant big profits. The goods were arriving. To me Berlin was like a distant suburb of New York, the plane was my streetcar. For months I went back and forth from continent to continent. I had discovered a demand for French goods: I stopped off in Paris. On Friday I would be at the Marché aux Puces before it opened, looking for goods for "Americans," bright objects with plenty of gilt. I soon got to know the Paris streets and sky. I bought without haggling: speed was my strength, time was money. On Monday, I would fly to Frankfurt and Berlin. Soon I added London to my round. I bought, made phone calls, raced from taxi to taxi, slept. Sometimes I hung about in a bar, torn between weariness and the need to talk to someone. I'd meet a girl. But I'd leave depressed. In New York, I'd met up with Margaret again, the student who'd worked with me in the Fallsburg hotel. She was gentle, she watched me as I smoked, sitting half naked on the side of the bed.

"Take some time off to live, Mendle," she said. "Don't run all the time."

I tried to lie down beside her. It was daybreak: I had all those goods at the warehouse to check. I preferred work to the peace which she was offering me. Maybe one day a woman would be able to slow me down, maybe one day I'd acquire a taste for repose. With her and only with her, I'd build my fortress. Margaret watched me leave.

"Try and learn to be happy, Mendle, you're always running away."

I kissed her and left, but her words worked their way back into me, troubling my sleep. Goldman's words came back to me. When would the day come when I could lay down my arms? Then work absorbed me again. One afternoon, in one of the auction rooms, when I was putting up my arm to raise a bid, someone tapped me on the shoulder: Jack Ellis, one of the guests at the Fallsburg hotel. Luck. I went back with him to the quiet shop on Third Avenue that he ran with his brother, Joe. I visited their cellars, I could already see my crates there, customers jostling around me. Luck: Jack and Joe Ellis agreed. I was the importer, I sold through their place, and they took a cut on my sales.

So my work gathered impetus: New York, London, Paris, Frankfurt, Berlin, Frankfurt, New York, the streets in those towns, the faces in those towns. The antique dealers who spoke Russian or Polish at the Marché aux Puces, the Germans from Berlin, the interior decorators following each other into the Third Avenue shop, Jurek meeting me in Berlin, taxis, sleep that overwhelmed me every night; and those few minutes every morning as I lay still, my eyes closed, and remembered them, my people, Father, Mother, my brothers, Rivka, whom I never forgot, and all the others. Then the rush, the telephones, the warehouses. Sometimes, to save money, I unloaded the truck myself on Third Avenue: eighty crates to take down, carry into the cellar, eighty crates to stack up to the ceiling, eighty crates to be opened. The customers were there, they came from Los Angeles, Houston and Memphis: interior decorators, antique dealers, wholesalers. They held out their hands: "You promised me." I'd wink, put the object to one side. I was still on the platform of the streetcar, lifting sacks of grain myself, holding them out to the porters. Then I set off again: New York, London, Paris, Frankfurt, Berlin, New York.

I always arrived in Paris on a Friday morning. I dashed around the Marché aux Puces: the Marché Vernaison, the Marché Paul-Bert, the Marché Biron. I'd bought a bicycle which a concierge kept for me, and to get around faster, I rode it — but parked it some distance from the shops, because I was a big antique dealer, an American antique dealer. Sometimes, on Sundays, before leaving for Frankfurt, I'd wander the streets, attracted by a passing woman. I was fond of the city, the river, the bridges. I sat in the sun, closed my eyes, it was May, the weather mild, that bridge was Poniatowski Bridge and I was going to meet Zofia. It was only in Paris I felt like wandering and dreaming. But I hadn't time.

In Berlin, the market was getting tougher.

"There's nothing left, Mietek."

Jurek greeted me with these words and with each trip it became truer. All the antique dealers in America had descended on Berlin, stripping the city and Germany of its china. Jurek showed me a set of dishes with a faded gold pattern.

"That's all," he said. "There's nothing left. Only what the others don't want."

"Buy away, Jurek, buy everything."

So the chipped inkstands and faded saucers piled up.

"You're mad, Mietek," Jurek kept saying.

I dragged him along; after a two-day search, we found an old craftsman willing to touch up our china; and there was no lack of buyers on Third Avenue. But once again Jurek threw his arms in the air.

"There's really nothing left."

It was true. I spent nearly two weeks in Germany. Jurek kept saying, "Let's pull out, Mietek. We've done it."

I hadn't reached my goal, not yet. I didn't want to give up. Ever. I looked around and in the end I found the K.P.M., the Royal China Works, a gold mine.

Jurek laughed.

"You're mad, Mietek, mad. The K.P.M.'s an official firm for kings and presidents."

I was as good as its founder, the King of Saxony; all of my people were as good as those German emperors, kings and princes for whom the K.P.M. had worked exclusively since the beginning of the eighteenth century.

"The K.P.M. will work for me, me, Mietek, a mere Jew from the ghetto."

It was a long haul. I saw the director, negotiated, paid, gave bribes. At last one day the huge cylindrical ovens of the K.P.M. began to heat up for *my* china, for me, the fugitive from Treblinka. That was a revenge too. And a master stroke.

The "antiques" which the K.P.M. turned out were genuine! So the dollars piled up and every thousand dollars meant another wall for my growing fortress.

But my motto was speed and the K.P.M. worked as slowly as it had in the eighteenth century. Once again, after a few months, I couldn't meet the demand: I needed other solutions.

I knew that there were factories in Bavaria and, on one of my trips, I hired a car and drove south. Woods, valleys, sky: countryside like that around Rosswein or Doebeln. But I was driving in another world: a few miles east, I'd left my comrades, the soldiers who'd turned up on a road in Poland shouting, *"Na Berlin!"* What had become of those friendly soldiers? I'd tried to live as I felt right, to be fair to men, to repay what I owed, to claim my due. All I wanted was to be on the side of men, and men were everywhere, both sides of the frontier. Like the butchers.

I stopped in Moschendorf and then in Hof. I saw the nearby mountains, the huge trees, the meadows. Here I was at the source: I visited a works in Moschendorf, saw the white-smocked workers bent over the china, checking the ovens. Here was the source. I asked to see the director. He received me in an office which looked out across the countryside.

"You have a noble tradition," I said.

He smiled and nodded his head. I was reminded of Schultz, in the ghetto, who made us work like slaves, Schultz walking through the workshops, complacent, prosperous; Schultz captured and then set free. Now they were going to work for me.

"Surely you can manage that?"

I had models, photographs, I put them on his desk. He resisted step by step. I cut him short.

"I'll pay. I'll buy everything."

In the end we struck a bargain all right; and I won in Hof, too. I wasn't just an importer and manufacturer of genuine antiques, but a copier as well! I drove slowly to Frankfurt, relieved: I'd set the machinery going, it was turning over. The first step was always the hardest, when the streetcar moves off, when you have to hang on and when you don't know how the Blue on the platform is going to react, when you've never crossed the wall before. Afterwards, everything's simple: you're risking your life but it's routine. I'd rounded the cape, cleared the breakers, now the current was bearing me along.

I stopped in Nuremberg: so this was the place where *they* had put it together, this was where the evil that had done violence to millions had erupted for the first time! I drove through the streets trying to understand, to envision what those days must have been like, when men here had let themselves be swept away. The town was noble, beautiful, in spite of the devastation. I crossed the bridges over the Pequitz, looked at the dark stone churches, walked through the old streets, the Hauptmark. Here, too, were worn cobbles, like those in Cherbourg or in Mila Street. I saw men the same as any others, and children: years before, evil had possessed them, they'd massed in the stadium in the searchlights, shouting. Such evil must never be allowed to rise again.

I took the plane to Frankfurt and returned to New York, to my grandmother, to Jack and Joe Ellis: the orders were pouring in. It wasn't long before the merchandise manufactured in Moschendorf and Hof turned up. As soon as the goods landed they were sold. I was amassing dollars, I invested, bought stock.

One evening, when I returned home very late after seeing Margaret, I found my grandmother in my room. She was lying on my bed asleep, a shawl around her shoulders, her white hair lying loose around her face. When she breathed, her chest barely stirred. I stood there looking at her, so thin and frail; she woke up at once. I put out my hand to help her up.

"I was waiting for you."

"You're crazy, Mama."

"You must hurry, Martin."

I didn't understand.

"If you want me to see your children. You're rich now."

"Mama, Mama."

I was aghast: it was true, her body looked like those of the old men I'd held in my arms back at Treblinka, in the *Lazarett*.

"Any day now, Martin, any day now. It could happen tomorrow. I'm old."

I clasped her to me and stroked her hair: "Mama, Mama." But she shook her head.

"Any day now, so hurry."

I couldn't sleep: I was now rich, an American citizen, an importer, a manufacturer, I was opening a branch in Canada and another in Havana. I owned buildings, bought stocks and bonds. I went from capital to capital, Paris and Berlin were my suburbs. Yet I'd achieved nothing of the results for which I'd built all this. I was alone. Mama could die any day now. I was alone, surrounded by inanimate objects, dollars, crates, goods. I couldn't even imagine my life changing now. I went from woman to woman, bed to bed, but none of them managed to still the voices, the names, the faces, the places that haunted me. I stayed with them long enough for an embrace, then lying down beside them, smoking a cigarette, I lost them, lost myself, they ceased to exist. Rivka and Zofia, my mother, my brothers, the yellow sand, that was what choked me as I lay beside those women after making love.

As dawn broke, I phoned Margaret. She was the only one I saw regularly: but why involve her in my existence? She didn't have much of a life either. Why bind her to my nightmares, sentence her to the agony of always knowing I was somewhere else? I went to see her in her small Brooklyn apartment over by Flatbush Avenue. She'd moved in there after I'd gotten her a job as a decorator with Wolker, an antique dealer friend of mine.

"Well, Mendle, what's wrong?"

I gave her a halfhearted kiss.

"Come here," she said.

She made me take off my jacket.

"Sit down, talk. Here."

She handed me her cup.

"Drink it, it's hot."

I made a long speech about myself. What was I, why the rush, the sudden void, my inability to get outside myself with a woman?

"Even with you, Margaret."

"I know, I know."

"I'll marry you," I suddenly said. "We'll have children."

"Drink up, Mendle."

She leaned over me, stroking my hair.

"You're looking and looking. But it'll either come on its own, or not at all. You'll either find a woman or you won't. But it's definitely not me, Mendle."

"Why not you?"

"It'll hit you, just like that. You're not the rational sort, you're not cut out for a marriage of reason."

She was talking like Goldman. She kissed me.

"You deserve to find someone, Mendle."

I clasped her to me, she was a good friend, a comrade, but she couldn't fill the gulf of misery which so often opened up in me. I slept a little, at her side, then returned once again to the inanimate objects with which I filled my existence. The factories in Hof and Moschendorf were providing goods for me; I went on buying in Paris, London and Berlin. I added more imports to my crates of art treasures: the wheels turned over, dollars produced more dollars. I was offered ideas; I bought and sold European cars by the hundred; I had period candelabra manufactured in Paris, and antique dealers from the West Coast, the South and the Midwest pleaded with me to set my candelabra aside for them. I was rich — but I was driven to work more and more to try and fill the gulf, to drive away the nightmares. My trips became even more frequent. Jurek kept saying, "You're like a runaway horse, Mietek. One day you're going to start foaming at the mouth."

I ran. Ran full speed ahead.

Landing one evening at Idlewild airport, outside customs, a stewardess handed me a message; but before I could open it I was flanked by two men with crew cuts.

"Mr. Gray? Customs check, if you don't mind."

Flanked by the two men, I left the line of passengers. I was subjected to a lengthy interrogation in an isolated office, then a thorough search. They had had all my luggage brought in.

"What are you looking for?"

They didn't answer. All I knew was that they were federal agents. They made me go with them to the warehouses: my crates had already been opened.

"All right," they finally said.

Then I had to go to the shop in Third Avenue. To show them my checkbooks, my accounts. I bore with it. I didn't say a word. They were power, silent, uncaring. They didn't find anything.

"Just a routine customs check," they said as they left.

It was normal, even insignificant, and yet I felt exhausted: at any time unknown forces could emerge, perhaps set in motion by a jealous rival, causing havoc in the arduous task of building a life. Forces such as an army, or a war. When would I be safe, free? Searching in my pocket, I found the message the hostess had handed me and I'd forgotten.

Urgent come 567 West 186th Street. Mr. Feld.

I fell into a grave full of yellow sand.

13

I Had Always Known Her

SHE was on her bed, already dressed, her hands folded on her breast. My uncle was sitting beside her. She was on her bed but her lips had stopped moving, they were thin and pinched, as if drawing inwards, as if they'd wanted to take a last breath at the very end. She was thin, so thin, in her best clothes, the ones she'd worn at the pier the first day, at the end of the corridor, in the crowd, when I'd been walking towards her ever since Muranowski Square, since the time my father had told me about her, that night, in the ghetto, on the eve of the battle. The ones she'd worn when she'd sat next to me, very straight, when we were driving towards Atlantic City in my blue Plymouth. They were her mourning clothes, her best clothes, thin, cheap material that I was rubbing between my fingers, poor material wrapped around her richness, her life. Oh, Mama, Mama, I'm always in mourning. I've touched so many dead people, seen so many bodies. Oh, Mama, Mama, you, too. I went and cried in the kitchen; I howled. With her, everything was dead, I was dead, too; oh, Mama. I touched the objects, the dishes, the table, went back into her bedroom. There she was on her bed, and I couldn't give her anything anymore, ever again. I'd left her, I'd gone off buying, selling, jumping from planes into taxis, I was rich, I'd lived for myself, I'd left her. I should have stayed by her side, lived with her, lived for her: I should have watched over her, held her to me, she was so thin and so frail, a child.

I couldn't stand it. I drifted off into the streets, the snack bars,

the subway. I left her. Goodbye, Mama, goodbye. I walked for
hours in the dust and noise. In the middle of the night, maybe
the second night, I went over to Margaret's. I didn't explain anything but started crying, in great sobs.

"Mendle, Mendle."

It was all she could say but it did me good to hear it. Sometimes I listened to myself crying, listened to my own despair,
stood outside myself and saw Mietek, heels beating, choking,
drowning. Then I began to get hold of myself again.

"There's nothing left for me to do here, Margaret. I can't go
on."

She didn't understand.

"Why live?"

"You're tired," she said. "You dare say that? Think that? You,
Mendle?"

Oh, Mama, her whole life, her smile, her hands kneading
dough, the questions she asked before going out with me on our
expeditions to Lakewood and Fallsburg.

"Do you think this hat's all right, Martin?"

"Just like a young girl, Mama, a young girl."

All that, an eternity of suffering, joy, love and knowledge, all
that squandered at once, scattered across the earth forever. I'd
never get used to death. Mama's death opened up all the graves
again, it was the death of all my people again, they were dragging
me with them.

"You've no right, Mendle, and you know it," Margaret kept
saying.

She was a sweet friend, a comrade. We went to Fallsburg for a
few days, then she left me alone there in the hotel, surrounded by
forest. I rowed on the lake, walked, walked until I was dead-tired.

The time had come for the reckoning: I'd fought to survive, to
stand witness, to avenge my people, perpetuate them, build a fortress, have children. I'd forged ahead, from goal to goal, I'd
jumped through windows, into cellars, I'd clung under a truck,
I'd buried myself in *their* sulfurous slag. I'd killed, hounded
beasts disguised as men, chosen risk, switched lives a hundred
times. Now I was alone. I'd forever been saying goodbye: good-

bye, my people, goodbye, my red-haired friend, goodbye, Mama. I was weary: always on your feet, Mietek, a rotten tree; the bark looks strong but the trunk is hollow. I was sick from too much loneliness and too much sorrow. Why bind a woman to my life; why give life, a life everything menaced?

I walked through rain and snow. Fallsburg was deserted, lashed by a cold north wind. Why build a fortress? Who for? Some days the sun shone but it seemed to freeze the sky, not warm it. Who was my fortress for? I'd no right to put an end to my life but I'd no right, with that gulf in me, to give life. All I could do was keep going, live from day to day, like those ants interminably setting off on their path. Father, I'll stick it out, but just now the game escapes me. I've done what I had to: I've survived, fought, avenged you, I've found Mama, helped her live, not well but as best I could, I've piled up stones for my fortress, I'm ready. But the misery is in me, the void around me. A fortress, but who for, why?

I became a machine, accurate, meeting interior decorators, phoning Clark, cabling Moschendorf, Hof. I operated efficiently, I missed no planes or auctions. Business was never better. I was just an importer, a manufacturer, a cog in the business world; imperturbable, punctual, active, resourceful. I could have gone on to the end of my life investing, buying, banking more money. It went on for months. Then, pains in my back, a throbbing tiredness at the base of my neck. My damaged eye had troubled me since Warsaw. Nightmares haunted me. Then another piece of grit: the federal agents wouldn't leave me. After every journey I was searched. Wasted hours. Crates opened, china broken. They apologized. I was compensated but they came back, apparently convinced I was trading in drugs, or giving false declarations of values. I got used to it. At Idlewild airport, I'd tell the customs inspector, as he was thumbing through the book with a black cover, "I'm there."

But there were other unexpected and painful incidents. I had taken the plane in Montreal for London; passengers were asleep, I was half-dozing, gazing out into the night. Suddenly I saw flames escaping from one of the engines. The hostess came over to me, drawing the curtain across the window, putting her fingers to her lips with a gesture towards the other passengers. I kept silent, fists clenched at my helplessness, at having to entrust myself to others. We landed safely back in Montreal. We left again hours later, but I forgot to cable Jurek, waiting for me in Berlin. I was going to be late, a day or two. I phoned him as soon as I arrived. I told him of the incident.

"Can't see you until this evening," he said. "I want to see you then."

He hung up without explanation. All day I was caught up in business. When I went to his place I had forgotten the barely concealed anger that had been in his voice. He was sitting down, a girl he'd known for some time beside him.

"Mietek, we've got to have a serious talk."

We'd been brothers. We'd run together through the streets of Berlin, embracing when the soldiers brandished the victory flag. He knew all about me, I was him. He was sweeping it all aside.

"You think only of yourself, Mietek. You're a dictator. You give the orders. I can't work with you anymore. Let's settle up."

"If you like, Jurek."

We sat opposite each other. The girl, insensitive and garrulous, inhibited us from finding the words that would reconcile us, from making the gesture reaffirming our brotherhood.

I was crushed between surprise, sadness and fatigue. I reproached myself. I'd buried myself in work, I hadn't found time to talk to Jurek, and we had drifted apart simply because of my tiredness and the pressures of my life.

"Let's settle our accounts," he said.

We had been brothers. We never counted. Now . . . Maybe one day, later, we'd meet again. Goodbye, Jurek. You're still me. Goodbye, Jurek.

Everything went on as before: the doctors diagnosed exhaustion.

One morning, Margaret phoned me. She was laughing.

"Mendle, I'm going to give you a nice present. From your *friend* Wolker."

He was copying my samples, the ones from Moschendorf, Hof

and Berlin, and had found manufacturers in Japan whose prices were sixty percent lower than mine.

"You're copying the Germans and the Japanese are copying you! It's justice, Mendle, justice!"

I was lucky: I sold off nearly all my stock in the days before the Japanese china arrived. The earth beneath my feet was crumbling, my people were dying, my brothers were walking out on me; I was sinking as I had in those potholes I'd feared so much in the forests of Poland. I wired Germany, stopped manufacture. Over in Moschendorf, in his large office looking out across the countryside, the director of production must have cursed the American and his vast markets.

It was a Saturday. It was joyless weather, gray and cold. Since Mama had died, I'd been living above the shop on Third Avenue. I was camping out in an apartment full of crates, empty closets and chaos. I dreaded the weekends, the loneliness. I was lying on my unmade bed when I suddenly remembered some originals I'd left behind in Moschendorf, very fine pieces worth a small fortune and which I had to get back. I couldn't leave before Tuesday. I had to write an urgent letter to Moschendorf, explaining the situation and letting him know I would be coming. I wrote German badly. The translation services were closed that Saturday. Maybe Margaret would know someone. I phoned but she didn't answer. I kept trying, dialing her number over and over. In my lonely state, being able to write that letter became a matter of life or death. All or nothing. I phoned again. In the end I went out, drove to Brooklyn, rang Margaret's doorbell and left a note. She phoned me later that day.

"How typical of you, Mendle. You've got plenty of time."

I didn't have time: that letter was my life. She began to laugh.

"I have an invalid with me now. I can't leave her."

"I'll be around."

I retraced my steps. It had begun to snow, occasional gray flakes that whirled endlessly before they settled. Just outside Margaret's, I slipped on the pavement and got up covered with slush. I rang. And met Dina. There she was before me: life. She smiled, then winked.

"You're in quite a state."

She smiled. We didn't move. I felt laughter surging inside, rippling up through my belly and neck. I was face to face with life. I'd reached the place where pain dies, after the iron band constricting your temples is loosened. I laughed. Margaret came over, smiling gently. I was hardly aware of her.

"You're crazy, Mendle," she said.

Dina started laughing with me. Then she hopped over to an armchair, her ankle in a plaster cast.

"I haven't introduced you," said Margaret.

"We're old friends," answered Dina.

I had always known her. Even if I knew nothing about her: age, religion, name, those were dead words, meaningless details. She was sitting there, suddenly serious, fluffing up her hair: she was life, strength, joy, faith. Having seen her I was a tree full of sap again. I began to talk, my words interspersed with roars of laughter. Time passed.

"How about your letter?" asked Margaret.

"Dina can come with me, I'll show it to her."

"I can walk." She got up.

She clung to my shoulder. It was still snowing. I enjoyed her weight, her touch; she was one of my people. Always had been.

"There's no hurry," I said.

Time no longer mattered. The streets of New York were empty, the tires of cars spurted slush. I talked on and on. Now and then she interrupted, asking a precise question, two or three words, which opened up another floodgate. We parked on Third Avenue in front of my apartment. I was still talking as the snow gradually covered the windshield, enclosing us. I told her about the ghetto, the graves, and then about Father, Zofia, Rivka, all my people. I told her about my dream, my fortress. Who for? Then it was her turn to do the talking: her divorce, her husband, a veteran of the concentration camps, her family scattered about Holland, Australia and Africa. She was a Protestant.

She had to go home. I got out, wiped off the snow, then I drove slowly through the streets. She lived uptown. She had to go to Holland, I to Germany. Her door. We leaned close to each other.

"What about your letter?"

"What letter."

We laughed, then fell silent. Cars passed, lighting us up at intervals. I listened to her breathing. It was as if I could hear her heart beating, see her breasts rising.

"You might like to go see my place while I'm away."

All or nothing.

I gave her my address and keys. She slipped the keys into her bag, tearing up the piece of paper.

"I've a good memory."

"I'd love to have my children with a man like you," she suddenly said, and hopped into her apartment.

The next few days were interminable: I was in a state. The hours dragged. I couldn't write. I didn't want to phone. I went to Paris, Berlin, Moschendorf, Hof. I recovered my originals, talked to the factory director, canceled contracts, approved orders. I was two people; one wandering the streets of Moschendorf and buying chandeliers in Paris, the other back with her on Third Avenue and in her apartment uptown. All or nothing. Maybe I was quits, maybe those last months had been the final test, as in Zambrow when I'd given up hope of climbing that fence, when I kept slipping against the wood, and then suddenly felt the boards that had enabled me to hoist myself up. The last obstacle before the forest.

I left Europe, underwent the usual search at Idlewild, joked with the federal agents, and took a taxi home.

It was night. Outside, on the sidewalk, I took out my key ring, slipped off the keys to my apartment and flung them away in the deserted street. The landing was silent. Not a sound of music, not a ray of light.

I knocked.

She was in front of me. She smiled, then winked. Behind her I could see some new furniture.

"I've moved in."

There was a nice smell, I had a home.

IV

Happiness

14

At Last, at Last, Peace and Joy

FOR twenty years I'd been running: for a sack of grain, to save
my life, to avenge my people, to sell my scarves and handkerchiefs from landing to landing in the Bronx, to earn dollars from
New York to Paris, Berlin to London. It was as if my life had
been a long uphill road but with my speed increasing, the turns
sharper and sharper. I didn't know how to brake; I couldn't! I
didn't want to; I had lost control of my life. It was running away
with me, I was going faster and faster; sometimes I had to fight
the urge to pull off the road, to explode, to give up that race in
which, after every turn, just when I thought I saw the flat, open
plain, there was another slope, a harder one, a fresh bend. Then,
just as I was probably really about to lose control, I met Dina.

A broad, peaceful, powerful, quiet river. She taught me to live,
she was life. I never tired of watching her: choosing a picture,
reading Rilke or Rimbaud aloud, putting on a record, catching
my arm and whispering, "Listen, close your eyes. Listen to the
music."

I'd lived in a world of groans, a savage world. I'd gambled
there would be another life, of real men. I had hurtled through
the years, a stone thrown in anger. Now, when she got up, there
was the smell of toast and coffee. Dina would pass me, and I could
pull her to me without fear. She wasn't menaced. Treblinka
wasn't around the corner. When she passed I always stopped, to
touch and rediscover; to know that she was there, supple and
lovely. When she spoke I watched her lips. She'd had her share of

misfortune: her husband, a former deportee, with whom she hadn't gotten on and for whom she'd left Holland. Finally, after a lot of wear and tear, divorce, a lonely existence as a model, homesickness for Europe, for simplicity and calm; reading, music, children, trees. She had dreamed of her fortress.

"I want you for me," she said.

I hid in her arms, she in mine, I was her father, she my mother; we were brother and sister; her head was made for my shoulders; her entire body for mine. When I touched her skin, when I lay beside her, I wanted to cry out, "At last, at last!" She gave me peace and life. It was a new birth. Everything was falling into place, life had a meaning. I'd been right to struggle, to keep on rejecting death, believing that one day I'd enjoy a time of peace. It had come late, when I'd given up hope, when Mama was no longer there to smile on my happiness. But Dina was there, I could see her, hear her, touch her. She was my peace, gentle, good-humored, and I could laugh with her, my body relaxed and appeased.

She was my shepherd. She helped me explore another world. I discovered books, those written voices singing alone for mankind. I discovered music. I discovered her friends, Grosz, Jacobi and others, many of the Berlin intellectuals who'd fled Nazi Germany at the same time as Brecht and who lived quietly in Huntington, Long Island. I studied them, came to know a new kind of face: to them the world wasn't violence or money. They created ideas, were nourished by them. Dina used to sit next to Jacobi: one of the clan forever talking about Bach, commenting on painting. I listened to them: full of jokes, ideas, laughter. "Champagne Dina," Jacobi used to say, winking at me. She was life.

We decided to get married quietly: our celebration was every day that we spent together. I phoned my uncle, Dina phoned Margaret. While waiting for them, we strolled through City Hall Park. The grass was covered with snow, the trees sparkled, we were holding each other by the waist.

"Do you remember? The first evening? I mentioned children, with you. Little Martins as stubborn as you."

We'd have daughters, too, like Dina. Half an hour later we

were married. We went back to Third Avenue, back to work; our Honeymoon.

Before Dina, I'd been a loner. I lived through a time when to misread a face meant death. I didn't like to owe anything, or to work with others: even in the forests of Poland I operated often alone, and later, with the Red Army, I still fought a private war. With Dina I shared everything. We did business, everything, together: she designed chandeliers, attracted buyers from all over the United States; she could pick the genuine from fakes. She engendered beauty. With her I could build an empire.

"But why, Martin? We've enough. Why?"

Of course: why? Money had only been a means. I gradually pulled out of my contracts and partnerships, and planned our retirement. No one around me understood. Wolker, my rival, thought it was a ploy.

"It's not possible," he kept telling Margaret. "You don't retire at thirty-five. Not with all the trumps he's holding. There has to be more to it."

There was: happiness.

We left for France. Paris with Dina was a different city. We stayed in a hotel on Boulevard Saint-Michel, and we were young. Dina despised luxury. At shop windows she'd give cries of delight and I'd lift her up off the ground. I settled my accounts in Paris and we drove south. Dina dreamed of the sea and sun. I loved the French countryside, neat and orderly, the forests, the geometry of the fields, the patchwork of colors. We explored towns huddled behind their walls, old women ambling down cobbled streets, ruddy-faced peasants drinking wine beside moss-covered fountains, the carvings over the porches; the stones worn by man. We sat under plane trees trying to understand the laughter and conversations around us but the six French lessons at the Alliance Française weren't enough. Yet we loved the voices, the country.

With Aix-en-Provence came sunshine; purple mountains encircling lavender-covered plains, then the red rocks of the Estérel. The Mediterranean.

"Here, Martin. Here!"

We stayed in a small hotel in Nice, every morning exploring

the coast and rocky hills. Dina laughed and sang, hair blowing around her face, and lay back in the car.

"I'm drinking in the sun."

We drove slowly, wandered about the countryside with our dreams. Sometimes, it would come to me in a flash that it was all make-believe, that I was going to be caught in iron bands again, thrown into a grave, and just as the yellow sand came pouring down to bury me, I'd hear Dina's voice. She'd put her arms around my neck.

"We'll find it," she said. "It'll be a house like a fortress, almost a castle, proud and noble, but simple and isolated. There'll be space, trees, fresh air and sunshine."

She was confident of both possible and achieved happiness. We visited dozens and dozens of villas.

"Not that one," she said. "We know what we want."

One morning we left the Route Nationale 7 at Mandelieu west of Cannes, to drive toward the solid mass of a mountain range, Tanneron. We moved slowly up through the golden sweet-smelling mimosa, high above the bright expanse of sea, the beaches, the islands like dark ships.

We stopped and walked along a narrow dirt road. A few minutes away was the sea, and here were the mountains, the pine forest, and here and there green and yellow patches of grass; and the mimosa. Then, on the crest of a plateau, we saw the house, rooted in the earth, broad, squat and strong. Dina gripped my arm.

"We're here."

It was the only place that could be home. It looked uninhabited.

"We must find out quickly," enthused Dina.

We drove down through the mimosa, and cork oaks, back to Cannes. I knew an antique dealer: Les Barons should have been sold by now, it had six owners, there'd be complications.

"Is it still . . . ?" asked Dina.

For the first time I felt she was anxious. But Les Barons was still for sale. I started running again. We had to have that house and we'd get it. I went from owner to owner, promises, drinks, goodwill: Dina followed me, kissed me.

"We'll manage, Martin. I'm sure. It's our house. I know."

We didn't even speak French. In that one day, from six owners, we bought Les Barons. In the evening we went back, stepping for the first time across the threshold of where we were going to live, visiting the thick-walled rooms about to welcome us.

"Our fortress, Martin. We *are* here."

Dina walked through the small rooms, talking; this wall would have to come down; here we'd have a large room with a fireplace; here some stairs, there another room.

"A music room, Martin."

I held her to me. I could see my dream in her eyes.

"I'll do the painting. I'll see to the decoration. You can look after the trees and plants."

I lifted her up, holding her in my arms, gazing at the sky through the damaged roof.

"We're going to live, Martin."

"We'll need children."

"Don't worry. Les Barons will be full of little Martins."

Yet I fretted: I wanted those children: they would be a revenge for all my people, the smiles of Mother and Mama, Father's strength; I wanted those children in Dina's image, to recall her, to recall them, to forge the links between my people, her, me and the future.

We stayed a few more days on the coast. Every morning we went up to Les Barons, letting our imaginations wander. We learned the moods of the sky, and of the air heavy with the smell of the sea and the pine trees, the harsh, warm, dry blast of the mistral and the lash of the wind from inland. We were already in love with the land. Dina was tireless getting to know the peasants, looking for a builder, drawing up plans. But we had to return to New York; you can't change life as quickly as all that. I had to prepare for all the years ahead at Les Barons. In New York, Dina and I saw Dr. Kugel.

"Children," he said, "aren't out of the question. But, there'll have to be treatment, an operation."

Dina was optimistic but I didn't want anyone to touch her. One evening, Margaret came with customers. When they entered the shop on Third Avenue, Dina and I noticed the little girl with them. She was tall and dark, and it seemed impossible the stout middle-aged couple could be her parents. Presumably an adopted child. But Dina persisted: she wanted to know everything about the couple. She phoned Margaret, found that they had waited thirteen years for a child; then, one day, they had discovered Dr. Gross. He prescribed a dietetic treatment, a strict vegetarian diet.

"That's it," said Dina.

I was a regular customer at Manny Wolf's Chop House. I used to bolt down hamburgers at P. J. Clarke's, the famous restaurant on Third Avenue. I'd lived on vodka, even drunk raw alcohol in the perfume factory. I was a red-meat eater. All that changed in days. Dina dragged me along to meetings and, in the mornings, read out loud from books on health foods and vegetarianism.

"Nature, Martin. Let's have a natural life."

We gave up smoking. We were happy, strong, united; we were building our own life, we were discovering it together. We'd sacrificed what had been meager, lonely pleasures to commune together, in certainty. We gave up meat and salt, and lived on nuts, grapefruit and bananas.

"I feel good, Martin. I feel light."

We were bringing each other back to life. Dina went on a two-week fast in Dr. Gross's clinic. I stayed with her, served her tumblers of grapefruit juice, watched her sleeping, saw her growing younger. A month later, she was pregnant.

"You see!"

She was up against me, so soft, her skin so smooth.

I kissed her; stroked her belly: life was there, her life and mine. I wanted to change myself, too. I began a long fast. Lying down, eyes half-closed, I felt transformed. Dr. Gross told me to sleep but how could I when my brain had never been so active. I sought the meaning of our life there, at Les Barons, in the sunshine, the children around us who would grow to be real men. I fasted for thirty-eight days. Colleagues phoned Gross, phoned Dina: "Stop him! He'll die!"

I was reborn. I shook off the dust of the ghetto, the yellow sand and sweat of Treblinka, the mud of the Polish forests and the dried blood that had stuck to my hands. I lost thirty-eight pounds. I never felt so young: my bones, my muscles, that had been beaten and wrenched so many times had gained another suppleness.

"You're very thin," said Dina, "all clean and new."

Nicole was born on November 27, 1960. We chose her name because of France, because of Les Barons, where she was going to live. We wanted her to be born there, but it was impossible. Later, when the other children arrived, in our home, we'd do it ourselves. Birth is both the most miraculous and simplest act in life.

I wasn't permitted to see Nicole being born. I waited with a few others in the large hall of Doctors Hospital in Manhattan. Hedy and Felix Gluckselig, Viennese antique dealers whom Dina had introduced to me, were there and tried joking with me.

"You're like all husbands," said Hedy.

She held my hands, tried to calm me, but she realized that this birth meant even more to me than to most fathers. Through it my people would live again.

A nurse came at last, with a big smile.

"It's a girl."

Thank you, Dina. From them, from me.

I followed the nurse repeating that name of a new life: Nicole, and that other name, Ida, which we'd chosen for her, so that Mother would live again through our first child. I saw Nicole, that life bestowed to mankind, that body which could grow only through others: Dina and myself. I couldn't leave the room, couldn't take my eyes off Dina and Nicole. They were my flesh, and in Nicole were all those lives, Mother, Zofia, Rivka, Mama, all of you, saved at last. Thank you, Dina, from them, from me.

I spent the next few days in a state of agitation and delight: there was so much to be done, for this new life to be protected. In fact, the world would have had to be changed, and if I could, I'd have set about it. But I had only the means to get my fortress ready for her, over there, at Les Barons.

A week later, I was called in by the senior doctor at the Doctors Hospital. He shook his head.

"Your wife can leave, but you've got to make her eat meat, otherwise your baby will die."

I reassured the doctor: Dina knew, Dina was right, and Nicole came from too far away, there was no danger. Dina went on with her diet of grapefruit and nuts, and our child was so beautiful, alive, like a part of Dina attached to her breast.

I hadn't survived for nothing.

This is your witness, all my people; this is your miracle, you who perished, this is your life.

15

So I Took a New Life in My Hands

WE returned to Les Barons. Wild mimosa was overgrowing
our land, almost up to the walls of the house. I began to
clear paths; Dina went from room to room holding Nicole in her
arms. I scythed, I dug: the dream was in my hands. It was here!
My land. My fortress: my people were singing, shouting, laughing
around me. A young Italian set to work knocking down inside
walls and putting on a new roof: we wanted a house of the countryside, a house roofed with old tiles, a house that belonged
wholly to the soil from which it had risen. We slept in rooms that
workmen drove us out of every day at dawn: I went off to cut
wood, to clear another section of our grounds. I recruited a team
of men who knew the land, then hired a bulldozer and we leveled
the soil, pushing back the earth and banking up the flower beds.
The engine panted, but here its jerky rhythm meant life.

We laid out an orchard and a garden to provide us with fruit
and vegetables, our only food. I planted my first peach trees. I
discovered a spring in a corner of our land. All three of us used to
sit by it: I'd look at Nicole and Dina, there they were, on *our*
land and *that* sound was the builder in our fortress.

From dawn to dusk we supervised the work, from dawn to dusk
we studied the changes of the sky, we were lost in the horizon and
the space around us. We began to know the faces of the peasants
of Tanneron: precise, sensible, calm men. They belonged to the
sea and the mountains. Within sight and reach they had opulent

Cannes but they had remained on their land, above the noise, the sights. We were like them.

Dina, Nicole and I walked down the road to the village. We were "the Americans" but Dina broke through all their reserve, she was "Champagne Dina." She made them laugh, she laughed at herself, at our stuttering French; she was alive. When I put my arm around her shoulders and she hugged Nicole to her, to me, I saw affection in the eyes of our peasant neighbors of Tanneron.

"It's good here," said Dina.

It was our fortress. In the morning, in the room where we were camping, we could hear Nicole; we would lie there, not moving, shoulder to shoulder, looking at our daughter, our life. Sometimes, before getting up, Dina would whisper, "Talk to me, I want to know, I want to know more about you."

Hesitantly, I sought memories and came forward with the savage past. I talked: but my wife and child were *here!* I defeated the butchers.

"I know you better every day," said Dina, "and every day I love you more."

Our fortress gradually took shape: we saw the beginnings of the large room and a huge fireplace; we could see the broad windows which Dina designed. The carpenter was hanging some old oak doors: but I didn't want a lot of doors, I wanted an open house where our voices and music could travel from room to room, enclosed only by walls and outside doors. We saw the stairs go in, and the tall cone-shaped fireplace in the music room, a room which went straight up to the roof, with only one support. Dina had wanted to do away with the floor above, too.

"Here," she said, "art must reign. It must be noble, spacious, like a castle, a chapel. We'll listen to the giants here."

We rebuilt the little rooms upstairs.

"We must be able to put the children here one day, if they want, later on, when they're married."

One of the rooms was already reserved for making a kitchen for the children. The laborers listened to her, laughed with her.

"Madame Gray knows what she wants. She knows how to do everything."

I looked at her, I never stopped looking at her: I loved the way she moved her arms, her voice, the way she moved her lips, the way she fluffed up her hair above her neck. She was life, strong and healthy, barefoot, bathing at the spring, naturally beautiful, as a tree.

We returned to the United States in late summer. Les Barons wasn't yet ready to be lived in during the winter, and I still had to wind up some odds and ends of business, organize our future, invest, buy, plan. But from the first day, New York was oppressive: we were no longer inhabitants of that great frenzied city. Dina and I couldn't bear to be apart. We could only live together in our peace, under our sky, in our fortress, following Nicole's exploring footsteps, laughing when she fell. All I was interested in now was planting trees, harvesting vegetables and fruit. We couldn't eat like others, or live like others anymore. We'd invented our life. Those were long months in New York. We often took off for the forests of Fallsburg and Lakewood, but those weren't our trees. We felt homesick for Les Barons, the space, the mimosa and the sea. When Dina told me she was pregnant, she went on to say, "He must be born over there, at home."

We arrived in the spring. The trees and grass were a soft, tender green; the road wound upwards, through the mimosa; we lost all words, we lived off that air, that silence, that sky merging with the sea. Beyond the turn, enclosed by the trees, we saw Les Barons. I stopped: our fortress lay before us, the pale hues of its roof, the stones in the walls almost white in the bright sunlight.

"He'll be born here."

Dina placed my hand on her belly.

"I want it to be you, you, in our house."

We moved into our upstairs rooms, Nicole close by us. We had read several books on childbirth and decided it would be best, for the first child whose birth I was to witness, that I was to deliver, to have the help of a midwife. Dina worked up to the last moment, shifting furniture, supervising tile layers, inspecting the kitchen. She was already a legend among the workers, as if she'd always been part of nature. Dina, child of the forest, living only on fruit and vegetables. A workman watched her making her salads in the wooden bowl. He was warming up his stew.

"I don't believe it," he said. "You never eat any meat?"

"But meat's dead. You have to kill to eat it."

He didn't understand.

One evening the midwife came and we went up to the bedroom. Dina lay down.

"I want my husband to do it," she said, "on his own."

So I took life in my hands, a trembling new life. I felt the movement, the first, with my fingers, and heard the nascent cry. I saw the face, this new tiny face made up of the faces of all my people. Death and the dead had ceased to exist; no graves had ever been dug in the yellow sands.

On that day in May, I took a new life in my hands.

By being born at Les Barons, Suzanne brought even more happiness to our fortress. It was never ending: the pink and lavender dawn, my conversations with Dina in the peace of the house, her whispers, our bodies side by side like one body, waiting for the children's cries, Suzanne demanding her breast, Nicole running, her bare feet pattering on the tiles, she snuggled between us, we were a body with four hearts huddled together. Nicole took my hand and solemnly inspected the trees; there was music, the giants I'd discovered, who sang with us. I'd installed speakers in the garden and the music came and went with the wind. Then there was the blazing midday sun, bursting with strength and joy; Nicole taking great bites of red watermelon. Then there was the sea, Nicole on my shoulders, Suzanne in my arms, plunging her in the water to shrieks of delight; then going back up to our dark-blue sky, the trails of stars, and Nicole, by her mother's side, guessing who'd first spot the shooting star falling towards us, disappearing into the sea. There was our fireplace, potatoes cooked in the ashes, as they'd been roasted in the Polish forests. Then music again, me carrying Nicole fast asleep to her bed, helpless in my arms, clinging to my neck; then the cool of the night and Dina's and my body coming alive again, for each other.

Every day similar, yet different: Dina painted the house, concocted new dishes from the same vegetables and fruits. I listened to her talking to Madame Lorenzelli, who used to come and help us, trying to persuade her to give up fats and meat.

"I can't, Madame Gray, I can't. You're different, you know

everything, if you decide on something you can do it, whereas
I . . ."

The children clung to Madame Lorenzelli, yelling, "Lelli,
Lelli, listen to Mummy."

She was one of us; and kind and gentle.

Dina wanted the best for other people. She helped the peasants,
gave them presents sometimes. I listened to her, never took my
eyes off her; she sewed, hung curtains, arranged flowers, every one
of her movements was an act of love. She loved creatures and
things: she *was* love. She talked to Nicole, taught her those first
ballet steps. Nicole went over them solemnly, and went on until
she'd copied Dina perfectly. I could have stayed there, not moving, just watching my family live. I sometimes thought about my
childhood, trying to evoke the years before the inferno; but I had
so few of those memories left. The savage whirlwind had swept
away my family and Senatorska Street. They were starting to live
again at last, here, with us, through the children.

"Martin, you must tell the children later on," said Dina. "You
owe it to your family, to your children."

Later on, when they were strong. In the meantime, I kept silent: our friends in France and the peasants of Tanneron imagined that I was one of those Americans who'd known only happiness, who inherited security. We were now all part of their
folklore.

They knew that, on October 10, 1964, I delivered Dina, on my
own, of our first son, Charles. They knew that a few hours later
Dina was out in the garden, holding this infant son. They knew
that we had renounced meat, salt, sugar, fats, vaccines, med-
icines and doctors. They discussed our midday salads, seasoned
only with herbs and lemon. They were conscious of our happiness: people who visited us didn't forget. They heard our music,
listened to Suzanne who could now play the piano in the big
room. Nicole danced.

"Are you vegetarians?" Nicole would ask our guests.

They'd laugh.

"But you kill to eat?"

We didn't want to kill. We were part of nature, it entered into us, we went barefoot in the sunshine, walked around our land, watched our trees grow, picked strawberries and peaches. We went down to the sea: Nicole and Suzanne starting dancing with Rosella Hightower in Cannes, and Dina took lessons too, to follow their progress. I loved Dina: among all those young girls, she was the youngest, most beautiful, most vital, and Nicole our daughter danced alongside her. We'd come back up at night, quickly tiring of other people, because they prevented us from being together in our fortress.

Every year for about two weeks, I had to leave my family and return to the United States, back to business, phone calls, harsh reality and loneliness. It was agony. They came with me to Nice airport, we kissed, then I was alone: I was terrified at the thought that I might never see them again, it was like a nightmare watching them vanish from sight. In New York I worked sixteen hours a day doing a month's work in two weeks. I buried myself in work to numb the agony. I met Hedy Gluckselig and talked endlessly about my family. On Sundays, at eight, I went down to the East Side to buy clothes for them all in the Jewish shops: I bought piles of blouses, skirts, dresses and toys. When I was buying, I was with them, living for them. At last I could go home to Nicole running towards me, Suzanne behind her, Dina holding Charles. They threw their arms around me, and I hugged them. We were one again.

When we got to Les Barons I was greeted by music: Nicole and Suzanne singing snatches from the Ninth Symphony, Nicole practicing new dance steps: they all had to show me what they'd been doing, what they'd learned. Suzanne offered me a drawing of a little girl, with her arms out; Nicole a marked exercise book in which the teacher had written that she was the best pupil in the Tanneron school. Then I got into my clothes of freedom and went barefoot to visit my land and my trees, Charles clinging to my neck, Nicole and Suzanne on each side of me. I told them about New York, opened my packages, took out all the colored materials and lace. Darling, Lady and Yellow romped around us: Nicole pushed them away but the three dogs wanted to be part of our circle too, especially Yellow, the gigantic police dog, acquired on a trip to Berlin. When I first saw him, bad-tempered and miserable, he immediately adopted me, following me through the hotel to my room, refusing to leave. After hours of persuasion his owner let me have him, and Yellow began living with us at Les Barons, playing with the children, all muscle and violence but curbing his strength and letting them ride on his back. When I came home, Laidak returned, too, as if he'd known I was arriving: a large cat, independent as the one on the banks of the Vistula, and he liked to go off on long forays through the countryside and then turn up, proud and disdainful. He kept his distance but if neglected, he'd meow, then one of us had to stroke him and cuddle him until he'd leap away and disappear for hours, or days.

So the years passed: happiness slipping quickly away. Around the house, in the fields and the flower beds the peach trees had grown, and the cypresses on the side of the road were thick and sturdy. We were healthy: Charles wrestled with me and ran beside me; he sat on the motorcycle and we went for walks in the fields. He was my son: one day I'd tell him about Father, Julek Feld, our struggle, the ghetto defended stone by stone, Treblinka and the forests. I felt his arms gripping my waist, he rested his head against my back: yes, my son, you can trust me. Yes, my son, I'm here.

We stopped in front of the house, I heard Suzanne playing the piano. I quieted Charles and listened to the clear notes. It was my daughter creating life through her fingers, my daughter once lifted in my hands while still damp, still linked to her mother. She was my daughter. I was proud.

Then Richard arrived. All of us were around Dina, watching her give birth to a new part of us, already crying. Dina was smiling, Nicole cut the cord. He was bound to us forever. Shortly afterwards, Dina got up and went out into the garden, baptizing him with sun and wind. I don't remember him out of her arms. He grew quickly, waved his arms, crawled in the grass, his face red with cherry juice, then she would snatch him from the earth and clutch him to her. I'd gaze at her: she'd never looked more beautiful.

Every day I went off with Dina and Richard to bring the older children from school. They couldn't have lunch there.

"The others eat meat," said Suzanne. "They eat animals which they kill."

"They don't know," Dina explained.

One day, we set off for Italy, Lelli's country; Nicole wanted a satchel she could sling across her back, maybe we could find one in Vintimille. Charles jumped into the car: to him Italy was a distant land. After we crossed the frontier, he slumped back in his seat.

"I don't see any difference."

He stubbornly repeated his words: he didn't know men or their violence, nor had he seen the scarred land they leave behind. He was talking like a child, like a true man. We had minestrone for lunch and the children tasted salty foods, which stung their mouths.

"But why, Daddy?" said Charles. "Why burn your lips? Vegetables taste so good. We must go home quickly."

They were sheltered. I had to realize that one day they would confront life in the world below Les Barons. So I bought some nearby land for them; later on they could live there, near us, as architects and builders. Dina and I had already imagined their future, our future. We began to prepare it for them, Dina drew up the plans, I supervised the work on the initial site. Charles came with me and watched rock being quarried, the first walls go up. One day, later, he and Richard, on that land where they were born, near where their parents and sisters had lived, would dwell there and then come back with their children to our fortress.

Some mornings, at dawn, I talked to Dina of my family, locked in that cupboard on Mila Street. My sons were my brothers too, all children of the ghetto, but saved.

"You must write it all down."

I went on my annual trip to the United States. It had been fine and dry for months. In New York I killed time, as usual, through work. On my return, they were there to greet me. Then Dina led me to a wing of our house.

"I've got a surprise for you."

She had fixed up a study in a sunny room.

"Now write what you've seen, for them, for us."

I held her in my arms, the children were jostling and knocking against the huge bay window which looked out over the country-side and the forest. Dina pointed to a white armchair, outside, in the lee of the wind.

"I'll be here, near you, all the time. I'll see you but won't disturb you."

Our happy summer seemed endless. Then the children went back to the village school.

The peasants were complaining: for weeks, for six months, some said, it hadn't rained at Tanneron.

V

Fate

16

Goodbye, My People

SATURDAY, October 3, 1970. The mistral was blowing, a dry wind that ripped through the orchard, lashed the peach trees and leveled the yellowing grass on the parched earth. In the distance, the sea was gray with white stripes.

It was just a windy day, like any other, the wind sweeping across the sky, scouring the coast and the Estérel.

"There are fires everywhere," said Madame Lorenzelli, "in Toulon, in La Garde. With this wind . . ."

She talked away. Dina was humming, she wanted to go down to Cannes. I looked over her shoulder at the card which she was writing to celebrate the birth of a friend's son: "Hello, Michel, welcome to this crazy world. I hope you'll do something good in this world and perhaps you'll add to its craziness. Welcome. Dina."

We left for Cannes. I had to cling onto the wheel, the wind was so strong. We got back about midday.

"What a wind!" said Madame Lorenzelli as she went home.

It was just a windy day.

We started lunch. Richard was on his mother's lap. Nicole was asking everyone questions. Suzanne was trying to answer; Charles wouldn't.

"It's always Mozart, why not Tchaikowsky?" he said. He liked the lilting way you said the name.

They were continually trying out their knowledge and Dina was the umpire. Suddenly, through the open window came a warm blast smelling of charred wood. I sprang to my feet: the hill behind the house was ablaze, columns of smoke filled with sparks were rising to the sky, red and yellow flames were whirling upwards. I saw the pine trees suddenly catch fire and a wall of flame bearing down on the house. The ghetto was on fire! I recognized those flames, the woman holding out her child at arm's length, I was yelling to her not to drop it, I could hear the walls crumbling. I could see a man, his clothes blazing, racing forward, stripped to the waist, his arms in the air: the ghetto was there, the inferno was closing in on us. The nightmare had returned.

The children began to scream, Dina comforted them one by one. I immediately remembered the car in the garage, the gasoline tank which would explode, the oil supply a few yards away. The children were shrieking. Their screams rent my head, the savage whirlwind was coming again. I'd never left the inferno. Here it is, Mietek, all around you.

"The oil!"

"I'll run with the children," shouted Dina.

She dragged them to her car beside the house; Yellow disappeared with them. Dina waved to me. I shouted twice.

"Mandelieu, Mandelieu!"

I ran to the garage and tried to start my car, but it was no use. I came out again: the wall of flame had drawn nearer. I could feel its heat on my forehead, the heat of the blazing ghetto. Our hill was a furnace. Down below was the Lorenzellis' house. Here, at Les Barons, there were only stones, my stones, but nothing mattered as much as life. I took the motorcycle and drove along a narrow path across the fields toward the belt of flames. The blast enveloped me, the smoke was blinding me; I drove on, then a gust of wind blew the smoke straight at me: I was choking. The ghetto, Mietek, the ghetto: I laid the motorcycle down on its side, dug a hole in the earth, buried my face in it and waited for a few seconds. The smoke vanished, only the heat remained. I picked up the motorcycle and arrived at the Lorenzellis' house. Lorenzelli had severe burns on his arm and shoulder; he shook his head.

"I'm blind," he said, "I'm blind."

I tried to reassure him: it was only smoke. I could hear the fire crackling, I could see the flames beaten down by the force of the wind, then suddenly shoot up, bright yellow with bluish-red tongues, from the sap of the mimosa. It was the whirlwind returning, here in our peace and quiet.

"You must go to the hospital. I'll run you down."

I shouted. Lorenzelli hesitated, agreed, then refused. Suddenly I saw that the wall of flame had almost reached my garage. I drove off, the motorcycle bouncing from mound to mound. In the garage piles of crates were burning. I got behind the steering wheel: the engine roared. I drove around in front of the house, but then, when I couldn't get the top up, I took the motorcycle again.

On the next hill flames were advancing, encircling a farmhouse. I drove on, hot branches whipping my shoulders, lashed by an electric cable that caught me across the base of the neck. I was back in the world of madness. I eventually reached the house.

"Cut across the fields!" I shouted to the inhabitants. "Come down and give me a hand. I'm going to get help for Lorenzelli."

I had to go to the Magnis. I set off on the road, giving the motorcycle full throttle to pass through a belt of smoke and fire, taking advantage of a gust of wind, accelerating again and driving the motorcycle through. The Magnis were there; they'd been spared too. I asked them to help clear the road so that we could bring help to Lorenzelli. Magni went off to raise men. I was exhausted, burned on the neck, hands and shoulders, my clothes torn. I took a breath; and suddenly the iron band gripped my temples, my heart, my entire body. No! No, Mietek! You're mad, Mietek! Calm down, Mietek! But the iron band had seized me. I was Mietek from the ghetto suddenly seeing Mother and Rivka in the column about to set off for the *Umschlagplatz*. I was back in Treblinka and I was laying my people in the grave. A cry racked my body. No, Mietek!

Madame Magni hadn't seen them. I took the motorcycle, tried to ease off the iron band: they'd reached Mandelieu, they were safe, it was just a nightmare. Maybe Dina and the children were waiting for me, thinking I'd perished.

I drove into the smoke on the road where branches were crashing, I yelled, yelled no to my torment, went along the valleys dotted with charred tree trunks, looking. I saw the house we'd started to build, the shutters closed: Dina must have given them a push as she went by. I felt hopeful, but seeing those dead trees, the chaos, the yellow sand filled my mouth, the grave gaped at my feet, I could feel the bodies around me, on me, I yelled, "No!"

I yelled as if someone might have heard me.

"Help me! Help me!"

I set off again on the road to Mandelieu. The air was filled with thick smoke, the smell of burned trees, a wind from the ghetto, from Treblinka. I was buried in a bunker, under the ruins, among my people. I noticed a car at the bottom of a ravine. I ran down, stumbling on clods of earth and burning stumps, crawling over the soil. The doors were open, the car hot. It was our car, with the luggage rack on top, that pair of spectacles in the glove compartment. I was in the grave. Night was falling, I couldn't see anything, no bodies. Maybe they'd run away, maybe the car had rolled to the bottom of the ravine by itself? I climbed back up the slope, the stones tearing my hands, and howled, "Help me! Help me!"

I finally reached the road: I flung myself on the motorcycle but the engine refused to start; so I ran towards our fortress: in the distance the fire was painting the sky red. Some policemen came to meet me.

"Help me! Help me! We must look for them."

I took them to the ravine. A helicopter came, propellers ripping through the air, and landed on the road. The engine pounded, pounded away, like the excavator back there. It was Treblinka again, the never-ending war. An old bus, full of SS men was burning; goodbye, my people, goodbye, Father, goodbye, Rivka, goodbye, brothers; I was trying to push off the sand that Ivan was throwing down on me.

The engine of the helicopter pounded away, then it began to scream, and the machine rose and glided towards the bottom of the ravine. From time to time one of the policemen said a few words to me, then one of them began to walk down the slope towards the car.

I could hear the engine throbbing, I could hear the excavator.

"I couldn't find anything," said the policeman.

He'd just climbed up from the bottom of the ravine. He wasn't looking at me.

"A dead sheep, a sheep, just a sheep. That's all I saw."

I wanted to believe him. They must be in Mandelieu.

I went there. In the town hall at Mandelieu it was agony; groups of men, faces blackened by smoke. They didn't know anything. I questioned them, they turned away.

So I went up to that ravine again.

On the side of the road a group of policemen watched me come and stepped aside. I wasn't shouting; my shouts, my yells, were inside me, only my head could hear them. No. No, Mietek! The policemen stepped aside, I walked forward, I was pleading with my eyes: "Help me! Help me!" and I fell into the yellow sand of Treblinka.

A man walked up to me: I recognized Augier, who grew mimosa in Tanneron. He caught me by the shoulders.

"Monsieur Gray, Monsieur Gray . . ."

I could see the tears in his eyes. I heard him speak but I didn't want to accept what I knew. I cried out for me, for them, "No! No!" And I wanted to snatch a revolver from one of the policemen and silence forever the voice inside me, the voice that had been saying for so many years, "Goodbye, my people, goodbye, my people, goodbye."

17

Day after Day

I didn't kill myself. I wanted to. Friends kept an eye on me.
Only inanimate objects remain of them. These three accordions, these toys, these exercise books. This drawing of a little girl with her arms out. Their clothes, my family's clothes. I still have some photographs; they're dead, meaningless.

Who'll bring them back to life? Who'll bring me back to life? I didn't kill myself. I talk, I eat, I do things. I've gotten past the mood when the urge to die was my only consolation. I've gotten past the stage when the only question was: "Why, why me? Why my people, twice! Hadn't I sufficiently paid my debt to mankind, or to fate? Why?"

I'm talking now, recounting my life so as to understand the chain of madness and chance, the misery weighing on me.

I'm alive, I eat, I do things. I wanted to know. I come from a world, my prehistory, which inured me to seeing death as it is. I pay no attention to those who tell me "they didn't suffer." I know they suffered horribly when they fled the car and ran from the flames, Dina ripping off the heels of her shoes to run faster, hugging her children as they clung to her, gaining a few yards on the blaze. Then suddenly killed by the fire. I still have those heels, a few buttons bleached by the fire, and Yellow's collar.

I'm alive, there's bitter sand in my mouth, sand tasting of death. Why?

It's not my grief that has shattered me. I know grief. It's for them, my children, Nicole, Suzanne, Charles and Richard: what did they know of life? Nothing. I took them in my hands, their mother held them out to me with all her strength, she thrust them to me. I followed in their footsteps, watched them grow, real men, beautiful women, killed before they'd lived. My family. I saw Dina thrive. I fought for it all, I lived through hundreds of years of savagery, and here I am, still crying out, "Goodbye, my people."

I'm speaking, trying to understand. Their lives had opened all those graves; they were my family brought back to life. Now, in their deaths my people died again. I'm talking, walking, pacing my home, my fortress empty, looking at the trees, the ravaged countryside. It was our fortress: the fortress is dead. My other giant police dog, Lady, ran away: she loved us, our happiness. Why should she stay? Laidak, the cat, doesn't come home anymore. Why should he.

I'm walking, listening to these cries inside my bursting head. I'm living. I've become two people again, here to the world, but dead inside. I look at the photos, thumb their exercise books, I'm sitting opposite their wooden urns, standing in front of the bay window Dina designed.

I'm crying. I'm not crying for myself. What am I? A man still alive. I'm crying for them, inside them, I am them, their suffering, their shattered lives, the future they'll never know. I can see them, hear them, oh, you, my people, all my people. Suzanne, the first life that I held in my hands; Nicole, Charles, Richard. I go into the room where they were born. I don't have to close my eyes: I see them, their bodies pulsing with life. I see them, their dead bodies.

Goodbye, my people.

I walk up onto the terrace and look at that surrounding sea of ravaged forest. There in the corner is the case of the gun with which I meant to put an end to myself, a few days after that Saturday, October 3. Now my friends have left: they trust me.

I'm walking, talking, I can't sleep, my head's bursting. I'm alive. The mayor came. He brought up the bodies. He knows. He's a fair, honest man. He doesn't mince words. Six others died that day. He's trying to find out why.

I sank for whole days into the depths of my misery. I was at Treblinka, in the hut, on the sorting lot, in the *Lazarett*. I remembered everything; my memory, under sorrow, disintegrated into a thousand details. I remembered the stench of the graves, the sound of the excavator, the expression of the officer with the pale eyes. I remembered Father, Julek Feld, all of them, my people, my friends. And the others, my sons, my wife, my daughters. I recalled their laughter, the way they ran through the meadows to the house, as their satchels flew in the air and Darling, Yellow and Lady romped about. I'd experienced both happiness and cruelty, life and death. I'd come to know, through my own eyes, that everything is possible, among butchers and men. Nothing is ever achieved finally. If you cross one wall, you find another. If you destroy one ghetto, another rises.

I know. My people are no longer here to learn, to hear my voice, and in this office I sit alone looking out at an ashen still life, at a white armchair that will remain empty, through a bay window where my children will never again come and lean. I know. But so many others do not know. Father once said in the ghetto that a *man* is someone with heart who sticks it out, and I told my children that a man is judged by what he does. That's what I wanted to teach them; and other words that now they will never hear. I am accountable to them now, all my people. Now, rejecting the gun in that near corner, I live to stick it out.

Once again I've left Treblinka. I've flung myself and my grief into the faces of the people of this land in which I've found peace and which had welcomed me. I take up the fight again, my war for my people, for those I loved, so that I can never reproach myself: "You knew and didn't speak out." I called a meeting of mayors, and talked about fire, about man's ignorance and lack of awareness, about what should be taught to children to put them on guard. I saw ministers in their offices, I had pamphlets and posters printed. I spoke on television, visited the major cities of France. Yes, I paraded my dead. I threw my people onto paper and screens. Yes. I proclaimed my grief and exploited it. I didn't want Dina and my children to have died in vain. I didn't want them to be forgotten. I wanted their loss to be a warning, a safeguard. This is my fight.

There are other evils, other struggles. I've endured them too. I've undergone them, for my people, my first family. Today it's this fight that matters to me because it's the fire which dealt me so cruel a blow.

I am living, doing things, keeping active. I escaped from Treblinka, I survived, I built my fortress. But all fortresses are frail, temporary. I'm still on the move; I don't want to live for myself. What's the point? Yesterday, I lived for my people, against the butchers. Today I'm still living for my people, through them, my family, and way back, way beyond it, I'm remembering that unknown people, my immemorial people, to whom I'm accountable for all my actions. I confuse all the faces. I'm nothing, except what they made me, what they gave me; I exist only by what I've given them. Alone I'm nothing.

I'm doing things. I got the Dina Gray Foundation off the ground in a few months. I held a meeting of journalists at Les Barons. I talked to them. My people are living on, my wife, my children are fighting on; what's life if not doing things for other people?

So I'm doing things, keeping active, talking; recounting this long story, my life. When I look at myself, I keep saying, "Why? Why?" But I want to talk on, carry on, keep faith. Live, stick it out, and one day, should the time come, give life again, to make my death, my people's deaths, impossible, so that forever, for as long as men live, there'll be one of them left to tell the tale and to bear witness, for those I loved.

This is my Fate.